SO
GAY
FOR
YOU

SO GAY FOR YOU

FRIENDSHIP, FOUND FAMILY & THE SHOW THAT STARTED IT ALL

LEISHA HAILEY AND KATE MOENNIG

ST. MARTIN'S PRESS
NEW YORK

First published in the United States by St. Martin's Press, an imprint of
St. Martin's Publishing Group

www.stmartins.com

The Library of Congress Cataloging-in-Publication Data is available
upon request.

ISBN 978-1-250-36136-3 (hardcover)
ISBN 978-1-250-36137-0 (ebook)
ISBN 978-1-250-41660-5 (signed edition)

First Edition: 2025

10 9 8 7 6 5 4 3 2 1

To the queers of every generation:
when you find your people, hold on tight.

Contents

SO
GAY
FOR
YOU

Prologue

| | |

Love at First Sight

I was at a barbecue in the Hollywood Hills talking to an ex of one of my exes (in keeping with gay tradition) when she mentioned the lesbian pilot. "Oh, did they finally find Amelia Earhart?" I asked. She chuckled, which made no sense to me, since I was genuinely invested in the aviator's whereabouts. The woman then explained that she and a handful of writers/producers were in development with Showtime for a TV series about chic lesbians living in Los Angeles. "You should audition," she encouraged. I took a bite of my vegan hot dog and wondered how I would even go about that.

Though I'd studied acting at a conservatory in New York City, I hadn't pursued it as a career. Instead, life had put me on a delightful detour into music. For almost a decade, I had been in a band, The Murmurs, with my best friend, Heather. We'd had some great success, but there were times, like this one, when I was broke.

Since my girlfriend of a few months, Robin, was the head buyer at a high-end retail store, she had kindly given me a job selling sunglasses. Shortly after the barbecue, I was at work, tightening screws on a pair of bug-eyed Miu Mius, when an influential record producer I'd worked with walked in. The last time he'd seen me I had a number 1 single, was signed to a major record label, and was touring the world.

"What are you doing here?" he asked, puzzled.

I tried to play it off like I too was browsing for a $350 pair of sunnies, which might have worked—until a customer asked if I could ring her up.

As I slunk away, I thought, *Something's got to change.*

The Showtime pilot suddenly sounded a lot more enticing, and besides, I did have a couple professional acting gigs under my belt. I had been plucked out of obscurity for a lesbian independent film called *All Over Me*. In the early 2000s, I had made real money when I'd randomly booked a national ad campaign for Yoplait. In the original ad, an actress who played my roommate and I are eating yogurt, then using similes to describe how good it is, like, "This is 'first kiss' good." I have a short brown pixie cut, and I just keep saying, "Mmmmm." The commercial feels gay-coded, and the subsequent ads in the campaign just get gayer. In one, my "roommate" and I are bridesmaids at a wedding (a super common place to enjoy a rich and creamy yogurt treat). My lines are "This is, like, 'burning this dress' good" and "'Not catching the bouquet' good." Thank goodness it's a thirty-second spot, because if it were a second longer it's possible my character would have put down her spoon and dived for a different snack.

Now, with visions of residual checks dancing in my head, I was determined to score an audition for this mysterious show. The problem was, I didn't have an agent or any idea how to get into the casting director's office. So, I whipped out my Motorola Razr and texted my band's manager, one digit at a time. She promised to look into it. Asking her was a long shot, but she came through. I was to read for a character named Shane McCutcheon on the curiously titled show *Earthlings*. Could I get to a fax machine to receive the audition materials?

The character of Shane was at a more successful place in her life than I was. Loosely modeled after A-list hairdresser Sally Hershberger, whose clients swarmed to get the "Sally Shag," Shane was a woman in charge, directing employees and kissing up to clients. To pull this off, I needed to project confidence and authority. I tried to butch it up for the audition but wanted to steer away from stereotypes. Apparently, the other women auditioning didn't share that concern: There was more flannel plaid in the waiting room than at a Scottish family reunion.

Two days later, I got a message from my music manager: "They want to see you again." I was ecstatic. The callback was in front of the casting director and the show's creators: Ilene Chaiken, Kathy Greenberg, and Michele Abbott. *Go Fish* director Rose Troche, who I knew from the New York lesbian scene, was also there. When I finished the audition, the executives huddled for a minute, then told me they wanted to bring me in to "test" for the network executives. They gave me some direction on what they'd like to see next time and sent me on my way. I didn't know it then, but this was the final step in getting the part.

I went through my wardrobe and curated what I thought was the perfect look for a hip, strong, sexy powerhouse hairstylist. To top it off, I put a comb in my back pocket that I could whip out as needed. I was so proud of my prop. My plan was to use it like the Fonz. *A comb*, I thought, *that'll be my thing. That'll be my Shane thing.*

The elevator soared up to the Showtime floor. When the doors opened, I waded into a pool of Jennys (did I just foreshadow?). I was sizing up the many frail women with long brown hair when an assistant greeted me. "Hi, we're so happy to have you. The producers are gathering, we'll bring you in soon. In the meantime, I have your contract. If you could just sign."

"Oh," I said, caught off guard.

With a smile, the assistant reminded me that I couldn't audition until the contract, locking in the terms and rate of my acting job, was executed. I grazed through the fat packet of legal jargon. Understanding almost nothing, and having no reps to call, I flipped to the last page, shrugged my shoulders, and signed my name.

As I waited my turn, a drop-dead gorgeous creature with the plumpest cherry-red lips sat down next to me. She looked like Mick Jagger. I thought, *Well, there's Shane.* Then, to psych myself up, I checked to see if she had a prop . . . she didn't. Maybe I still had a shot?

We could hear the Jennys auditioning. Since it was clear that it was just the two of us going up for Shane, I introduced myself to this beautiful stranger, whose name was Kate. We made a little small talk, but I was reluctant to get into a long conversation, because I was up next and didn't want to lose focus.

The network test itself went quickly. The view out of the conference room window was stunning, looking out over the Hollywood Hills. I stood in front of a long oval table with about twenty people sitting behind it, staring at me. I did each scene twice, adjusting my performance to notes the executives gave.

On the way out, I told Kate the producers were really nice and to break a leg. Then I said goodbye, sure I'd never see her again. After all, only one of us could get the role.

KATE

I was in New York City, hungry for work. I'd fallen into a predictable pattern, shuffling between "being in the mix" to "it's not going forward" more times than I could count. I was accustomed to the disappointment by then and told myself this was part of paying my dues. Only four years deep into trying this professionally, I was painfully aware that rejection was 99 percent of the job. Then one afternoon in the early summer of 2002, my manager called.

"Showtime is making a pilot called *Earthlings*. It's not what you think it is."

"Is it science fiction?" Instantly I imagined tight onesie space suits, lots of expositional dialogue with million-dollar words, all said with a straight face. The one major network show that I'd been on at that point was The WB's *Dawson's Creek* spin-off, *Young Americans*.

Only eight episodes had aired before *Young Americans* was shelved. Following that, there were some random indie films that don't need to be named, a music video, a *Law & Order* episode—every New York actor's rite of passage—and some off-off-off, not-even-close-to-Broadway theater in and around New York. To feel somewhat creative during the lulls, I would hang out with my other actor friends, getting stoned and making improvised home movies in our apartments and around our neighborhoods just to play different characters, regardless of how off the wall it could get.

"It's not science fiction," my manager promised. "Give it a read." By the middle of the first page, when a character named Bette says to another character named Tina, "Let's make a baby," it was glaringly obvious that spaceships would not be involved. The concept of a gang of gay girlfriends hanging out in Los Angeles, having active sex lives, was intriguing but did kind of read like a fantasy in a faraway galaxy. It certainly didn't resemble my own life. I didn't have my own gay group who gossiped at brunch. I spent a lot of my nights playing pool at random Irish bars with friends and rarely discussed my dating life with anyone. At the time I was dating guys and girls, both kind of half-assedly.

"Are you comfortable with nudity?" my manager asked.

Huh. I'd never been asked that question. The role required it, and I had to decide before I even went through the trouble of auditioning.

"Sure?" I said. Truth is, I didn't give it much thought. Who was I to turn down anything at this point?

My manager sent me the script and sides, the pages I'd perform at the audition, for a character named Shane McCutcheon. I'll never forget the character description. It's usually no more than two sentences long, just enough to give you a broad idea of who you're dealing with.

This is what I saw:

A womanizing serial monogamist

First, what was a monogamist? I looked it up in a dictionary but still didn't quite get it. I even called my mom and asked her, "What's a monogamist?" When I realized what the definition was, I thought, *Well, that description makes no sense.* How can you be a womanizer and a monogamist at the same time? It confounded me. I ruminated on that nonsensical Shane description. The local lothario, serial monogamist. Wasn't that a contradiction? How was I supposed to play that?

I was told they were under the gun to cast this Shane part, and I was asked to audition on a Saturday afternoon. The office building was empty, so it was just the casting director in the room, which was comforting, since usually there would be a hundred other people who looked like me waiting their turn.

After we read through the sides once, the casting director looked me dead in the eye and said, "You know, you could do this part. You'd be good for it."

I thanked her and took off. I was so used to not getting the job that I didn't allow her compliment to overshadow reality. I knew my chances were slim and they were casting out of LA, so I figured they had a laundry list of girls up for the role.

A few days later, to my pleasant surprise, I got a call that they wanted me to test for the executives in LA. "I don't know what your chances are," my manager said, "but I do know that you're going to be testing with a lot of girls who are reading for another part, Jenny Schecter. There's one other girl reading for Shane. I don't know who it is. Do you want me to find out?"

"Nah, I'm good. I don't care." I preferred not to add stress to an already stressful situation. More importantly, I didn't want to self-sabotage by playing casting director before I even got there.

Showtime flew me to LA and put me up in a hotel in Century City, across the street from their corporate office. A friend of mine from drama school in New York was also flown out to LA to test for the role of Jenny. We walked over to the audition together, having no clue that nobody walks in LA.

We rode the elevator up to the fourteenth floor and were guided through frosted-glass double doors into a crowded scene that reminded me of the cattle calls during my short-lived modeling days. What looked like a hundred girls with long brown hair milled about the lobby. I did not have long brown hair but rather a very dark choppy mop.

A handler came over to my friend and me. "Jennys to the left, Shanes to the right," she said, ushering us to different parts of the waiting room. My friend disappeared into the sea of Jennys and I walked over to the quiet Shane section. There was a lone person already sitting there—Leisha. *Hey*, I thought, kind of excited, *it's the girl from the Yoplait commercials.*

Leisha had a wispy, Weedwacker-looking haircut that I would liken to JC Chasez's from NSYNC. She was wearing a red corduroy blazer with an embroidered tiger leaping across the chest, Levi jeans with patches all over them, and combat boots. *Is this how people in LA dress?*

It was clear that the handler could spot the two major homos that looked like Shanes, so they stuck us in a corner while they plowed through all the Jennys of the day, who wouldn't be hired. I was sure I wouldn't either. Not only had Leisha done the yogurt commercial, but she'd recently been in the indie lesbian film *All Over Me*. She had name recognition, *and* she sold probiotics. She had Shane in the bag.

Leisha was very colorful and light, while I fell into the dark and broody category. I was wearing a vintage denim blazer with a navy-blue tank, black Beatle boots, and Henry Duarte jeans my cousin had gifted me. I had really liked hers, and she had generously bought me a pair. So, I wore them for good luck.

As they were filtering out the Jennys, going through them like Pepsi bottles on a conveyor belt, we sat there waiting for the doomsday clock, knowing our names were going to get called eventually. The cavernous waiting area grew emptier and quieter by the minute. Pretty soon it was just the two of us sitting in that echoing hallway.

For a palate cleanse, Ilene Chaiken, Kathy Greenberg, and Rose Troche took a fifteen-minute break and stepped out into the hallway. Ilene, a petite, soft-spoken woman, made a point of introducing herself, kindly thanked us both for coming in, and we exchanged pleasantries while trying to hide our nerves. It felt like she was welcoming us into her home. I'd never seen a show's creator treat potential cast members like that and I've never seen it since. She humanized this very unnerving experience with warmth and grace. Soon after, Rose pulled us aside individually and gave us notes to go in the room with. She had the ability to instantly get on our level and make the nerves and awkwardness fade away with pitch-perfect wit and humor.

Leisha was called in first. When she stood up and walked into the room, I looked at her butt and I saw a little comb peeking out of her back pocket. *Goddamnit.* I never would have thought of that. As the door shut, I heard the handler say, "Hi, everyone, this is Leisha Hailey." *I'm done*, I thought.

I couldn't help but see what she was doing through the partition in the glass doors. She whipped that little comb out like the Fonz, and I knew I had blown my shot. I had gotten flown all the way out to LA only to lose another job over a plastic comb. I was too busy trying to make sense of how to be a lothario monogamist and a prop was the last thing on my mind. As Leisha passed by me on the way out, I was sweating in my denim-on-denim Canadian tuxedo. I literally sweated through my jacket and was hoping nobody would notice the armpit ring. Finally, I got called into the conference room, which, yeah, had a great view, but was as bright and fluorescent as a chemistry class. I hoped I didn't look like I had jaundice.

Ilene casually studied me as I settled in and said, "Whenever you're ready," in that comforting voice of hers. In the sides, a client was sitting in the chair while Shane was barking orders at the people around her. So, I asked the reader to sit in the chair for me and I turned it to face me. I proceeded to subtly seduce "the client" while simultaneously bossing around the imaginary staff. The scene wasn't long, maybe a page and a half, and Rose gave me a slight adjustment that I didn't really listen to because my adrenaline had taken over my hearing.

They gave no indication whether they bought what I was selling, and before I knew it I was flying back to New York on a red-eye. I had a bartending job lined up for a private party that I was going to work with two of my friends to make some easy money. That night, as I mixed endless vodka Red Bulls, a few drunk girls kept insisting I looked like that girl from that WB show *Young Americans*. Then another would say, "Would you shut up already, why would a WB actor be bartending?" Um, because we got canceled two years ago? But thanks for watching!

In the suspenseful week that followed, my manager would check in with me, repeating, "You're still in it" over and over. They say patience is a virtue, but it's not mine. How much longer was I going to be "in it" for? With every day that passed, the more the character made sense to me, and the more I wanted the part. I later learned the delay was because Ilene and Rose had to fight for me to get the job. The straight male network executives, unsurprisingly, didn't get me.

About ten or twelve days after we tested, the call I had been endlessly thinking about finally came in. I was officially offered Shane. I'll never forget answering the phone and hearing my manager and agent on the line. Relief washed over me: I not only had a job, but one I actually wanted. I always feel like working is the vacation and trying to find the job is the job. For the first time in I couldn't remember how long, it felt like I could take a deep breath.

Apparently, after the auditions, the room was split: the president of Showtime wanted me as Shane, but Ilene wanted Kate. Imagine for just a second what a radically different show it would be if I was Shane. It just doesn't make sense . . . I mean, with this voice? Thankfully, Ilene knew better, and explained to the heterosexual men in the room why Kate was the only choice for Shane. "We'll bring Leisha in for another role," she reassured them.

I didn't know any of this, only that my phone wasn't ringing. Then, a week later, I got a call to read for another part. This is pretty rare. Usually, if you don't get the role you auditioned for, it's over. I was sent new sides for a character named Alice Pieszecki. The scene was set in a Korean spa, and Alice was interacting with Tina. They were catching up in the mineral pool, naked, and as they got up to leave, they ran into Tina's ex . . . with her new lover. There we were, the four of us, trying to navigate an already awkward moment, with nothing to hide behind, not even a towel. The scene was so Alice: it had physical comedy, was a little cringey, and her quick wit ultimately rescued Tina from the embarrassing run-in. I really wanted this role—being Alice felt right. It's the closest to Cinderella I'll probably ever feel; the shoe just fit.

The sides described Alice as "bubbly," the comic relief character, so I wore something very colorful to the audition, borderline clownish. As I was waiting, Rose, the director, pulled me aside. "Listen, I'm sorry you didn't get the other part. I'm glad you're back. They really like you in there, but I have to tell you . . . this is too much," she said, waving her hands in front of my outfit. "How far away do you live?" Everything in LA is thirty-five minutes away, minimum. I told her

I wouldn't be back for an hour and a half. "No problem," she said, smiling. "Go home, change, and come back."

"But—" I started.

"Wear all black," she ordered.

I jumped in the car and raced home. I borrowed the blandest thing my girlfriend Robin owned and returned out of breath and a little self-conscious. Immediately, I was shuttled into the audition. Channeling my own nervousness and discombobulation into the character, I could feel my lines landing. The room was with me, smiling and laughing.

My bandmate, Heather, was at my house a few days later when the casting director called and offered me the role of Alice. I wish I could tell you I dropped the phone and screamed and jumped up and down like the lottery winner I was. But that's not what happened.

"I'm going to need a minute to think about it," I heard myself say. Turning down a role at this point in the process is unheard of. What was I doing? The casting director was stunned. "Okay, um, do you want a minute to think about it?"

The Murmurs was all I'd known. Heather and I had built the band with love and imagination and a mutual desire to avoid getting a real job. We had shared so much. In the last decade, even though we'd each been in romantic relationships with other people, we'd become codependent. The "us" was all-encompassing. I wanted to play Alice more than anything, but what would happen to us if I took the job? Heather was scared of finding out, and I was terrified.

The casting director called again, sure I would have come to my senses.

"I can't thank you enough. You guys have been really sweet," I said, then looked at Heather. "But I'm going to have to turn it down."

"Are you sure?" she sputtered in disbelief. "Are there questions or concerns that I could answer? Do you want to talk to anybody?"

"No, I'm sure. But thank you for the opportunity." As I put the phone down, I knew I had let go of a once-in-a-lifetime opportunity. I desperately wanted to run toward it, but I felt paralyzed.

The phone rang yet again. It was one of the main producers of *Earthlings*. "I hate that I put you guys through this," I explained regretfully. "But I'm in a band, and I can't leave."

I hung up the phone for the final time just as Robin came home from work. We went into the bedroom, and I filled her in. "What are you doing?" she howled. "Call them back right now!" Sometimes you need someone else to push you out of your own way.

KATE

A few weeks later, on the flight to Vancouver to film the *Earthlings* pilot, I thought of the *All Over Me* / Yoplait girl. *What was her name again? Will she be there too? Did she sew that tiger on her jacket or did it come that way?* I had liked her a lot, though we'd barely spoken.

About an hour after I landed, I walked into the production office, and the first person I made eye contact with was the girl I had been thinking about. Leisha, with her big smile and a guitar case on her back, shouted "Hey!" and we gave each other a huge hug like we were long-lost friends. In that second, I knew this was exactly where I was meant to be.

1

||||

Learning the Ropes

LEISHA

On the outside, the Haileys, who hailed from Bellevue, Nebraska, looked like your typical seventies Midwestern family. My dad, Robert, was a navigator at neighboring Offutt Air Force Base, my mom, Jane, was a nurse, and my older sister, Kaydra, and I looked like poster children for the 4-H Club.

Surrounded by cornfields, our town was small and safe. There were a lot of cows and trucks and guys who liked cows and trucks. The sign as you entered town read "Nebraska: The Good Life," which was basically true. Football was king, and the team color, red, was a staple in everyone's wardrobe. As kids, Kaydra and I were encouraged to run wild with our friends, building forts and climbing trees in the Fontenelle Forest behind our house, or playing hide-and-seek throughout the neighborhood. We might be gone from dawn until dusk, but when my mom rang her big brass bell, it was time to head home for supper stat. My family revisited the details of our days over dinner together every night, no matter what. Even when my parents worked multiple jobs, they made it a priority to not only share a meal but handwash, dry, and put the dishes away together.

Our tiny house was on the main boulevard, smack-dab in the center of town. It was less cookie-cutter, more fixer-upper. We were a DIY kind of family. We all chipped in and helped with what seemed like endless projects: raking the leaves, painting the house, shoveling snow, and throwing epic garage sales. Whatever needed to be done, the four of us learned how to do it.

I was a major tomboy. Picture me with short hair and rainbow suspenders, wrestling, building Legos, or zipping around on my Flint- stones Big Wheel. My look was in stark contrast to my sister, Kaydra, an accomplished gymnast with the most beautiful long, straight hair you've ever seen. We shared a bathroom. I'd sit on the toilet with the lid down and watch, mesmerized, as she spent an hour brushing her hair with a hard pink plastic brush and perfectly placing her ribbon barrettes. If they weren't aligned just so, she would have a total melt- down. Why in the wide world of sports did she care so much about this? But Kaydra was never mistaken for a boy, while I was, constantly. After a soccer game, if we went to get ice cream, someone would coo to my mom, "Your son is so cute." I hated it, but I had no interest in changing. I felt comfortable the way I was.

In junior high, the All-American Soap Box Derby became my ob- session. Before racing, I'd buy a kit with some of the necessary parts and materials, then spend the next few months designing and fabri- cating the fastest, lightest, most badass car you can imagine. During math class, I would set aside the equations—I didn't understand them anyway—and sketch. Then every night after dinner, my dad and I descended into the basement, which smelled of sawdust and his oc- casional cigar. We'd measure, cut, saw, and sand. He taught me how to use all the power tools. My mom and I collaborated on the design, which was insanely important to me. I wanted to light up the track with sparkle and flash. Matte paint? Why, when there's metallic?

I was the only girl racing, but my competition treated me like one of the guys. I had a lot to prove on that hill every summer. We'd race down the Strip, a long, steep road lined with the town's fast-food restaurants. I knew that stretch like the back of my hand:

veer left at the Goodrich Dairy, start braking at Long John Silver. I'd
be screaming the whole way down . . . not because I was scared of
hurtling at speeds upward of twenty miles an hour, but because I'd
read that if you scream inside your car, the vibration of your voice
makes you go a nanosecond faster.

As much as I cared about being the fastest, I cared even more
about taking home the trophy for best design. For example, Ms. Pac-
Man was my theme of choice for the junior division car because
I was going to gobble up the competition! My pièce de résistance,
however, was my senior division car. It was always important to get a
local sponsor, like Lyle's Tires, to offset costs. In return, you splashed
their logo across your car. That year, the shape of my racer looked
like a high-top sneaker, so I used that as inspiration for my design.
Naturally, at thirteen years old, my first thought was to approach
Nike. I made a tiny model of what I was envisioning and mailed it
along with a handwritten letter to the president of Nike, seeking a
national endorsement. Weeks later, a giant box landed on our front
porch. It was filled with swag and a lovely letter from the president
saying he had the model car on a shelf in his office. While he couldn't
send any money, he gave me permission to use the trademark. I'd
struck a major deal and went on to win best design. Tragically, in all
my years racing, I never made it to the World Championship in Ak-
ron, Ohio. Yes, if you're wondering, it's a thorn in my side to this day.

Living in rural Nebraska, a red state, you might assume my
parents were conservative. Quite the opposite—they were super
liberal. Although my dad was in the military, he was a guitar-
playing, chess-loving bookworm who was also a proud atheist.
And while I don't think my mom would have referred to herself
as a feminist, she instilled in me and my sister competence, independence, and a belief that we could do anything we put our
minds to.

Ours was the house where people dropped in anytime: chatty neighbors, angsty teenagers seeking advice from my mom, coworkers to watch the Democratic National Convention when Walter Mondale announced Geraldine Ferraro as his running mate. But the town's few gays were the main staples. My parents were so accepting of same-sex relationships, I actually wasn't aware at first that outside our home it was judged. In our living room, Jay, the high school drama teacher, and his longtime partner, Tim, acted like any other couple. Aunt Maureen, a nurse and my mom's best friend, would hold hands with Ladonna . . . then, a few years later, Kathy . . . then Mary (Maureen was very popular with the ladies).

It wasn't until I started becoming aware of my own sexuality that I understood the whispered conversations about Tim not attending the high school play because Jay might lose his job. Or that Maureen's second, unused bedroom at her house was to justify her current female "housemate." Despite my parents' open-mindedness, I got society's larger message loud and clear: *Don't be yourself.*

So, I kept my burgeoning lezzie crushes a secret. But by fifth grade, they were undeniable. That year, I tagged along with my friend Suzy to an audition for *The Sound of Music* at the high school. They needed a bunch of kids to play the von Trapps and I ended up getting the scene-stealing part of Gretl.

There I met CJ. She was older, a senior, had short hair and a killer smile, and quickly became one of my favorite things. When I was around CJ, I felt a rush, an excitement. When I wasn't around her, I thought about her. My parents had put me in an oil painting class. My amazing teacher, Mrs. Lawshi, assigned us an outside project where we could pick any subject to paint. There was only one choice as far as I was concerned. Painting CJ's portrait meant I could analyze the details of her face. I'd gaze at it before and after school— agonizing over how to accurately capture her radiance. Closing weekend of our smash-hit production of *The Sound of Music,* it was time to present the painting. I was so nervous I asked my mom to walk me through it. She assured me that CJ would love it and see how much effort I had put into it. When I unveiled my tribute to her, CJ was so sweet, complimenting it like a parent would a homemade clay ashtray from their kid. To me, it was everything: *Here are all my feelings on a canvas. I can't stop thinking about you and your face.* And thus began my tradition of overgifting my crushes. (Incidentally, the following year, I heard CJ had jaw alignment surgery and had to get her teeth wired shut. *How awful!* I thought. I prayed it wouldn't change her beautiful smile. I tossed and turned at night worrying about her having to drink her meals through a straw. I would have done anything to be the one to hold that liquid dinner up to her lips.)

There was another pivotal discovery I made from this experience: a love of performing. In seventh grade I got the lead role in the high school's production of *Oliver!* I hadn't gone through puberty, so I had the physique and vocal range the role required. Finally, my boyish looks and charm weren't a drawback but a strength. I threw myself into honing a Cockney accent, while my mom sewed my intentionally ratty costume. I loved the community of a stage production, the spectacle, the camaraderie. In the theater wing, I was surrounded by people who were more committed to being themselves than conforming. Among the drama geeks I felt I had permission to be different.

Then came the boobs. They came out of nowhere and they got in the way. On the soccer field, they slowed me down and made chest trapping painful. But more than the physical inconvenience, my boobs marked the end of my childhood. It wasn't that I didn't want to grow up, it was that I now felt expected to care about things like lip gloss and curling irons. Clothes fit differently, and the ones I was supposed to wear seemed like they belonged in Kaydra's closet more than mine. As a tomboy, I had felt I could do anything. Now I was undeniably a girl . . . and that was uncomfortable, limiting, and totally foreign.

Crushes on girls around me, which before had been exciting but harmless, now felt taboo. *Besides*, I thought, *there's no way they'll be reciprocated*. To spare myself inevitable heartache, I relegated those thoughts to fantasy: lesbian celebrity crushes only. Since it was the eighties, my options were Martina Navratilova or Martina Navratilova. So I did what so many other gay teens must have been doing at the time—projected all my queer visions on to straights.

Oh, Molly. Molly, Molly, Molly. She had me all kinds of upside down. Anyone who walked into my bedroom and saw the collage of photos from *Sixteen Candles* and *The Breakfast Club* could see I had a bad case of Ringwald. That ginger hair, that pouty mouth. In order to join the Official Fan Club, I had to send a letter. I wrote about how Molly and I had soooooooo much in common: We were both actresses and even looked alike. I enlisted my sister to take a Polaroid of me so Molly herself could see the striking resemblance. The photo went into the envelope along with my letter, which ended, "I can't wait to work together some day!"

Of all her masterpieces, it was her portrayal of Andie Walsh in *Pretty in Pink* that had the greatest impact on me. At the time, labels were a big thing: You were a jock or a nerd or a stoner, etc. Andie refused to fit neatly into any box, and she let people know with her clothes. One day she'd wear an oversized men's blazer, the next a dainty cardigan with what might now be called a Ruth Bader Ginsburg collar. Her outfits were not only self-expression but an act of rebellion. At the end, when she shows up to prom in the dress that she's upcycled, Andie sends a clear message: I was special the whole time, you just didn't see it. At that moment, her classmates finally do, and she's celebrated.

Most people like that Andie gets the guy in the end of the movie, but I loved that she got herself. I was so far from self-acceptance in high school. Some people saw me as an athlete, others as a girl who did plays. I was both of those things and so much more. But no one—not even my parents—saw all of me. How could they when I was hiding part of myself?

Cue the identity crisis.

KATE

I always looked at my childhood as something like an inconvenience. I was ready to be an adult by the time I was eight. If I could just get the growing-up part over with, I was convinced everything else would work itself out.

Like Leisha, I too was surrounded by fabulous gay men growing up, but it didn't help me tap into who I was any faster. My mother, Mary, was a Broadway dancer who had done seventeen shows during the sixties and seventies, which is considered the most prolific era in New York City theater history. One of my favorite stories about her: In 1962, during the Cuban Missile Crisis, she was about to take the stage for the 8:00 p.m. performance of Richard Rodgers's *No Strings* at the Broadhurst Theatre, starring Diahann Carroll and Richard Kiley, when she got a call backstage from her then boyfriend, who was in the military. "Look, I'm breaking protocol by telling you this," he said urgently, "but you need to get out of town, now." Maybe some, hearing that warning, would panic and run out of the theater screaming. My mom simply said, "No. I have a show to do," and hung up. She chalked it up to him being a drama queen. One of the reasons she retired was because she got pregnant with me. My mom is an only child, so a lot of my "aunts" and "uncles" were her old dancer friends. She met my godfather, Uncle Geoff, when they were doing Noël Coward's *The Girl Who Came to Supper*, directed by Joe Layton. Geoff was the stage manager, and their first interaction was when he barked at her to "move your ass" so she wouldn't miss her cue. Naturally, my offended mother snarled back, "I know my cue, thank you very much." Not long after, my mom saw that Geoff had fallen asleep during morning mass at St. Patrick's Cathedral, which they both frequented. "You better move your ass," she said, as she nudged him awake. They shared a taxi to rehearsal after the service. From that moment on, two of the crankiest people I have ever known became the best of friends.

When the AIDS epidemic hit, I remember my mother being deeply affected, as the many gay men who were significant in her life tragically passed away. She always read *The New York Times* obituaries—which she referred to as the "Irish sports pages"—during the eighties and nineties, and practically every day she recognized yet another name of one of her old, dear friends. My Uncle Geoff and his longtime partner, Uncle Jerry, survived, and continued to be constants in my life. They owned a vacation house out in the Poconos, and we would go there for a couple weeks every summer and see theater with them in New York. They were my first exposure to a gay relationship, yet no one ever directly acknowledged that they were a couple. To me they were just Uncle Geoff and Uncle Jerry. It never crossed my mind that girls could be together like that too. Who knows if Geoff and Jerry saw in me what took years for me to see in myself. I'm sure my wearing a Viking costume to greet people at the door when I was six, challenging visitors to sword fights, spoke volumes. All I know is that my Uncle Geoff wasn't the least bit surprised when, years later, he found out.

My mom to this day claims that she had absolutely no idea I might be gay. I suppose it was easy to ignore the signs. Like the ballet leotard with the Superman logo on the front, the skateboards, the obsession with *The Dukes of Hazzard*. Not to mention my constant conviction that if the boys could do something, I could do it too. My mom is the definition of a lady—standing with perfect posture in third position, in her five-inch stilettos and color-blocked outfits, because according to her "it makes me look taller." I've always been the exact opposite, and early on, I don't think she knew what to do with me.

I was born and raised in Philadelphia, ironically considered a very "gay" town, though back then I didn't perceive it as such. I grew up in a neighborhood called Center City, right in the heart of Philly. We lived in an apartment, and my backyard was a park called Rittenhouse Square. My grade school was down the street from the Liberty Bell (years before it was hit with a hammer and put into a visitor center) and my school bus stop was practically on the steps of Independence Hall. Much of the city is gentrified now, but thankfully the people are still direct and speak their mind with little filter. I got off the train from New York once and the conductor yelled out, "Welcome to the City of Brotherly Love . . . sometimes!"

In Center City, I was surrounded by history, museums, theater, music, and plenty of places to skateboard. My dad, William, or Bill, as everyone called him, was a violin maker—Isaac Stern and Itzhak Perlman were loyal customers at what we referred to as "the shop." As a kid, I would listen to classical music every night to fall asleep, and my mom took me to the children's orchestra on Saturdays at the Academy of Music to help balance my musical palate, which otherwise primarily consisted of Madonna, Michael Jackson, Whitney Houston, and the Beastie Boys. The sound of tuning violins, though, was the soundtrack of my childhood, and I've always found them to be the most perfect-sounding instrument.

My father's shop was one of the longest-running string shops in the world. It was the family business, which originated in Germany and carried on through thirteen generations. When it moved to Philadelphia, it lived in a humble town house on Locust Street, with a small wooden sign hanging out front in the shape of a violin that read "William Moennig & Son." Walking through the door was like walking into Geppetto's factory. The guys in smocks hunched over their workbenches, surrounded by mason jars of hand-mixed stains and resins, and every chisel and carving tool known to man.

Although it was the Moennig birthright that every male not only be named William but also make violins, it was never my dad's dream to take over the family business. He would have been most satisfied if left alone to be an artisan. He could create anything he saw—whether through oil painting, wood decoys, or even furniture. He was a true artist.

However, he married young to his first wife, and with two kids and a family to support, his plans shifted. I came along years later when my father had remarried and was my parents' only child—my two half siblings, Pam and Bill, were old enough to be my parents when I was born. I don't know if it's true or not, but I always got the sense that my father didn't really *need* another kid. The man was forty-eight when I arrived, and now that I'm closer to his age, I can't say I blame him.

I always wished for a sibling to grow up with so I would have a teammate and someone to confide in. I often found the direct energy and questions from my parents challenging, and would love when people came over for dinner, which took the spotlight off me. At the very least, being an only child taught me independence and to enjoy my own company. Early on, I found that I preferred to figure most things out on my own.

When it was time to have me enrolled in school, my dad let my mom call most of the shots. She was and still is proudly and devoutly Irish Catholic, which meant that her only daughter's school would be as well. Cultivating a young person's individuality didn't feel like a priority in the Catholic school system, nor did creativity. So, I spent my childhood trying to find other outlets. School didn't come easily, and I had such a difficult time in practically all my classes that a teacher once called my mom to ask if maybe I had a hearing problem. I didn't. I just wasn't paying attention.

Throughout, my grades were barely passable, and I found it

challenging to retain information. Reading came easily enough, but the words would get mixed up in my head and I would get the answers wrong during quizzes and tests. When I was six, I remember being pulled out of class multiple times to take "alternative learning." A very nice woman who I had never seen before would take me into a makeshift classroom in our gymnasium to play learning games, and I would take tests with cartoon animals on the pages. No one explained to me why I was there or what the point was, but it felt like my private recess. The outcome was that everyone in charge thought it would be best for me to repeat the second grade, which was an experience that turned out to be more traumatizing than I would have imagined.

The kids from my original class were a tough crowd to say the least. When the next school year started and I didn't move up with them, their teasing became relentless. It happened during recess, in the hallways, at lunch, and in front of everyone including the teachers, who to my recollection didn't do much to stop it. My former classmates would point and laugh, asking, "Why are you in the same class again? What are you, stupid?" It felt merciless.

During class one day, I either spaced out or answered a question incorrectly, and in front of everyone, the teacher suddenly screamed, "You're going to have to repeat second grade a third time and by then you'll be so big!" Her anger was harrowing, loud, and solely directed at me. I feared the other classes heard it through the thin, retractable walls. For a long time after that, her words hung in my brain.

On top of all that, I was constantly being mistaken for a boy. It probably didn't help that I had a short bowl haircut, wore boyish clothes, and climbed anything I could. I was usually the fastest during impromptu Big Wheel races in the park, or on a skateboard, which I rode with abandon, no fear of getting hurt. During the summer, I'd stay with my sister Pam at her beach house down at the Jersey Shore so I could surf, and I loved when a storm front or potential hurricane rolled through, since the waves would get bigger. For a period of time, girls thought I looked like Joey McIntyre from New Kids on the Block. Which is a fun throwback now but back then was embarrassing. It was not the kind of attention I ever wanted.

I'd regularly get called out in public places, by random people who didn't know any better. For a few summers I went to Oak Lane Day Camp. They'd bus us out there from the city to some wooded area, and there was always a kid throwing up in the van. Our first day was orientation, where they announced the cabin assignments. There were girl bunks and boy bunks. They called out our names one by one, and we'd go stand with our new group. Inevitably, when they called my name and I walked up to be sorted, the counselor with the mic said, "No, no, no. Boy, boy, no, not you."

"That's me," I mumbled quietly. "I'm a girl." Being misgendered as a kid made my ears turn bright red and my cheeks flush. Kids would stare, laugh, and whisper to each other.

The eighties were a binary world, and I always seemed to fall into a gray, in-between zone. I don't know how I would identify if I were a young kid today, but back then, I just thought of myself as a tomboy. I rebelled against the feminine dress code at school, the jumpers and skirts that were my uniform. Why did the boys get to wear warm pants but I had to wear a kilt in twenty-five-degree weather? Why did the boys get to wear comfortable black shoes while I was expected to wear saddle shoes? They hurt and had no arch support.

When I was around seven years old, my first act of independence was deciding that my personal style didn't involve my mom's opinion. Her idea of what her daughter was supposed to look like soon went out the window. In 1985 I wanted to dress like Marty McFly.

My first real foray into fashion was the Z. Cavaricci era, the

Starter jackets and high-top Travel Fox sneakers, which could have been part of the reason why I was mistaken for a New Kid on the Block. A few years later, I ditched the high-tops when I discovered Kate Moss and the gang from those CK One ads. It was part of what the adults called "the unwashed grunge era," or what I liked to call Utopia. I was fifteen when movies like *Reality Bites* and *Singles* came out. Mainstream fashion started to become androgynous. Before that, girls' fashion was overtly feminine, with off-the-shoulder tops, stirrup pants, and miniskirts. Now, used Levi's, flannel shirts, vintage T-shirts, and Doc Martens were embraced, and gender norms started to blur.

I met my first best friend, J, when we were maybe six years old. I think our moms became friendly at the neighborhood park where all the kids would play. The mom group would convene over on the benches by the goat statue and smoke cigarettes while the kids ran wild. The neighborhood was small enough that everyone who was roughly the same age knew each other. I don't have a specific memory of what made J and I click. All I know is that we were inseparable. We only lived a block and a half away from each other, and I could see his house down the street from my bedroom window in my parents' twelfth-floor apartment. Our landline numbers were identical except for the last two digits.

The best way to describe J is that he looked like a splinter. He was unusually small and skinny for his age, while I was gawky and a few inches taller than him through most of our childhood. J was incredibly funny, book smart, and naturally talented. One of those gifted kids who would be considered an artistic prodigy today. At fifteen, during our Tori Amos era, J started taking piano lessons. After a day or two, he was able to play "Winter" beginning to end without missing a key. In twelfth grade, J won an award for a play he wrote about Holocaust survivors, and Temple University performed it in their theater department. In addition to his talent, there was something different about J that no one could figure out.

J wasn't flamboyant by any means. He just had a quiet softness and wasn't like the other kids. Everyone assumed he was gay and would ask me, like I was his keeper, though as far as I knew, he wasn't. Throughout high school, all of J's friends were the cool, pretty girls, who loved hanging around him because they somehow knew he was safe. Since J and I were always the same clothing size, we constantly shared our vintage Levi's, plaid pants, and motorcycle boots. On some level, we knew each other's secrets too, without ever saying them out loud.

J and I were two creative idiots together. We would write two-person plays and perform them for anyone who would watch. Without realizing it, I suppose I was carrying on a family tradition, but at that age, I didn't really pay attention to what my family did. In addition to my mom's Broadway career, I knew my Aunt Blythe was an actor. I remember seeing her perform in Shakespeare in the Park and on Broadway in Noël Coward's "Blithe Spirit." My uncle Bruce was something called a producer on a TV show about doctors called *St. Elsewhere* that my parents watched.

I didn't even realize my aunt also acted in movies until my teacher had us watch a film in guidance class one day. I spent the whole hour puzzling over why the actor playing the wife looked so familiar. It got to the point that I wasn't even paying attention to what is inarguably a phenomenal film. That night at dinner, when my dad asked me how my day was, I told him we watched a movie called *The Great Santini* "and this woman looked so familiar, but I couldn't figure out why."

He just stared at me in disbelief. "That's your Aunt Blythe."

I suppose what solidified my understanding of what my family did was when my older cousin Gwyneth suddenly blew up into stardom out of nowhere. There's a six-year gap between Gwyneth and me, so

I had always been the baby cousin tagging along after my three cooler and older cousins. I think they tolerated me like you would a puppy in the middle of potty training. When we were little, they convinced me that an alligator lived in the pool and threatened to throw me in. I would crawl on my cousin Hillary's back and she would carry me everywhere. Other times, they would wrap me up in blankets and roll me down the stairs. During family gatherings for the holidays, Gwyneth's younger brother Jake and I would always find ways to get a rise out of her, like taking everything out of her room and putting it in the bathtub while she was sleeping. I remember us bonding over Bon Jovi's new single "Livin' on a Prayer." She gave me hand-me-down clothing that she didn't want and taught me to put lemon juice in my hair during the summer to make it blond, though that never worked. She held my hand during the scary parts of the Matterhorn ride at Disneyland and didn't get mad when I accidently peed in her roll-out guest bed when I was ten. Years later she kindly invited me as her date to the Met Gala.

Having said all of this, I can't really give credit to my extended family for piquing my interest in performing. Their world felt far away from mine. Instead, it was bonding with my dad over movies he introduced me to that spurred my curiosity. He introduced me to *Alien* and *Jaws* when I was five years old. I was six or so when we watched *Cool Hand Luke*, *The Godfather*, and *Yojimbo* together. He would carve an apple with his pocketknife and pass me slices while I asked him, "What happened?" during the parts that went over my young head. I remember not understanding what the lead character was taping to his body at the beginning of *Midnight Express*. When I asked he just said, "Don't worry about it." It was hash.

More than anything else, it was my friendship with J that first gave me the confidence and the curiosity to give acting a try. We'd been doing it since we were very young without even realizing it.

We could have made an award-winning, eight-season arc of *Melrose Place* with our Barbie characters' drama. When we were twelve years old, J said, "Come do a play with me, we'll have fun together," and got me involved with the neighborhood playhouse theater Plays and Players. First, I was on the crew, which then quickly led me to playing my first androgynous role of many—Christopher Robin in *Winnie the Pooh*.

In eighth grade, my school—despite being one of the least artistic environments you can imagine—decided to do a musical with the graduating class. From what I understand, it was the only time it happened. Since it was an interparochial Catholic school, *Do Black Patent Leather Shoes Really Reflect Up?* was the obvious choice. I got cast once again as a boy—the troublemaking goofball character— and my mom volunteered her services and choreographed the show. I had the greatest night singing and dancing, and this time I wasn't made fun of. Instead, I was getting congratulated for doing a good job playing a gender-nonconforming role. St. Mary's didn't realize how ahead of the curve they were.

J and I also wrote together prolifically—plays, short stories, movies we made with broken handheld cameras that his dad owned. We performed sold-out shows, a reboot of *Winnie the Pooh*, that we wrote, directed, and produced ourselves at the free library for a limited run. We were industrious twelve-year-olds, working with what we had. Our play even got a positive review in *The Philadelphia Inquirer*.

We had a horror-movie phase and felt inspired to write our own scripts that involved mutual friends or kids from our schools. We would read them out loud to each other, laughing so hard and gasping for breath at how ridiculously everything we wrote unfolded. All these years later, I stand by how good some of the things we wrote actually were.

For the most part, J and I were each other's muse but could also be each other's fuse. It didn't take much to be bad influences on each other. One summer, an older girl in the neighborhood, Sophia, volunteered to chaperone the two of us to 7-Eleven, which was only a block and a half away. Over the course of the twenty-minute field trip, we managed to knock over the entire candy aisle, almost get hit by a car, and nearly get mugged. Poor Sophia returned us to our parents with a harrowed look in her eyes, like the lone survivor of a horror film, and never offered to take us anywhere again. We tested people and boundaries constantly without even realizing it. It's not that we wanted to cause problems or try to make anyone's life difficult. We were just curious to see how far we could push these seemingly arbitrary rules that had been instilled everywhere we went. I remember getting in trouble for asking "why?" a lot.

It was also easy to become a bit destructive if we had nothing else to do. J's kitchen window faced the street. When it was raining or snowing, and J's parents were out to dinner, we'd fill buckets of water or run outside to collect pails of snow, run back upstairs and wait for someone to pass by, then dump it out the second-floor window onto people's heads. Or we "borrowed" J's parents' credit cards, called the toll-free numbers on mail order catalogs as outrageous characters we had created. We would find ways to incorporate random, nonsensical movie quotes that we had memorized into these phone calls and feel proud when we did it seamlessly. The chances of the person on the other end believing us were slim to none but some were clearly amused since they'd stay on with us for up to forty minutes.

After we ran out of catalogs we would get a hold of J's older sister's school directory, create a character, and call other kids as that person. J's talent was putting on a hot-girl voice. We would usually call the boys since they were easily manipulated into believing that this imaginary girl that just transferred to Central High wanted to come over while their parents were out. Other times we would find the number of someone who knew someone we knew and pretend to be their dementia-riddled grandmother. J's interpretation of his Jewish Bubbe Betty was second to none.

Shelly was a Rax Girl. She and my sister Kaydra and their two best friends, Kathy and Kathy, had given themselves that name because they would go to Rax Roast Beef every day before Thunderettes practice to eat fries, drink pop, and gossip. They were seniors and I was a sophomore, so they never paid me much attention. Then I joined swing choir. If you just conjured up an image of risers and a Christmas concert, you've got the wrong idea. This was the world's nerdiest extracurricular: pairs of boy/girl couples in fancy dress doing jazz hands and boogie steps while singing the hits of yesteryear. One rehearsal, I was in the arms of my partner, Mark, singing "You give me fever," when Shelly locked on my gaze and raised an eyebrow as if to say, "What a lovely way to burn."

Our connection was charged from the jump. Shelly was my height and had a dark brown bob and a complexion that was downright exotic in Bellevue. Even at eighteen, she was confident, fearless, and knew what she wanted. Impossibly, what she wanted was to be the alto to my soprano. Around the Rax Girls, Shelly would flex her status as a senior, exude this energy like she owned me. But when it was just us, we'd flirt and joke like the only two people left on earth. Her gaze rendered me powerless, and she knew it.

I'd had boyfriends, one of whom I genuinely loved, but I'd never felt like this. Shelly was dating a guy, yet she'd keep me company for hours while I was working concessions at the movie theater, or I'd go hang at the public pool while she lifeguarded. Shelly had a hot touch. If she casually put her hand on my arm, I'd feel aftershocks for days. The air between us was thick, like a muggy summer afternoon begging for the rains to come and bring some relief.

"I want to kiss you," she braved one night. "Me too," I admitted, spellbound. We stared at each other, unable to narrow the seven inches between our faces. A plan was hatched: We'd score some tequila from her dad's cupboard and bring it to the barn party that weekend. In a sea of friends, I sat on the open tailgate of a pickup, Shelly circling. Drunk enough, we took cover in the field and made out in the grass. It was a hungry kiss, pure desire. I'd waited my whole life for this, and I couldn't believe it was real. Waking up the next morning, I felt for the chigger bites up my shins . . . proof that it had actually happened.

If you were to flip through the photos from the disposable camera of my relationship with Shelly, you would see:

- Shelly and I making eyes at each other while slurping noodles on a "friend date" at Spaghetti Works.
- Me giving sweat-glistened Shelly a victory piggyback after she'd won the 200-meter dash at a track meet.
- A close-up of my blissed-out face after me and Shelly fingerbanged on my waterbed.
- Us in matching stone-washed jean jackets—hair teased to the heavens—posing for a professional portrait (don't bother flipping to the photo insert because there is no freaking way I'm letting anyone see that).
- Me in the auditorium during the end-of-the-year pops concert . . . the only person in the audience wise to the reason for Shelly's inspired rendition of Anita Baker's "Caught Up in the Rapture."

What the glossy stack of four-by-sixes would not show is the longing, the confusion, the heartache. I was infatuated with Shelly, compelled to share every waking minute with her. I was sure she felt the same, so why was she spending so much time with the Rax

Girls or her boyfriend? She was leaving for college, and we had a finite number of days to trip on this incredible love drug. It wasn't like I expected her to break up with her boyfriend and be with me—that literally was not an option for two Nebraska girls in 1986—but being a side piece was unhealthy. Our undercover relationship had me whiplashed between euphoria and worthlessness. I was madly in love, an unreliable protector of my own heart.

Lonely doesn't begin to describe how I felt starting junior year. Not only was Shelly gone, but my sister was off to college as well. I belonged in Bellevue less than either of them, so how was I the one left behind? Shelly had tried to make a clean break before heading to school in Texas. I was devastated, of course. But even worse, just when my feelings began to scab over, she called. For the next few months, we mailed each other long letters—twenty handwritten pages at a time—and elaborate care packages. One of hers included a bootleg calling card. Shelly would ring me at the house, I'd hop on my bike and tear down the hill to the Kwik Shop, then call her from the pay phone for privacy. The whole time I was saving up to go visit. I couldn't wait to be swallowed up by her.

I got a plane ticket to go see her, but before I arrived in San Antonio, Shelly told me she had a new boyfriend. *Big whoop*, I thought. She'd had boyfriends while we were together. I bounded off the plane more excited than I'd been for anything in my life.

Shelly snuck me into a honky-tonk bar. We were soaking each other up, right back in our bubble. Then her boyfriend arrived. He had blue eyes and a headful of tight blond curls and was studying to be a doctor or something impressive. I watched Shelly lay her hot hand on his forearm and, like the tide going out, felt her pull away from me.

The rest of the night is a blur of beer and bad choices. Her boyfriend had a friend. I hooked up with him, maybe to make her jealous, maybe to distract myself from knowing she was hooking up with Pre-Med, maybe to feel something other than pain.

I returned to Bellevue a hollow shell of myself. The despair of losing Shelly was unmanageable. Worse, I couldn't talk to anyone about it. I'd get on my bike and, for hours, ride in circles around the school's track. My thoughts were also on an endless loop: *Why didn't she let me go when she went to college? How could she let me visit her? Why had I hooked up with that guy? Why didn't she stop me? How will I live without her?*

What's that part of the world that gets zero hours of sunlight for all of winter? That was me. One day my mom picked me up from school and I burst into tears. "Leisha, what's wrong?"

"Nothing."

"Honey, you have to talk to me."

I couldn't. I didn't talk for weeks. Months. But my mom never wavered in her resolve to reach me. Calling on her experience as a nurse, she gently asked if I thought about hurting myself. I stared at the floor.

My mom took me to a therapist, which was almost unheard of at the time. After two months of treatment, I mustered the courage to tell my psychiatrist that I thought girls were pretty. The doctor responded that my feelings were natural. I brightened, hope forming that someone actually understood. Then the trained, paid professional continued, "Don't worry, it's a phase. You'll grow out of it."

In that instant, somehow, my shame and self-loathing were kicked to the curb. In their place was just one thing: survival. I knew I wasn't safe in this room, in this town, and vowed to find a way out. Until then, I committed to playing my best straight-girl role. And, for the next year and a half, I succeeded . . . with just the occasional slip. Like when I made a boyfriend fool around with me while listening to the new Indigo Girls tape my sister brought home from college. Oopsie.

I knew that there was only one place for me: the great Broadway. It was NYC or bust. No, I had never been there, but I could see it so clearly: me, dancing through the streets like the kids in *Fame* or hanging with the outcasts in *The Rocky Horror Picture Show.* I researched acting schools and found the American Academy of Dramatic Arts. My audition had to be perfect. At the local library, I flipped through volumes of monologues. Like every musical-theater kid, I worshiped Barbra Streisand. Her pipes, her face, her timing. She was uncompromisingly herself. I scoured Barbra's body of work. After feeling out passages from *What's Up, Doc?* and *Funny Girl,* I tried on *Yentl.* "If we don't have to hide my studying from God," I asked the mirror, "then why from the neighbors?" I liked the idea of exploring secrecy and dressing like a boy for the audition, but pulling off Orthodox Judaism was a stretch, so it was back to the drawing board. Except for my parents, everyone thought I was crazy to pursue this New York dream. *Maybe they're right,* I thought. Aloud, I muttered, "Maybe I'm nuts." And then it hit me—Barbra Streisand's monologue in the movie *Nuts!*

In front of the stern headmaster of the academy, I delivered Babs's courtroom speech. "I know I'm supposed to be a good little girl for my mother and father. An obedient wife to my husband. Stick out my tongue for the doctor, lower my head for the judge. I know all of that." I set my voice aquiver to drive it home. "I know what you expect me to do. But I'm not just a picture in your heads. Do you understand?" There was a stillness in the air. When I peered up to gauge the reaction to my performance, the gleam in the headmaster's misty eye let me know I was right where I belonged.

My acceptance letter arrived three months later.

KATE

In high school, trouble increasingly found me, whether it was wearing motorcycle boots with my uniform and defying the dress code, cutting class, or talking back when I thought teachers were condescending. Truth is, I couldn't keep up with the curriculum in this polished prep school in the suburbs. In senior year, I was suspended for getting caught smoking on the school's campus. The friend I was with managed to flick her cigarette away at the right moment and I was the only one they saw. The dean of students offered a lesser sentence if I came forward with anyone else who was enjoying that midday American Spirit break with me. Since I didn't take their bait, they gave me a full in-school suspension. Which amounted to sitting in someone's office after school each day for an hour. The punishment lasted less than ten days, and I was let off with a warning. It was all pretty counterproductive since the school itself smelled like an ashtray. The day of my crime, the dean called my mom, expecting her to have a breakdown over the phone, but to her credit, all she said was, "I know, I'm watching." Her opinion was that since she started smoking at seventeen, why should she be a hypocrite with me? It was the mid-nineties after all. When it came time to apply for colleges, I was encouraged by my parents to investigate drama conservatories instead of state schools. When I landed on the American Academy of Dramatic Arts, my "college prep counselor" was inconsolable. She told my mom I was making a horrible mistake. What that teacher didn't know was that the woman she was lecturing also never went to college and it didn't stop her from following her passion, training in her craft, and living her dream. As my mom has said throughout my life: "I was a dancer, honey, that's what I knew."

In fact, my mom was constantly surprising me with what she

tolerated. She didn't seem to worry that J and I were going off to raves in our teens either. We always told our parents where we were headed and then took off for New York City or New Jersey for a full twenty-four hours, diligently getting home by Sunday. Truth is, I never gave her a reason to mistrust me. We weren't doing drugs or even drinking. I recall she was more disappointed after the time years earlier when she spent hours helping J and me choreograph a dance routine for a talent competition. After two weeks of rehearsals with her, we got on stage for our big number, but we broke down into a fit of hysterics, never taking one step she taught us. We just stood on stage laughing uncontrollably, tears rolling down our cheeks, while "Heart" from *Damn Yankees* played in the background to a very confused audience.

That happened often. At Plays and Players, the in-house director always had to separate the two of us in rehearsals. We had our own language and would laugh endlessly over something that only made sense to us. In one play we were in together, J's character had to pass stage right, by the bed my character would crawl into at the end of the play. Throughout the show, during his cues, J would grab whatever he could get his hands on backstage and place it on the bed without anyone noticing. Masking tape, a flashlight, a wrench, a screwdriver—anything solid and preferably heavy. At the end of each performance, during the play's most poignant moment, as I climbed into the bed, all you would hear in the dark was the clattering of tools falling on the ground and the masking tape rolling downstage and into the front row. My young understanding of performing was that it was an outlet to release pent-up energy, and why not have fun while doing it?

J and I were just two kids who didn't really know who we were, only that we were safe with each other. We would have sleepovers practically every weekend and sleep in each other's beds. If we had nothing to do on a Saturday night, we would visit our friend Chris on Thirteenth Street, which was considered the gay street in town, with nondescript bars lining the block. We'd sit with him on a stoop and keep him company while he waited for customers. He would then disappear to do his thing, only to return twenty minutes later and wait for the next car to stop.

There was never anything romantic between J and me, however. Though I was a late bloomer, I had some boyfriends throughout high school, and a few were considered popular. I dated them out of a sense that it was expected of me and with a vague sense of guilt that I genuinely didn't care if we lasted even a week.

Girls were different. I think I kissed my first girl when I was five years old. We were playing Snow White, and I was, of course, the prince, because my hair was shorter. She leaned in to kiss me and my immediate feeling was fear and fascination. I remember backing up and almost falling, literally, into the closet, but I do think our lips touched briefly. Not long after that, she abruptly stopped talking to me and fell into a different group of friends. She was in my first second-grade class—before I got held back—but we wound up going to the same high school. When I was a freshman, I recall her acting like she had just met me and didn't know my name.

I had small girl-crushes growing up. Like the lifeguard at our swim club who nonchalantly swung her whistle cord back and forth around her finger like a Western gunslinger, aviator glasses perched on her head as she sat on top of the lifeguard stand. Or my day camp counselor, Dawn, who wore blue eyeshadow and reminded me of Nancy McKeon. I remember thinking my fifth-grade teacher was cute in that eighties-yuppy kind of way, but when someone in my class secretly put a stink bomb in her trash can as a joke, she had a meltdown and became so frenzied that my crush faded.

Jo Polniaczek from *The Facts of Life* was a gateway drug. Every week, that show was my escape. I was convinced she and Blair Warner were in a secret relationship, which makes sense when you think about their circumstances. I think at one point in the show Jo had a boyfriend come visit and I was left confused—it didn't seem right to me. The other girls in my fourth-grade class had photos of Kirk Cameron and *21 Jump Street's* Johnny Depp taped in their desk cubbies. I had clippings of Nancy McKeon and Sigourney Weaver as Ripley in mine.

The other unattainable crush that sticks out is Helen Slater in *The Legend of Billie Jean*. Her platinum pixie hair, the one dangling earring, and the cut-up wet suit made into a shirt. The Pat Benatar anthem "Invincible" playing in the background wherever she went. I wanted to be her when I grew up. One of my closest friends, Hillary (not my cousin Hillary), and I would endlessly watch that movie together, and during the end credits we would run around the living room pretending to be Billie Jean Davy as we jumped over the furniture.

In real life, the experiences I had with girls were far subtler. There was one girl in high school who I got to know toward the end of senior year. The unspoken energy between us just felt a little bit different compared with anyone else. It was never brought up or acknowledged, so who knows if I'm right about this. Even if I was, my instincts knew that was not the time or place to do anything about it. I only had a few months of that chemistry with her, then she went off to college in who-knows-where, Pennsylvania.

Years later when I was living in New York, my friend Leslie would always say, "Chemistry is a two-way street. If you feel it, they feel it." From those few experiences I had, I knew something was going on. A few stolen glances, lingering maybe a little too long, the silence louder than what's spoken. It's the perplexing gray zone that can make a lot of gay people write themselves off as just being delusional. I spent four years at an all-girls Catholic high school—I couldn't be the only one.

When I dared acknowledge to myself that I might be gay, I weighed the pros and cons of my circumstances, and the cons far outweighed the pros. I knew I wasn't ready to live my authentic life in my hometown.

J was a grade above me and had left for New York University a year earlier. That became my get-out-of-jail-free card, which I played almost every weekend. J was staying in the NYU dorms, and we would do what we always did, share the bed. J took me around and introduced me to all his new friends. A bunch of eighteen-year-olds from all over the country, living on their own in New York. It was heaven. One of his new friends was openly bisexual, and no one batted an eye when she talked about her girlfriend back home.

If I could get up there on a Thursday evening, we would go to the gone-but-not-forgotten bar Don Hill's in the West Village. We were all underage but still managed to get in every time. After a while, the bouncer and DJ Frankie got to know us, and we were on a first-name basis. One Thursday, we somehow became friends with Parker Posey for the night. I wasn't even eighteen, yet here were Parker and her fabulous group of friends, inviting us to join them at their table without any judgment. She always reminded me of Lady Miss Kier from Deee-Lite. It could have been the carefree attitude mixed with the platform boots. In 1995, that bar felt like the epitome of the New York I sought out. This fantastic artistic, eccentric, amazing group of people were purely and unapologetically themselves.

Considering I had to be back in uniform on Monday morning, I was hesitant to celebrate my own individuality, but I basked in everyone else's. I figured one day, I would do the same for myself. I had only a few semesters left before graduation and had already been accepted to drama school in New York. My plan of escape was ready to go. Since my grades had always been an issue, to counter that, I became quite proficient at cheating. By that point, I think my high school and I had had enough of each other. I justified the cheating by telling myself I was doing us both a favor. By the end of senior year, I had a mental countdown leading up to graduation and it felt like time was crawling by. Four more months, one more month, ten more days . . . until I threw that unflattering hat in the air and I was free.

2

||||

Like Fish out of Water

LEISHA

I can't imagine how impossibly brave my mother must have been to deliver me to New York in the fall of 1989. Fueled in large part by the crack epidemic, the city was riddled with crime. A woman had been brutally raped while jogging in Central Park, three Black teenagers were beaten with bats by a mob of white youth, and the streets were teeming with petty thieves and robbers. AIDS had claimed the lives of nineteen thousand residents, by and large gay men. Somehow, my mom still got in the taxi and headed back to Bellevue after making my bed in my girls' dormitory and kissing me on the forehead.

The American Academy of Dramatic Arts is a small, two-year school without housing, so I lived with the dancers studying at Juilliard. Our house mother was a coarse Russian woman who cooked dinner every night while complaining about Gorbachev. To say I stuck out among the tall, toned, tight-ponytailed ballerinas is an understatement. Maybe that's why my housemate Debbie zeroed in on me. A student at Hunter College, she wore her hair slicked back and had a round, makeup-free face and masculine energy. We became friends. One night I felt safe enough to show her a photo of me and my ex, Shelly. "I know just where to take you," Debbie said and grinned, as if she'd won a bet with herself.

I tossed Kaydra's old driver's license in my wallet and followed Debbie onto a graffiti-covered subway. We emerged in the West Village. The buildings were older and smaller than around Lincoln Center. People were dressed funkier too. I had no idea what to expect as we crossed the threshold of the Cubbyhole into my very first lesbian bar. There was no shower of rainbow balloons, no drag king placing a crown on my head, no dream girl looking up coyly from her vodka cran at the end of the bar. There were only about eight women atop stools, chatting casually, but I felt a rush of excitement, nerves, and a touch of scandal. Dee, an ex-sailor in her fifties with more charm than Baltimore, served me a Rolling Rock and I retreated to a dark corner to soak it all in.

School, meanwhile, was everything I'd imagined. On the first day we had to stand up and introduce ourselves, say where we were from, and share one personal fact. When it was my turn, I clutched my stack of books about the Stanislavski method and said, "I'm Leisha. I'm from Nebraska, and I'm here to learn the craft." My ambition was to receive training on how to be a serious actor, the kind who starred in productions of Tennessee Williams and Eugene O'Neill. I expected everyone else to approach our studies with a similar level of earnestness, which is why I felt instant disdain for the girl who stood up and said, "Hey, I'm Heather. I'm from Lawnguyland, but I've been in Flahrida, and I want to see my name in lights." Eye roll. *Not my people*, I thought.

By day I would throw myself into vocal warmups and repetition exercises: Actor 1, "Your eyes are blue." Actor 2, "Your eyes are blue." Actor 1 (different delivery), "Your eyes are blue." Actor 2 (responding accordingly), "Your eyes are blue." But the minute the bell rang, I threw on my backpack, said goodbye to my school friends, and slunk downtown to the Cubbyhole. I was there several nights a week. I know this because I still have my pocket calendar from this era and many days are cryptically labeled with "CH" in marker. The legend-ary bouncer Liz would give me a friendly wink and wave me in. I'd show up at happy hour and wait for the thirty-year-old professionals to get off work and meet up with their friends. They'd look over at this kid pretending to be twenty-one and give me a sweet smile. It wasn't like I was cruising or trying to meet someone; it just felt good to be there. Like I was whole.

I don't know how I mustered up the courage, but eventually I sent a beer to a woman across the bar like I'd seen someone else do. The recipient of my romantic gesture and her whole posse came to sit with me. They were affectionately called bridge-and-tunnel dykes because they came from New Jersey. With their thick accents, big hearts, and bigger hair, they looked after me in a maternal way, their little stray pup. When we were at the bar together, they bought me drinks and shared their relationship dramas. I would listen in fascination. When I got the flu, one of them made me chicken soup and brought it to my dorm.

I didn't tell anybody about my solo excursions, not even the people becoming my closest friends at school . . . one of whom, shockingly, was Heather. She was growing on me, Ms. Long Island by way of Florida. Not that my burgeoning sexuality was much of a mystery. After seeing a girl in a Gap ad, I'd torn out the picture, brought it to Astor Place, and instructed the stylist to chop off all my hair. My jeans had slipped from my waist to my hips, and I was pair-ing them with grungy T-shirts. Sinead O'Connor was in constant rotation in my dorm room. I knew my classmates were speculating, but I wasn't ready to talk about it. I was, however, ready to hook up with a girl—any girl—as soon as humanly possible.

That's how I found myself in bed with a possible Mafia princess.

Gianna was also an acting student. Despite her blond hair and blue eyes, she was certified Italian. She'd been straight up until this point but homed in on me like a nonna on a cannoli. At school we'd play it cool, but on the weekends, Gianna and I would hit the Cubbyhole, which was wall-to-wall women holding hands and making out to Lisa Stansfield's "All Around the World." When we were hot and bothered, we'd head back to my new place—I'd ditched the dancers and moved in with Tom, an aspiring actor from a dairy farm in Wisconsin who, like me, was "out about being in the closet." Then, like generations of young lesbians before us, Gianna and I figured out sapphic sex.

I'm calling her Gianna for safety. Even at acting school she had a fake last name and I'm pretty sure it wasn't a stage name. She brought me on some wild adventures: We met her father at a casino in Atlantic City, and I got the feeling he ran the joint. Another time, Gianna told me to throw on a dress because we were being picked up after school. A black stretch limo pulled up, and when we climbed inside, there was her dad surrounded by his right-hand men. We drove to an Italian restaurant in New Jersey that had been shut down for her father and his entourage. It was like a scene out of *Goodfellas*, the wise guys none the wiser that Gianna and I were sneaking off to the bathroom to make out.

From dinner we went to a club, partied into the wee hours of the morning, then rode to a dark alley. We waited in the car as one of the henchmen knocked on a nondescript door. In true speakeasy style, a Dutch door slid open, revealing an eyehole. It slid closed and the door opened into a tiny, exclusive after-hours joint. As our drinks arrived a man sidled up to me, "Nice to meet you, where are you from, sweetheart?" He then kissed me on the cheek, and I got a whiff of his scent: Grey Flannel cologne with notes of Sunday gravy. It was only after he pulled away that I realized I'd been kissed by John Gotti.

Gianna and I had chemistry, but as I'd complain to Tom and

Heather, she wasn't serious enough about acting for me. "Uta Hagen isn't serious enough about acting for you," Heather quipped. Toward the end of freshman year, Gianna and I burned out and she didn't come back to school. It's a cliché that lesbians stay friends with their exes, but in this case, it was impossible because I think she literally went into the Witness Protection Program.

One of the most important aspects of that relationship was that it led me to come out to a few of my friends at acting school. Integrating my two lives felt right. I wanted to be all of me all of the time but knew once I was out of the closet, there was no going back in. Terrified, I took the leap and asked my mom to come visit. I knew she was accepting—two of her best friends were gay, after all—but I couldn't quiet the doubting voice, the one that made me fear rejection. The whole weekend went by, then ten minutes before she had to leave for the airport, "I have to tell you something," I blabbered. She waited patiently for me to continue. I couldn't and started sobbing.

"Honey, I'm not going to leave until you tell me what's going on . . . are you pregnant?" she asked.

No answer, just crying.

"Are you in a cult?" An excellent question, and not totally unreasonable. I shook my head no.

My mom ran down a list of everything that could be wrong. Finally, out of guesses, she was quiet. "Are you gay?" she asked softly.

"Yeah," I eked out.

"Oh, honey," she said visibly relaxing. "C'mere." I fell into her and she wrapped her arms around me. "I love everything about you."

Thanks to my stalling, my mom was about to miss her flight. We rushed downstairs, I hailed my mom a cab, and I loaded her suitcase into the trunk. "LaGuardia Airport," I instructed the driver. Then, before closing the door, with my immaturity on full display, I casually asked of my mother, "Hey, by the way, would you mind telling dad and Kaydra for me? Awesome, thanks."

My father couldn't have been more accepting, and Kaydra and I grew closer overnight . . . finally able to have the sister relationship I'd previously kept at arm's length. With the veil of secrecy lifted, I could now share all aspects of my life with my family. It was liberating.

By the end of my first year of school, I had a raging crush on Heather. When she played guitar, she was the brightest light, and everyone flew to her. *I gotta get me a guitar*, I thought.

Maybe I could entice Heather to hang out with me second year if I took up an instrument, I thought, so I spent the entire summer learning guitar. When I returned to school, I rented my very own studio apartment in the East Village. On Fifth and A, it was maybe two hundred square feet, with only enough room for a twin bed. There was a bathtub in the main living area that doubled as a kitchen counter when you threw a piece of plywood over it, and the "bathroom" was a closet with a toilet. It was perfect.

I'd invite Heather over to hang out and play music. Eventually, my master plan worked, and we started dating. Heather was the kindest, happiest person I'd ever met. Everything was more fun with her, but she wasn't ready to come out and I wasn't willing to go back in. We ended the affair but started a band. We called ourselves The Murmurs and feverishly wrote songs whenever we weren't in acting class.

One day, the light on my answering machine flashed, and I hit play. "Hey sweetie, it's Dad. Mom and I have something to tell you. Call us back when you're home from class." I lit a cigarette, dialed their number, and tried not to sound like I was smoking when my dad picked up. "Hey Dad, what's going on?" I asked cheerily. I heard him call to my mom to pick up the line. This was standard—it was rare I'd speak to one on the phone without the other. My parents broke the news that she had been diagnosed with multiple sclerosis. "What's that?" I asked, with the innocence of a child. They explained it is a degenerative disease that attacks the central nervous system. It can cause muscle weakness, problems with balance and coordination, cognitive issues—"So what do we do? How do we fix it?" I interrupted. There was silence. Then my mom, the nurse, cut in, "There is no cure, honey, but symptoms can go into remission."

I was crestfallen and confused when I hung up. I also was overcome with the feeling that my family had been robbed . . . like the most precious possession we had was being ripped from us. I was twenty years old, on the precipice of my adult life, looking forward to nothing more than getting to know my mother as her own, whole being. I wanted to eat goya champuru with her on the Japanese island where I was born, wave to her in the house seats while bowing on opening night of my Broadway debut, laugh at the inside jokes she'd form with my life partner. I was not ready or capable of accepting this information.

Dread began to pool in the pit of my stomach. That's when a new and ever-so-useful tool named denial—one I would come to use quite often—introduced itself. I kept putting one foot in front of the other, as I knew my mom would want me to. When Heather and I graduated from the academy, we and our British friend Nick got an apartment together. Heather and I played music constantly. Our writing was inspired by the musicians of the early 1970s but informed by our lives at the time in New York. With each phrase, each verse, we were finding our sound. We cobbled together a meager livelihood from odd jobs, including my gig as a coat-check girl at the lesbian club Crazy Nanny's. That job didn't last long, however, after I accidentally ruined an entire closet of black leather jackets. While the patrons were dancing and drinking, I'd sit in the coat closet and read *An Actor Prepares*, propping my feet up on a giant fire extinguisher. One night,

I put my feet up too fast and set off the fire extinguisher. The entire coat closet was sprayed white with foamy retardant. Everyone was pretty cool about it, except for these two women who came after me, screaming "You owe us money!" I obviously couldn't pay for one leather jacket, let alone two, so I quit just to avoid the shakedown.

One Christmas, walking through Penn Station, Heather and I saw a group of musicians playing violins with their cases open and piles of money pouring out. That's when we took up busking. We threw our guitars over our shoulders, found a subway platform that didn't already have a guy drumming on an upside-down paint tub, and played. People would stop and gather around us, tossing money in our case until their train pulled up. Then the next crowd would roll in and do the same. We'd roam between Times Square and Grand Central Station, playing for hours until the cops chased us away. It wasn't what I'd come to the city to do, but I couldn't imagine doing anything else.

We played anywhere we could, including a backyard party in Brooklyn, where a super-skinny white man with dreads seemed to really dig us. When we finished our set he approached, "Do you want to be recorded?" Uh, yeah. His name was Billy Basinski. In a beautiful domed loft in a converted Coca-Cola factory, he produced The Murmurs' first album. With our demo, we landed a gig in Manhattan at the Pyramid Club on Avenue A. It was electrifying . . . and contagious. We booked more bars and clubs around the East Village, often opening for the drag queens who were headlining. We became their paper dolls. They'd slather our faces in foundation and plop a beehive wig on our heads. We were still finding our signature style as we warmed up the crowd before Mistress Formika appeared on stage in all her glory. She was an unstoppable, undeniable example of out, proud, loud, and fabulous. Being embraced by the drag queen community pushed me to fully celebrate my queerness.

Years later I asked my mom how she found the strength to send her baby girl to New York City. She confided that she and her own mother had long talks about it, my mom saying, "I'm scared to let her go," and my grandma wisely countering, "Jane, if you don't let her go, it will be a lot worse." How right she was. There, on those streets, I had found a version of me that I truly loved.

KATE

Shortly after graduation, I rushed to join the summer pro-
gram at the academy in Manhattan. The same one Leisha started
out in, but just a few years later. I could tell my mom didn't like the
fact that I wanted to move out so quickly, but she kept those feelings
to herself. She knew that I wasn't going to abide by her timeline. I
had started packing my things weeks before and everything sat in
bags, waiting.

Once I began the summer program, I'd be lying if I said I was
as committed as Leisha at first. I was too busy getting high every
day and running around the city. J was going to start his second
year at NYU, and our plan was to be roommates and split the rent.
We moved into an apartment a block away from Penn Station on
Thirtieth and Ninth Avenue, above a fast-food chicken spot. That
studio apartment we shared felt like our kingdom. We picked up
right where we had left off, except now we were let loose into the
wilderness of New York.

At this point we were both eighteen, and we didn't stop to catch
our breath. We would wander around exploring different parts of
the city, vintage shop at Cheap Jacks on Broadway, go dancing at
Don Hill's and the Limelight. We bought weed from a grumpy,
monosyllabic guy named John who also went to NYU. He lived on
Broome Street in Chinatown in what I thought at the time was a
swanky loft. It was completely empty except for a few skateboards,
collapsible tables, chairs, and gaudy neon lighting everywhere. For a
period, J and I even DJ'd together. We borrowed this girl's equipment
under the agreement that she would come with us to make sure we
didn't break anything, and in return we'd all get paid in drugs.

My time wasn't spent wisely in those first few months, but I jus-

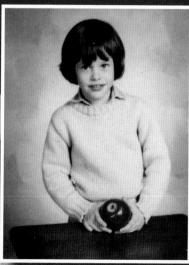

THE DOWNTOWN RESIDENT EDITION

Vol. 2, No. 3
April 9 - 23 1998
One Dollar

girls

meet the murmurs pg

GET FIT
pp. 10-12

A DAY IN DC
p. 8

Serving Battery Park, Chelsea, Lower East Side, Soho, Tribeca and the Village.

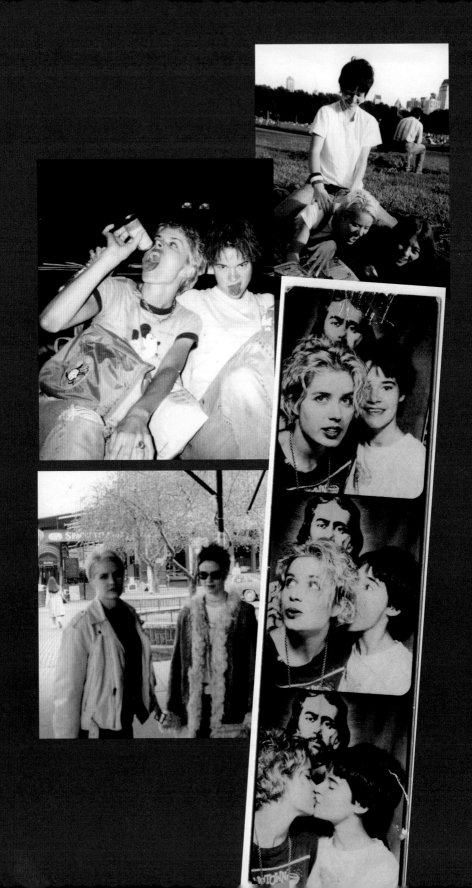

tified it by rationalizing that I'd rather fuck off now so I could be emotionally present for the official fall program. I just needed a minute to emotionally purge whatever was in my system. After that, I knew that I would be ready to wholeheartedly commit while not ever taking the opportunity for granted.

When the official school year started, it was refreshing to finally have a focus. I read as many plays as I could get my hands on, curious to learn the different acting techniques and discover which ones I preferred. The professors were godlike to everyone, and they each had their own approach. The renowned Jackie Bartone had one note throughout every scene study regardless of the characters' relationship: *"You want to fuck them!"* Within weeks, I met so many interesting and talented people from all over the world that I didn't really stop to think about anything else—and I didn't want to. School consumed me, though I somehow did manage to have an on/off boyfriend during my first year. A very talented guy who was a year above me, he had great hair and beautiful eyes and wore his sensitive feelings on his sleeve. I didn't mean to but I must have driven him crazy, always one foot in and one out. I made the mistake of telling him I loved him once while high on ecstasy. Later that same night, he started to perform a Jim Morrison poem for me in front of everyone. By that point my drug-induced feelings had faded, and the only solution was to pull an Irish exit with my friend Shari out of secondhand embarrassment. The relationship didn't last long.

You had to be invited back to attend a second year at the academy. By then the classes had gotten smaller, the work more concentrated, and we all took our craft very seriously. The workload became so intense that we would find ourselves easily spending twelve to fifteen hours a day at school, whether it was for rehearsals or research. It was a magical place to be a theater nerd.

Some assignments were tougher than others. Like when they

thought it was a good idea for me to play Anna Karenina. Even back then I knew I was terribly miscast. Another time, I played a grandmother riddled with dementia, and my friend Lauren played the distraught daughter. Somehow our performances went off without a hitch. Maybe I channeled all the prank phone calls from years earlier. Shortly after, I was more fittingly cast in the play *A Late Snow* by Jane Chambers, about five gay women trapped overnight in a cabin during a snowstorm. I played Pat, the self-destructive ex of the character Ellie, played by Lauren again. We went from geriatric relatives to ex-lovers in a span of weeks. The casting choices made at this school were entertaining and often bizarre.

Prior to me starting second year, J and I had our first growing-apart pains. We moved out of our lair on Thirtieth and Ninth to a loft on Horatio and Washington Streets, in the Meatpacking District, with a mutual friend of ours, Maya. Our duo had become a trio, and we needed more space. Aside from the diner Florent, the bar Hogs & Heifers, and some sex workers milling about, it really was just a meatpacking district. This was years before Pastis, Gucci, and Hermès moved in, which was why three students could afford it.

For practically thirteen years, J and I had been so enmeshed, so codependent, always planning on moving through life together. Suddenly we were both trying to find our footing as individuals. Initially, Maya moving in with us felt organic and familial. Yet somewhere in there, our dynamics began to fray. One night, pent-up frustrations came flooding out into an epic, soul-crushing, hours-long fight. It's hard to say exactly what it was about, but I remember feeling trapped by the expectations J and I had unknowingly established with each other. I wanted to be my own person and not be tied down. I wanted to be selfish and only be responsible for myself. I didn't want to smoke pot and watch TV anymore. Between the academy and Maya, who I found myself increasingly drawn to, the world was opening a little bit more and I didn't want to miss a second of it. I craved independence. The fight was a perfect shitstorm and absolutely devastating. J eventually moved out, and for the first time in a long time I was emotionally on my own. I have always considered that my first heartbreak.

In hindsight, our separation allowed us to become who we were supposed to be. I was able to spend more time with friends at the academy, socialize outside of school, and meet new people. And for the first time ever, I began to recognize that part of myself I'd pushed aside and kept hidden for so long.

After J moved out, it was just Maya and I in the loft. We had clicked from the moment we were introduced a year earlier. At night she would often crawl into my single bed, curl up, and spoon me as we slept. It felt natural and no one thought twice about it. Technically, she had a boyfriend, and I guess I sort of had one too, but I rarely if ever slept over at his place. I had, of course, a litany of reasons why I couldn't.

I'm sure it's not surprising that Maya was the first girl I ever kissed, aside from the incident in elementary school. I recall a few friends were over one afternoon, vodka or tequila was involved, and at some point, Maya and I had disappeared into the kitchen to get more ice or limes or something. One of us was opening or closing the refrigerator when suddenly, we were up against the wall. It was passionate and electrifying. The voices in the other room grew quiet as the moments clicked by, and somewhere inside of me a seal broke. We looked at each other, a little shocked yet exhilarated by what we had finally done. I now understood the feeling I had heard everyone talk about.

After that fateful day, the naive part of me figured we might be more than friends? We got along well, had inside jokes, loved and hated the same things, borrowed each other's clothes, had similar sensibilities, and made each other laugh. I thought we were a great match. The only problem was that Maya was straight—something she continually felt the need to reiterate to me after our encounter. She started to stay over at her boyfriend's place more often, not coming home for stretches of time. The days of roller-skating around our empty loft blasting Foxy Brown and Lil' Kim while sharing a joint were a thing of the past. We slowly drifted apart, and I missed her.

I was very good at internalizing any pain I felt, and there were bigger issues at hand. Like what I was going to do once school was over. The academy was only a two-year program, and for the first time, I had no plan. I'd achieved my goals up to that point. As if life weren't confusing enough, a few days after graduation, my father was diagnosed with cancer.

My aunt Blythe swooped in with excellent timing and suggested I spend the summer up in Williamstown, Massachusetts, at the Williamstown Theatre Festival. It's the theater camp of all theater camps. Sigourney Weaver, Richard Dreyfuss, Olympia Dukakis, Nathan Lane, Christopher Walken—the list of who has performed up there goes on and on. My mom was relieved I'd get out of the city. She had enough to deal with now and knew her nineteen-year-old child having no guidance in New York City in the summertime would not add up to good decisions.

As an apprentice at Williamstown, you basically do everything but act. I assisted the lighting department, helped with set design, was a stagehand, and acted as a dresser in the costume department for Becky Ann Baker and Bobby Cannavale. It was typical to pull all-nighters breaking down and building up full sets throughout the season. It was not uncommon to operate a forklift to move pylons or be sent alone to northern New Jersey four hours away in a run-down minivan to pick up equipment, with bad directions written down on the back of a napkin. Nobody cared about car insurance. I had the time of my life.

It was equally inspiring to be around the other young actors in the program who were just starting out as well. The bar was set high, with people like Kathryn Hahn, Sterling K. Brown, Charlie Day, and Jimmi Simpson—who is still a dear friend to this day. I've always considered Williamstown my graduate school because I learned more from that hands-on experience than I think I would have anywhere else.

I returned the following summer to Williamstown and was a part of the non-Equity company. This time I developed a slow-growing crush on a girl who was proudly bisexual. She was effortlessly captivating, self-possessed, and one of the sexiest people I'd ever encountered. She turned heads. We knew each other a bit from the season before but became better friends that summer, and I got the sense her boyfriend was possibly a bit threatened by our interactions. I would look at her and wonder, *Why him, out of everyone?*

A year later or so later we finally wound up sharing a night together in New York. It was like a dream come true, but I was so nervous after, I couldn't find the words to express myself. We lost touch for a while, and when, months later, I finally found the courage to say how much she meant to me, she already had a new boyfriend she was crazy about. It was too late.

After that first summer in Williamstown, I came back to New York and a new living situation. Maya had moved to Los Angeles, and we gave up the loft. With no place to go, I temporarily moved in with Lauren, who lived in a cute ground-floor railroad apartment in the West Village over on Bedford Street. The day I got back to the city, I walked in the door to Lauren, with her thick Manchester-English accent, excitedly announcing a casting director had just left a message for me.

"Kate, she wants to send you a movie script!"

"What? Why?"

"Because you nutta, she wants to meet you."

"Am I supposed to call her back?"

"Are you mad? Yes! Call her now or I'm doing it."

The company was Hopkins, Smith & Barden, which cast films like *Good Will Hunting* and *Shakespeare in Love*. They had heard about me through the lovely Matt McGrath, who I'd met through my family years earlier and became reacquainted with that summer. He was doing a play that I was working tech for—meaning I was pulling a large scrim back and forth at certain cues. Matt had been cast in this movie and suggested me for a part. I was left a little speechless and offered to pick up the script the following morning, but they wanted to messenger it to my apartment immediately. The movie was called *Take It Like a Man*. I was completely dumbfounded. Having only been back in New York for less than an hour, this was the last thing I was expecting. I asked the casting director what role I was reading for, and she gave me the character's name, Brandon. Who happened to be the lead. *Okay*, I said to myself, *stay in the moment and don't psych yourself out.*

Take It Like a Man later became *Boys Don't Cry*. The movie was based on a true story about a transgender boy's murder in Nebraska just a few years ago. The script was brilliant, and I couldn't believe I hadn't heard the story before. It haunted me for days.

I put on my vintage gingham button-down and loose jeans. I had medium-length hair at the time, so I threw it up in a sloppy man bun.

I walked into the office, and there were a couple people sitting there, including Lecy Goranson, who played Becky on the sitcom *Roseanne*. "What role are you reading for?" one of them asked me.

"The Brandon role."

"Oh my god."

"What?"

"Wow, congratulations. This is the final callback for the movie."

"Holy shit. This is my first time reading." I started to wonder what the hell was going on. Final callback? I didn't know how any of this worked. But I went in and that's where I first met Kimberly Peirce, the director, and Christine Vachon, who ran Killer Films, home of indies like *I Shot Andy Warhol*, *Safe*, and *Happiness*. I had been a fan of Killer Films and saw every movie they put out. I was a little starstruck to meet Christine, but she and Kim defused any intimidation by being so kind and grateful to meet me. I remember them thanking me profusely for coming in on such short notice, and all I could think was, *You're thanking me? I wouldn't miss this for the world*. We chatted for a long time before we even read the scenes. Looking back, I can now tell they just wanted to get to know me, since I came out of left field. I can't remember what we discussed. I was just trying to keep up and take everything as it came.

I liked Kim instantly. Her passion for this story was contagious, and I felt unprepared in comparison. I'd only received the script a couple days prior, and the extent of my experience was doing scene work, plays at school, and community theater. "I'd love to bring you back to test again for the rest of the company," Kim said. "Would you mind making yourself more masculine?"

That was a first. She suggested I wear my hair back, maybe a baseball cap, and looser-fitting clothes than what I had on. She wanted to see how passable I could be. *Should I show them my childhood photos?*

For the second audition a few days later, I put my hair up in a cap, rubbed a tiny bit of eyeliner on my fingertips to accentuate the hairs on my upper lip, and borrowed clothing from Lauren's boyfriend. After that final audition, I heard nothing for what seemed like ages. I didn't have a manager or agent, but since everyone I met over there was so nice, I was emboldened to call up the casting director myself to check in and thank them for the opportunity. She was apologetic and said they loved me but ultimately felt I was too young and possibly too green.

It was disappointing, but I understood. I was grateful for even getting that close, and for the biggest twist-of-fate opportunity in my life so far. It gave me a boost of self-confidence. The movie came out a year later and it was a masterpiece. I saw it opening night and the theater was sold out. I went with my friend Steven, who has a habit of talking during movies, but thankfully we couldn't find seats together. I just wanted to concentrate and see how Kim brought it all to life.

If you're thinking that *Boys Don't Cry* led me to some grand epiphany about my own queerness, well, it didn't. Told you, I bloomed late. I was still loosely dating guys, including one incredibly gorgeous model. One night, he took me to dinner at an underground sushi restaurant that only cool people knew of. "You should model," he said to me. "Do you want to come and meet my agent?" At that point, I had been back in New York for only a few months from Williamstown with nothing going on. Why not? He took me to his agency a few days later. I figured I would have to give them some song and dance, but instead they just took my picture against a pristine blank wall and assigned me a booking agent. It was like getting a flu shot.

LEISHA

The day I first laid eyes on Kimberly Jan Dickens is high-lighted in my calendar with a big heart drawn in thick green Sharpie. A friend of mine from the American Academy of Dramatic Arts, Katherine, worked at a Southern-themed restaurant called Cowgirl Hall of Fame. Located in the heart of the West Village, Cowgirl was the United Nations of homosexuals: Big groups of all different kinds of queers would gather to eat and drink with no inhibitions. A table of leather daddies would be seated next to a drum corps of women wearing WAC (Women's Action Coalition) T-shirts who were right by a group of self-identified "cross-dressers." Wednesday nights RuPaul would come in for the all-you-can-eat catfish fry. "Lei-sha, I'm working with the cutest gay girl," Katherine raved one day. "Come to one of my dinner shifts so you can check her out."

I two-stepped into my red cowboy boots, grabbed nine of my closest friends, and dragged them on my reconnaissance mission to see if this Kim was all Katherine had talked her up to be. Looking sharp and rolling deep, I arrived at Cowgirl, only to find that Kim wasn't working that night. Not wanting to waste a perfectly good outing, I went hog on a Frito pie, paid the check, then led my crew down the street to the Cubbyhole. Sipping my Amstel Light, I was convincing myself Kim and I weren't meant to be, when the door opened. In sidled a Marilyn Monroe look-alike in a beat-up white leather motorcycle jacket and lived-in Levis. Since everyone in New York wore black head to toe, this beautiful blond cut a ray of light through the sea of darkness. As I was picking my jaw up off the floor, I noticed her footwear . . . black cowboy boots. That's when Katherine turned to me, and over Madonna's "Vogue," whisper-yelled, "That's Kim!"

She and I chatted shyly. I was delighted by her Southern lilt and asked where she was from. "Huntsville, Alabama," she replied. "What brought you to New York?" "I'm an actress," she said. Kim had also graduated from the academy. As we continued to talk, I angled my ear unnecessarily close to her mouth, just to get my nose near her neck. She smelled so good. My friends cut in; it was time for us to head to a party. I wasn't ready to leave this gorgeous woman, so I asked if she wanted to come along. Miraculously, she did.

We moved around in a group that night like Scrubbing Bubbles, slipping and gliding from one hot spot to another, and ended up in her apartment. I left Kim a flyer for my band's next gig and was certain she'd come. When she didn't, I was disappointed. We didn't have cell phones so it's not like I could text her and find out why. We'd shared such a great night, but I figured she was lost in the wind. The universe thought otherwise. Just a few days later, I stopped by Ludlow Street Café . . . and there she was. Kim explained she'd been rehearsing a play the night of my show and was sorry she'd missed it. We talked and danced together; her moves were sexy in an understated, confident way. Then we walked the late-night streets of New York City. It was one of those nights you never want to end.

Kim was out and comfortable with herself. For the first time I could be open about my relationship anywhere and with everyone. It was so freeing. Our friend group was full of dancers, painters, actors, writers, performance artists, and musicians. Creativity reverberated between us like sound waves, bouncing and multiplying from a hum to a roar. We all had menial jobs that paid almost enough for our shares of the rent, beans, rice, and the occasional six-pack. Central Park was free, so we'd spend days there exploring, lounging, playing Frisbee. We'd religiously support each other's shows and whatever bands were playing in the East Village haunts, grumbling when there was a one-dollar cover. If we went out to eat it was a big deal.

Angelica's Kitchen had these macrobiotic bowls with brown rice, steamed veggies, and tempeh. Dojo's had a carrot ginger dressing that must have been laced because we'd have physical cravings for it. The cheese salad at Florent was so expensive it had to be split and was reserved for special occasions.

Transportation was the expense I was constantly trying to work around. Heather and I got roller skates and would clomp our way into Cowgirl at the start of Kim's shift to take advantage of her employee-discount lunch. Eventually, Heather upgraded to a peppy little scooter. We tore through the city on that thing in a truly irresponsible fashion, whizzing between cars and over interborough bridges. Sometimes I'd borrow it and, to Kim's chagrin, drive her to work going the wrong way up Hudson Avenue. A little older and a lot more responsible, Kim was inclined to obey the rules of the road since we were on a motorized vehicle. I didn't think they should apply to what felt like a toy. The playful dispute was made moot when Heather's scooter was stolen. In the rare instance we took a taxi, our ragtag gang of six would illegally squish and stuff ourselves into the back. Only then would someone think to ask, "Hey, does anyone have money?" We'd beg the driver to pull over and wait while we played ATM roulette to see whose balance could cover the fare.

Kim and I were a feedback loop of encouragement and action, invested equally in making our own and each other's dreams happen. I'd see every show her acting class put on and she was a devoted roadie, carrying equipment to and from my many gigs. When it was time to take headshots, I curled Kim's hair, did her makeup, and suggested poses on the roof while a neighbor with a camera snapped away. Kim didn't have representation, so she printed a hundred "mailers," postcard-sized composite headshots, and we spent hours addressing them to agents and managers, licking stamps, and walking them to the post office. Kim was the perfect lab assistant in the invention of myself. If I said it was time to change my look, she'd show up with a deli bag full of plastic barrettes, Manic Panic, and false eyelashes.

After two years of dating, we moved in together. Our building was across the street from the fabled Chelsea Hotel, home to legends like Patti Smith, Arthur Miller, and Sid Vicious and Nancy Spungen . . . until Sid stabbed Nancy. Next door was the McBurney Young Men's Christian Association, which is the exact one that inspired the Village People to write "YMCA." Our studio was puny so we had to make every inch count. Since we never used the oven, we hid Kim's tips in there . . . just in case anyone ever tried to rob us. When I got a job at Taylor's bakery next to Cowgirl Hall of Fame, Kim and I would walk to work together and stop at Dot's Closet, where colored corduroys from the seventies went for five dollars a pair. We collected the rainbow and took turns wearing them. A vintage Snoopy sweatshirt for a dollar? Yes, please. If Kim worked nights, she'd bring home a barbecued beef sandwich or honey-fried chicken plate that I'd eat at midnight. We were making it work.

There's a temptation to romanticize one's twenties, but this truly was a period of boundless freedom. There were no fences. As long as I paid my half of the rent and utilities, I could run as far as possible in any direction. My parents told me they were proud of me for being safe and self-reliant in the big, bad city. I beamed. Using all the skills I'd learned growing up, I had found a way to be responsible in my own scrappy, Technicolor way.

That is not to say there weren't challenges. With Kim's hair bleach blond and mine bright pink, we looked like strawberry shortcake walking down the street. "Disgusting dykes!" a man yelled and spat on the ground as we passed by holding hands. We could have let it affect us, disentangled our fingers, cowered and shrank. But we learned that the way to keep power in an exchange like that was to stand tall in the face of it. So, we kept walking and held hands a little tighter.

Three of Kim's closest friends, servers at Cowgirl, died of AIDS while she was working there—one was just twenty-seven years old. For those of us coming up on the tail end of the epidemic, and those who had lived through the crisis, there was a defiance in simply being queer. There was an in-your-face-ness to the movement. It was at once political and aesthetic. We were the opposite of mainstream but more than a subculture. We weren't seeking acceptance—gay marriage wasn't even on the agenda—we were fighting for survival. Take the chant, "We're here, we're queer, get used to it." There's no asking permission in those words—we were saying, "If you have a problem, that's on you because we're not going anywhere." I was emboldened by being part of a community with such vitality and rebelliousness.

The Murmurs were playing shows almost every night in and around the East Village. We had amassed a loyal following at venues like Sin-è, Brownies, and Max Fish. In 1993 we noticed some straight-looking white dudes in the audience. They were hard to miss in our typical crowd . . . and they kept coming back. Then they began introducing themselves as A&R guys, scouts from various record labels sent out to discover emerging bands. Heather and I had never played music with the intention of getting signed to a major label. I don't even think we knew what that meant. We just enjoyed writing songs and sharing them with like-minded people, yet we found ourselves in a bidding war between MCA and RCA. The labels wined and dined us, and we ultimately decided to go with Michael Rosenblatt at MCA because he had signed Madonna a decade before.

Heather and I got flown to Los Angeles (the first time visiting LA for both of us) to "meet the team." We walked the floor, shook hands with the president of the label, and were taken to Nozawa for sushi. I had no idea what I was eating, but I wasn't about to waste a single morsel. Then we were handed VIP tickets to Universal Studios and nearly lost our minds with excitement.

The Murmurs' debut self-titled album was released. Our song "You Suck" landed at number 89 on the Billboard charts, broke the Top 20 on alternative radio, and was number 1 in Norway. Our video was in constant rotation on MTV's alternative show *120 Minutes*. Heather and I trotted the globe, playing hundreds of shows and opening for bands like Bush and Adam Ant. Heather got to see her name in lights, and I got to see more of the world than I ever imagined.

When I was home in New York, Kim and I were strong as ever. Smoke show that she was, she'd tried her hand at modeling, booked a Calvin Klein runway during Fashion Week, and landed her first movie role in *Palookaville*, starring opposite Vincent Gallo.

One night, lying in bed and dreaming about our future, I made a declaration. I wanted three things in life: an awesome bike, to go to the clubs, and to get a pug. I was going to name her Tulip, she'd wear a hot-pink spiked leather collar, and we'd look really cool together. Kim was like, "Okay," and went and bought a book about pugs. After doing some proper research, she had follow-up questions. Would we be able to afford Tulip? Would a dog have enough room in our studio apartment? Most importantly, she asked, "Who will clean Tulip's clam bog when you're on tour and I'm on location?"

"Clam bog?" I questioned, already sure I didn't want to hear the answer.

"'Pugs collect feta-cheese-like stuff in their wrinkles,'" Kim read. "'If not swabbed daily, it can turn into a yeast infection.'"

We put the pug on hold, but I got the bike, a boys' vintage Kent in robin's-egg blue. She was a thing of beauty that I tweaked and customized: a black banana-boat seat, tape on the bars, streamers off the handles. With my bright pink hair, uniform of vinyl clothes, and eight-inch platform combat boots that I had specially made by a cobbler down the street, people would point as I zoomed by. Then I'd have to leave the bike, the girl, and the onlookers behind and go back on tour. It was a constant ping-ponging between life on the road and life at home.

In 1996, when I was in Manhattan, a woman named Alex Sichel approached me in a coffee shop. "Would you consider auditioning for a movie I wrote with my sister? You're exactly what I'm imagining this character to be." I told Kim what had happened, and she'd heard of the casting director who I was supposed to meet. The project sounded legit, so I tried out and got the role of Lucy in the indie lesbian feature *All Over Me*. Finally, I'd get a chance to put my acting education to use. At the same time, Kim booked a network sitcom pilot written by Michael Patrick King.

It's said that a goldfish grows to the size of its bowl. Ours was tiny, and I wanted us each to be able to swell to our maximum potential. Kim felt we could do it together. After all, there was nothing wrong with our relationship. But I was only twenty-four and a half years old, a goldfish who longed to hydroplane and breach like a dolphin. So, after five nurturing and expansive years, Kim and I returned each other to the wild.

Healing from heartbreak, it helped having a new job to throw myself into. I started production on *All Over Me*. Acting with Alison Folland, who played the lead, Claude, was a rush. Plus, I got to sneak my beloved bike into the film . . . she appears in the final scene while Claude and Lucy eat ice cream on a date. But the most inspiring thing about this experience was that the crew was disproportionately made up of gay women. Alex the director, Victoria the second assistant director (AD), Linda the second second AD, Andrea the head of props, Lori the producer's assistant, JoJo the stills photographer, and even Sam, a female grip! The script supervisor was Jamie Babbit, who would go on to direct *But I'm a Cheerleader* and so much more. My transpo girl, Lara, would pick me up and always knew to have Advil or American Spirits on hand (depending on what kind of night it had been). She remains one of my best friends. All of these badass women, in slouchy jeans with chunky belts, working together to make what would become a lesbian cult classic.

When the movie wrapped, Heather and I flew out to Los Angeles to record our second album in the famous Capitol Records building. We loved LA so much we moved across the country to live in sunny California.

The move changed everything. The Murmurs became LA's little gay band. We played all around town at clubs like the Viper Room, Silverlake Lounge, and the Troubadour. We released our next album, *Pristine Smut*, and I immersed myself in the lesbian scene, going to parties and all the playgrounds where the ladies congregated: Little Frida's, the Normandie Room, Milk Bar, Cherry, and the Abbey. It was like a Beach Boys song come to life.

On my twenty-fifth birthday, a mutual friend brought k.d. lang to my party at the Dresden Room. She was so striking and charismatic. We talked all night while the iconic lounge duo Marty and Elayne performed. Channeling my early Cubbyhole fearlessness, I got her number and called her the next day to ask her out. She said nobody had ever had the guts to do that, and yes. k.d. picked me up on her Harley and took me for a ride, and that's an understatement. We began seriously dating and moved in together within the year.

The Murmurs toured again, and this time the crowds knew our songs and sang along. We were invited to play Lilith Fair and shared the bill with our musical heroes. We found ourselves on tour buses hanging out with Chrissie Hynde, Bonnie Raitt, and Sheryl Crow, or stealing golf carts with members of Luscious Jackson—I'm talking to you, Schellenbach. It was a dream come true, to say the least.

In parallel, k.d. and I had a whirlwind five years together full of love and adventure. Eventually, her iconic, giant life and our ten-year age difference became more than the relationship could handle . . . "So It Shall Be."

Two years later, I found myself at that fortuitous barbecue, hearing about the pilot that would change everything.

I appreciated that the modeling routine gave me something to
do every day. My agent handed me a pocket calendar notebook with
CLICK MODELS printed on the front. Every day, I would run around
town for "go sees," model speak for general appointments to show
your book—a portfolio of work you've done—to clients. In the back
flap were six-by-nine postcards with your best photos, listing your
height, weight, and eye color. A real glimpse into the soul. There
were usually six to ten of these things a day all over the city, and I
got to know the subway system like the back of my hand. Then, at
the end of the day, I would call my booking agent from a pay phone
and get the list of appointments for the following day. On and on it
went. The meetings lasted less than five minutes with people who
barely looked up. Some just stuck their hand out for your book without saying anything, and then handed it back unimpressed. Waiting
for the appointments always took longer than the actual meetings.
The lobbies would be full of beautiful people smoking in the fire
escapes, waiting, and the appointment times were always delayed.
Instead of saying "nice to meet you" or "what's your name?" the
models would ask, "Can I see your book?" as an icebreaker.

My illustrious modeling career lasted about twenty minutes. My
timing was off by about four years—I didn't realize that the whole
ck one waif vibration had passed. When I showed up it was the
beginning of the "glamazon" era, led by Gisele Bündchen. The popular models of the day were leaning very tall, very feminine, and
could fill out gowns. Sometimes the client would ask me to put one
on and I looked like a five-year-old playing dress-up with Mom's
makeup.

As fate would have it, my agency shared the top-floor loft with a separate management company for actors. Amid my modeling and not doing very well at it, a TV pilot was being cast in LA. I guess they couldn't find the right actor to play one of the roles, so casting resorted to filing through a Rolodex of models. My booking agent knew I had just graduated from drama school and said, "You fit this, do you want to read for it?" Absolutely. He then tossed me over to Peg Donegan, who ran the management company, and she's been my manager ever since.

I went in to read for a WB pilot called *Young Americans*, a spin-off of *Dawson's Creek*. True to what was starting to be a theme, the character, Jacqueline "Jake" Pratt, was a girl posing as a boy who secretly enrolled in Rawley Academy for Boys, the preppiest of East Coast boarding schools, to get back at her negligent mother—a rather exhausting revenge tactic. I went in to read for it and the casting director looked at me, relieved, and said, "You should play this part." A few days later I was on a plane to LA so I could test for the studio and network. I was twenty-one when I got my first job and had to join SAG (before it held hands with AFTRA). One piece of advice my mom gave me was to drop the *O* in my last name and use Mennig, the proper phonetic spelling. "You're going to spend the rest of your life correcting people with that ugly mispronunciation if you don't," she warned. I flatly refused, and she has never been more right about anything.

The other main girl hired on *Young Americans* was the darling Kate Bosworth. On the surface, Kate and I were opposites. Although her character had her own set of problems—involving an incestuous relationship with her secret half brother—she was the all-American girl with straight blond hair, made to grace the cover of *Teen Vogue*. I had my dark hair cut short to play Jake so I could pass as a boy, by, ironically, the show's creator Steven Antin's good friend Sally Hershberger, who did it as a favor. The opening credits featured gorgeous close-ups of all the main characters—and a random medium shot of me, which they snagged from a scene we had filmed earlier.

A year after filming the pilot in Atlanta, we were given eight episodes to air during the summer months, and production took place in Baltimore. While my character, Jake, is going through all the trouble of masking her identity, she befriends and falls in love with Hamilton, played by Ian Somerhalder. During the pilot and throughout the series, Ian and I instantly bonded and became like brother and sister. When my mom met him, she exclaimed, "He's prettier than you!" She wasn't wrong. We were like long-lost siblings and got along so well that it made sense to become roommates in Baltimore. Our easy dynamic added to the chemistry of our characters' confusing romance, which involved Hamilton having a sexual identity crisis. Credit to Steven Antin for mixing Shakespeare with *Dead Poets Society* and getting it to air on the prime-time slot.

One early morning during rehearsal for the first scene of the day, another actor and I witnessed one of our costars violently throw himself down a flight of stairs. I assumed he was either still drunk or too hungover from the night before, I have no idea which. Maybe his goal was to get some sleep in a hospital bed instead of freezing outside like the rest of us. What I do know is that just minutes before, he whispered to us "watch this" like he was about to do everyone on set a favor. As we watched him hurl himself with abandon, we stood there stunned and speechless. The commitment to that level of physical harm was nothing short of heart stopping. Neither of us could believe what we were seeing, as he lay there motionless while everyone around us came frantically running from every direction to help. It was so believable I genuinely thought he had hit his head or damaged his spinal cord. After getting his wish and being whisked away in an ambulance, word got around that it wasn't an accident. It was clear he was now a marked liability and was required to have a guardian on set with him every day following. Maybe that contributed to the demise of our little show.

Young Americans was a short-lived summer event brought to you by Coca-Cola. After it finished airing, I naively thought other jobs would immediately follow. Instead, I went through a dry spell. Small, low-budget films that never saw the light of day helped pass the time. Blink-and-you-miss-me parts in larger ones. I joined some friends from the academy, and we put on plays in theaters that would have us. Mostly, I was dealing with lots of rejection. Through the disappointment, I developed a tendency to dissociate. It was the only way I knew how to keep going and not get discouraged. *Everything happens for a reason* is what I would say to myself on a loop. I even started to treat auditions like personal tests. As in, what can I try in the room that I haven't done before? I had nothing to lose at that point and used the opportunity to challenge myself, even if I failed miserably.

Around the same time, J reached out to me. We hadn't really spoken in almost three years, aside from wishing each other happy birthdays or him calling to ask about my dad, who at the time was going in and out of remission. I had heard through the grapevine that after J graduated NYU, he had moved back to Philly, which surprised me since we both were so adamant that we would never go back home. Now, J was calling to share some news. I heard the seriousness and slight panic in J's voice, which is always a terrifying way to start a conversation.

J wanted to let me know that she was in the early process of transitioning. She had never been clearer about anything in her life and she wanted me to be one of the first people to know. I was shocked that I wasn't shocked. It all made sense. A flash roll of memories we had together ran through my brain as we spoke. All the curiosity that our friends and even I had at times around her not dating but never coming out. The questions people would ask us about why we never dated. The Barbies, her obsession over Shannon Doherty and her Levi's, the collection of *Vogue* magazines, dressing me up and doing my makeup for photo shoots, the notepads she filled with sketches of women. There were so many details I had never questioned over our yearslong friendship that now suddenly made more sense than ever.

After all those years of knowing each other, I had never heard her speak with as much pride, confidence, or emotion as I did that night. We found ourselves talking for hours. She told me about the aha moment that made her realize who she really was. How she told her parents, who were surprised but supportive, and what she now had to do in her process to transition. We laughed about the random double dates we went on together as kids that always ended in disaster. We laughed about the girl who had a massive, multiyear crush on J when we were little. If only she could see her now. We laughed and cried over the memories, distance, and loss we both felt after we parted ways.

One thing J had in spades was courage. When she wanted something, she made it happen. She has always had the ability to show me that in life, you must create your own opportunity. That was what she was doing, creating the life she deserved, by being the person she really was. Through all the laughter and tears I finally remembered to ask, "What should I call you?"

"Jenna."

When writing this, I debated on how to use Jenna's pronouns while referencing the past. When I texted her and asked, she insisted I use *he*, since she had finally made peace with and found respect for that time in her life and has grown to love who she was then.

As destiny would have it, Jenna had been living in the shadows of herself and made a choice to change that. What she didn't know was that I too was hiding. Where she had courage, I had fear. I don't think my group of friends had any idea of the struggle going on inside of me. They weren't homophobic at all, but I didn't trust that they would understand, maybe because I didn't understand. We were in New York of all places, and we were each artists in some form or another, but I was too caught up in my own self-loathing to seek out support from those around me. So, I stayed quiet and ruminated.

I would have loved to go to lesbian bars, but without a coven of gay women to go with, I spent more time at gay boy clubs with my friend Steven, my darling movie talker. There were many nights he would drag me to an all-male club on Seventeenth Street called Splash. To this day, I have no idea why I was ever allowed in. Maybe it was my short hair from *Young Americans* that was taking forever to grow out. We would go on field trips to a go-go dancers' bar up on Forth-Fifth Street, with gorgeous sweaty men grinding on the bar tops. I felt like his nonbeard beard, even though he had long been out and proud. Porn always played on the TV in these bars, so while Steven was off mingling and when I got tired of people watching, I'd watch the TV to see if there was any plot to follow besides the fucking. Sometimes a cute girl would show up to one of these testosterone-fueled events with her gay boyfriends, and Steven would nudge my arm and raise his eyebrows as if to say, "She's your type, go talk to her." Though I never took his bait, ever so slowly, I was growing into myself.

I was wandering around the Lower East Side one night with my friend Brad when we found ourselves close to the renowned lesbian bar Meow Mix on Houston Street. For some reason I had the instinct to suggest we go in for a nightcap. I'd heard about it but imagined it as a mythical foreign land where all the cool girls lived. I don't know what I was expecting but as we sat at the bar, I found my intimidation fading away. The place looked normal, like the bars I would frequent. There was no halo around it or golden orbs floating over people's heads. It was much smaller than I had imagined, plus it was practically empty. This was the mecca that I'd heard so much about? Why hadn't I ever come here before?

I looked right next to me, and there, sitting at the bar, was Kimberly Peirce, the director of *Boys Don't Cry*, who I had met a few years earlier when I read for Brandon Teena. She was having a drink with a blond woman who I didn't recognize at first. There was a break in their conversation, so I said, "Hey, I don't know if you remember me . . ." I was ready to be completely brushed off, but the opposite happened. Kim instantly remembered me and was so gracious and lovely. "Of course I do, it's so great to see you! This is my friend Courtney." Courtney Love.

Kimberly asked what I had been up to. Which is usually code for "what are you working on?" I told her about *Young Americans* on The WB. "Oh my god, I love The WB, I love *Dawson's Creek*!" Courtney exclaimed. I was floored. I would never have taken the lead singer of Hole for a *Dawson's* girl.

I don't regret that it took me longer to find my footing in the gay world. Yeah, maybe I missed a moment or two, but I was operating at a pace that made sense to me at the time. As with my acting career, I was realizing that for every missed opportunity, there was another, equally special one that would find me when I was ready. Which is what happened a couple years later, when I got sent the script called *Earthlings*.

3

| | |

Lights, Camera, Action

LEISHA

Boarding my flight to Vancouver to shoot the *Earthlings* pilot, I took my seat next to a gorgeous woman. Naturally, I looked anywhere but at her, pretending to busy myself with the barf bag. Suddenly, Hot Girl was talking to me. "Hi! Are you going up to shoot the pilot?" I nervously met eyes with Erin Daniels. "Um, yeah, I got cast as Alice." She let rip that laugh that would forever be etched into my heart. "I'm the tennis player!" she enthused. For the next two and a half hours we talked and talked. Well, Erin talked. She does that. And I was grateful because I was too nervous to do anything other than listen. I heard all about her audition and how she'd gone out for Tina, then they brought her back for Dana, but the network wasn't sold on her in the role until she read for it in a miniskirt and ponytail. "Wow," I responded, before she launched into her next story: She had just broken up with her boyfriend and was thinking about moving, but then got this job and . . .

Swoon. *Keep talking*, I thought. This was my kinda girl.

I was dropped at the front door of the production office with one suitcase and two guitars. I figured there'd be plenty of downtime while filming, and I was committed to making good on my promise to Heather that this pilot wouldn't interfere with our band. Just as I was about to step into this strange, new world, I heard a husky "Hey." I turned. "We met at the audition." A giant smile overtook my face upon seeing Kate. "I'm so psyched you're doing this," she said. "Me too," I said, beaming. It felt like fate.

A production assistant led us inside and sent us down different hallways. I was handed a school binder filled with cast names, set locations, and call times for wardrobe fittings. I had never seen anything like it. It was all so official and more than a little intimidating. Then I was whisked away by Paul and Joanne, the department heads, for hair and makeup. They were already at work rotating through actors and brainstorming looks. They plopped me in a chair and flitted around my head. "Maybe we should make this asymmetrical," suggested Paul. He ran his fingers through the hair above my left ear. "Or we could add some pieces here." *Pieces?* I wondered. Little did I know how significant that innocent-sounding word would become in all the actors' lives.

I was sent back to the lobby and excitedly greeted by a Southern accent spilling out of a massive grin. "Hi, I'm Laurel!" she sang. "So nice to meet you." "Hi," I offered meekly. "This is Jennifer," she said and gestured to her right. As an eighties kid, I had cut an asymmetrical collar on multiple sweatshirts after seeing *Flashdance*. I'd never imagined a scenario in which I'd be meeting, let alone working with, Jennifer Beals. "Welcome to the show," she intonated, her big, warm eyes dispelling my nerves.

I felt a presence beside me and spun to see a dark-haired woman who, despite her small frame, exuded a big intensity. *This must be Jenny.* "I'm Mia," she purred. As we shook hands, it was as if we'd met before. There was a kinship, a familiarity. "Have you seen the sets yet?" I shook my head. "Follow me," she said bewitchingly.

The one movie I had done was independent, shot entirely on location and on a shoestring budget. It was the same for all the gay movies I'd watched in small art-house theaters . . . usually with only three other people in the seats. I assumed *Earthlings* would be the same. I'd wear mostly my own clothes to play Alice, as a skeleton crew with a single camera would steal shots on the bustling Vancouver sidewalks. A few bags of Cheetos and some peanut M&M's would constitute craft service and maybe Ilene would get some cool riot grrrl bands to lend us songs for the soundtrack. I couldn't have been more wrong.

Mia flung open the doors to the soundstage and I walked into West Hollywood. It was like they'd flown in a full residential street from Los Angeles. Immaculately detailed Craftsman houses surrounded a Mediterranean-style pool. "It's eight feet deep," a guy from set construction beamed proudly. It was then the illusion was broken and my ears were filled with the roar of saws and the pounding of hammers.

Mia led me down Bette and Tina's driveway, and we peered into Jenny's living room. I was in awe. Like Charlie Bucket, I surveyed my Wonka-like surroundings, unable to believe I'd drawn a golden ticket.

KATE

Our first night in Vancouver, the whole cast met in the hotel
lobby. The producers were taking us out to dinner at Cioppino's, a
chic Italian restaurant in Yaletown, and we thought it would be fun
to walk there together. Little did we know this foreshadowed the
next six years of our lives doing everything as a collective.

At the restaurant, we all were seated in a private dining room
at a long table. The meal was served family style, which suited the
energy we had started to form with one another right off the bat.
We each had smiles plastered across our faces. Jennifer sat at the
grown-up end of the table with Ilene and the producers. She not
only glowed but radiated authority, and it was clear that she was our
star. I had met Jennifer in the elevator of our hotel with her husband
earlier that day. Since we're both very shy, there was an awkward,
quiet moment as the floors dinged by. I finally said, "You're doing
the *Earthlings* pilot, right?" She said yes and we introduced ourselves.
In a future interview with *Vogue*, she said that as soon as I got out
and flashed them the peace sign, they turned to each other and said,
"Shane." She was so impressive that it took the rest of us a moment
to feel comfortable to call her and invite her out with us. We would
try to coax each other to do it. "I don't want to call her! You call
her." Erin, who is 180 degrees from her Dana character, finally said,
"Gimme the goddamn phone," and bravely invited Jennifer. After
that ice was broken, we synchronized and became a family.

Pam, who played Kit, is known to be a badass on camera but was
one of the kindest people I'd ever met. This icon of the seventies lived
on a horse ranch in Colorado because, as she said, "Girl, I left Hollywood years ago. I fly in, do my thing, I leave. That's how I survived this
whole time." Nothing anyone could ever do would make her blink.

Laurel was sitting at the other head of the table at Cioppino's, opposite Jennifer. She had a pink pashmina scarf draped around her neck. She'd just gotten married and had to cut her honeymoon short because she'd gotten this job. Laurel had a body of work prior to the show and she referenced her past projects with nicknames, like, "When I did *Two Girls* . . ." for *The Incredibly True Adventure of Two Girls in Love*. Or "During *Boogie* . . ." for *Boogie Nights*. At first, I wondered if that's what experienced actors do—abbreviate everything. Next to Laurel, and directly across from me, was Leisha. I remember thinking that I wanted to sit near Leisha and finally get to know her more. The energy she put out was happy, light, easygoing. Little did I know Leisha has another side to her. Under the mask of a Funshine Care Bear, she's a drillmaster.

Before I knew it, Leisha had zeroed in on me. "I want to know about you," she started, then proceeded to grill me about who I was, who I was dating, where I lived . . . I could barely answer one question before the next one was asked. It was rapid-fire: *Where are you from? And why is that? What are your parents' names? How old are they? Where are they from?* I felt like a turtle on its back, trying to flip over. It was like she was working double time in trying to see through me and into my soul. Leisha has this curious quality—she says she just loves the mysterious ones, which is great, unless it's directed at you. I thought I was pretty good at keeping people at bay, and it took time to earn my trust. Not Leisha. She cut through the skin and the muscle and the fat.

To her credit, when I told Leisha I had been dating a guy back home (I really was!), the look on her face was stunned confusion, but she did not interrogate me about it. It can be a little humiliating when older gays who have made it through their journey and have accepted who they are talk down to the young ones who haven't gotten there yet. Leisha could have been condescending, like, oh, we're gonna play that game? But she didn't, and that helped earn my trust.

Mia and I snuck out to smoke cigarettes during that first dinner. I found her intriguing, with her big, captivating eyes that quietly take in whatever room she walks into. She clearly didn't mind uncomfortable silences, and in fact I think she found them entertaining. I quickly learned that her brilliant sense of humor comes from observing people's smallest nuances. Not only that, but her level of intelligence felt a cut above mine. This job wasn't the only thing going on for her. In fact, she had just got back from some faraway land that she was researching for a book she was in the process of writing. Simply said, Mia was utterly fascinating.

Finally, there was Erin, who looked like Cindy Crawford and had the most perfectly broken-in pair of cowboy boots. She was the second person I met in the production office on that first day. As intimidated as I was by her, I found out she was equally scared of me and thought I was the cool girl from New York. Meanwhile we were two nerds who quickly bonded over nightcaps at the hotel bar since we both were night owls. Within hours, it felt like I had known her my whole life.

The Sutton Place is like a Hollywood dorm in Canada. The hotel is divided into two sections, the apartment side and the hotel side. The apartment side is where production people and actors stay long term. During the pilot shoot, there was another group of actors staying there as well, shooting a rival Showtime pilot called *The Ranch*, which was about a Nevada brothel. We would run into them at the hotel bar and lobby, and each cast knew only one would survive. Although all of us were friendly and got along, it did feel like *West Side Story*. Back in LA after we finished the pilot, Erin and I were crossing the street when a woman in a car at the stoplight rolled down her window, hung out of it, and yelled, "Hey, lesbians! It's me, the whore!" It was one of the girls from *The Ranch*. That felt like a good omen.

LEISHA

I was working out in the hotel gym, replaying the events of the previous night's amazing cast welcome dinner. *Yes*, I thought, *I really did meet the icon Pam Grier, and yes, she did regale us with stories from her* Foxy Brown *days.* She was so inviting and generous and leaned over to us younger actors to impart wisdom. I couldn't believe I had shared Sunday lasagna with such a stacked table of accomplished women.

Kate hopped on the treadmill next to me and snapped me out of my thoughts. Breaking the ice, she said, "I really like your shirt." Not only was I flattered that the cool girl with good style liked my T-shirt, but I was especially flattered because it was from my old band, Gush. Then she asked, "Do you want to go grab lunch?" "Anything to get off this machine," I replied. "I don't really exercise, I just thought this is what actors do." Who knew we would spend the next four weeks hanging out together . . . except for when Shane had a sex scene.

My first official task as Alice was to go for a wardrobe fitting. It was held in a large truck parked by our cast trailers. Without much conversation, the costumer handed me a pair of pants with a stampede of horses across the legs and declared, "These are great!" I walked the slacks back to my trailer with the enthusiasm of someone walking the plank of a pirate ship. Staring at myself in the full-length mirror, I panicked. Was I allowed to say no? I didn't know the rules, but I knew for certain that Alice was not a rodeo-riding cowgirl. I mustered all my courage and suggested to the costumer that we put the horses out to pasture.

It was only right that a full ensemble scene at The Planet would be the first one shot for the pilot. The cast had been hanging out during preproduction, forging friendships and familiarity, but I was still incredibly nervous. Alice's lines were about butts: to wax or not to wax, that was the question; how to promote bush confidence; and "squirting in a jar." The women on *Sex and the City* had conversations this explicit, but I'd never seen them between gay characters. In fact, I couldn't recall seeing any film or TV show with this many lesbian characters interacting, let alone exchanging dialogue so frank. As Rose called "Action," there was a feeling in the air that day, like we were deliberately and bravely stomping over a line. I let that thrill propel me into the scene. I rode the wave of defiance and let it influence my delivery. When I opened my mouth to speak Alice's words, they came out more "in your face" than I ever had been. I didn't even know that was in me until I had an excuse, a reason to try it out. Playing this character was showing me other sides of myself.

After shooting the group scene, Kate, Erin, and I weren't working again until the next week. So I took that opportunity to set up my Pro Tools rig. Rummaging through cords—music equipment splayed across the bed and snaking into the bathroom—I called Robin to tell her about the day's events. My new girlfriend and I had gotten pretty serious right before I'd booked the pilot, so we were figuring out the rituals of a long-distance relationship. Bored, Kate Kramer'ed into my room. I hung up with Robin and listened to Kate describe all the fun we could have outside. She can be very persuasive and, honestly, I was easily seduced. Adventures with new friends sounded way more fun than trying to fix the bridge on a song. So, I started playing hooky on my band stuff.

We had all kinds of escapades. One day we drove an hour and a half to a ski resort in Whistler, bought two double-scoop ice-cream cones, then got right back in the car and returned to Vancouver.

After these outings, Kate and Erin and I would run into Jennifer, Mia, and Laurel in the hotel lobby, weary from a fourteen-hour day.

"We're so tired," they'd sigh. "And we have a 5:00 a.m. call time tomorrow." We would listen with concern, then jump in the car and zip off to the trendy neighborhood Kitsilano to try on vintage clothes and skin creams.

On the days I did film, I was learning in real time the diplomatic protocol on set. It was like being in a foreign country with its own language, so I put on my observation hat and learned the lingo: "Back to one" meant we were starting the scene over and to return to my original position. "Last looks" prompted a flurry of activity from hair and makeup, meaning shooting was imminent, so make sure no hairs were out of place or unwanted sweat was beading on an upper lip. "Turning around" meant we'd finished shooting one actor's side of the conversation and had to reposition the lights and the camera to capture the other actor's side. I also learned by watching the more experienced actors that when the camera wasn't facing their side of the conversation—and therefore only the back of their head would be seen—they didn't give their all with every take, rather just enough to support the actor whose face was being shot. *Hot tip*, I thought. I couldn't let on that I was figuring all of this out in the moment, so through discreet trial and error I got to know how many takes you got for your coverage, what different lenses were picking up, and what kind of blocking helped or hindered camera moves. I was a human sponge taking it all in.

I also learned about the hierarchy of a call sheet and the importance of the number one. Each character is assigned a number, with one being the main lead or most prominent actor. This person sets the tone, priorities, and energy for the set. As our leader—and first actor daring enough to sign on to *Earthlings* and play a gay character—Jennifer commanded the set with strength and grace. The tone she established on the pilot let us know we were in the hands of someone who cared deeply about the project.

I was so excited when I read the scene between Jenny and Alice. I'd already picked Mia out of the crowd of actors as one to learn from. As she worked, she had this quiet confidence that took up just the right amount of space, and I would watch her from the sidelines. Mia's performance was subtle yet demanded your attention. Through the smallest movement or inflection, you could sense so much was going on for her character. I was really looking forward to our first one-on-one interaction. Jenny and Alice are guests at Bette and Tina's sperm-catching party. I'm wearing an oatmeal-colored pleather jacket that Kate described as being made of regurgitated wet dog food but is actually a coveted vintage Courrèges item. To this day I like to say to Kate, "Girls in halter tops tricked out with flames and low-rise flare pants shouldn't throw stones." But I digress . . . Jenny and Alice are sitting on the couch, Alice is all coy hair twirls and active listening, doing her best to flirt, when Karina swoops in with her alluring accent and hoity-toity literary references. It's immediately clear that Alice is outclassed, so she tries to save face as Jenny and Karina explore their budding attraction.

With her friends at The Planet, Alice is bold, even brassy. She's witty, smart, quick, a little neurotic, and loyal. I discovered a different side to her while shooting this scene with Jenny. Mia is a fascinating collaborator; acting opposite her is a fencing match, where you can't be caught off guard or she will strike. I was a little intimidated by Mia and therefore Alice was by Jenny. So, when Alice is flirting with this cute girl, I learned about her insecurity, the feeling that she's out of her league. She tries to appear confident, while melting on the inside. "I'll leave you two alone to get married," Alice says before ultimately skittering away. To nail the scene, I tapped into my inner teen, back when I would flirt with the pretty straight girl I was never going to get. I used all that flustered energy, and that's the exact moment I found my way to Alice.

KATE

Initially, my reps didn't really want me to take the *L Word*
job because the salary was so low—$15,000, to be precise. That's be-
fore taxes and commissions. I later learned Leisha also had the same
deal. The more credits you have, the more your quote goes up, the
more money you make. I had only one TV series credit to my name
at that point, and it never dawned on me to turn down the low offer
in confidence that they would come back with a little bit more. Still,
$15,000 was more than I ever had seen, so I figured that was good
enough. Little did I know that would come back to haunt us years
later. But I loved the character, and I had a funny feeling this was
going to be a special opportunity—there was nothing like it being
made. Of course, it was far from a sure thing that the show would
get picked up.

When I got to Canada to film the pilot, I was broke. I didn't even
have a credit card to put down for incidentals, just an ATM card with
maybe forty dollars on it. Per diems were the saving grace. Production would give each of us our precious manila envelopes filled
with cash at the beginning of each week. I survived on The Sutton's
chicken Caesar salads, which luckily came with additional carbs in
the form of pretzel rolls.

We shot the pilot from the end of June 2002 until mid-August.
Leisha, Erin, and I likened ourselves to the Greek chorus, and we became the comic foil to everyone else's straight man. Right away we
found that lived-in banter only close friends have with each other.

We were in a new city, on our own, we had a job, and we had
more days off than we could count. We devoted full days to making
customized iron-on T-shirts with ironic phrases and made-up words,
trying to sound punk. We thought we were onto something with

this endeavor, but we never wore any of them. However, we were very committed to our short-lived craft.

We had movie nights in our rooms. After watching *Election*, starring Reese Witherspoon, we constantly quoted that movie to each other, and it quickly became an inside joke. Our contracts required that we had rental cars, so we would drive around Vancouver with the windows down blasting The Cars' "My Best Friend's Girl."

I felt an instant loyalty to my new friends. One night, we had come back from having dinner with Erin when suddenly Leisha stopped dead in her tracks and said, "That's my ex-girlfriend, look down, look away." They hadn't seen each other in years, and Leisha had less than thirty seconds to fill us in. The woman in question, Kim, was filming another Showtime limited series called *Out of Order*. Erin and I were forbidden to talk to her, forbidden to like her, forbidden to look in her direction. We protested—she seemed so kind and friendly, not to mention gorgeous. However, being Leisha's loyal new friends, we diligently followed our marching orders—almost entirely. Days later, when I was in the elevator with Kim, and Leisha wasn't there, I admit I snuck in a hello.

When it came to understanding my character, I initially thought a lot about how to play "cool girl" without being a gagging cliché. Shane's origin was inspired by an amalgamation of every angsty and complicated guy that I grew up watching. Paul Newman in *Cool Hand Luke*, Steve McQueen in *Nevada Smith*, Dallas Winston from *The Outsiders*, Dylan McKay in *Beverly Hills 90210*. I realized the key to all those characters is that they didn't have to try, they just were. From there I worked backward and realized that all the walls Shane had up stemmed from the pain and hurt she had experienced and only blamed herself for. Slowly I began to see that there was more under the surface to this so-called monogamist lothario. Ilene wanted me to watch *Shampoo* starring Warren Beatty. She sent a copy over to the hotel along with a DVD player. After watching, I realized there was nothing monogamous about this character.

The first scene I ever filmed on *The L Word*, I'm standing next to Leisha at the counter in The Planet, the neighborhood coffee shop, which was the hub for all the characters to hang out. Later on, it also became a bar, dance club, live music venue, and even a funeral home, but during the pilot it was just serving coffee. I'm wearing a gray Western shirt with cutoff sleeves and a black leather wrist cuff that I had made myself. I was supposed to be half asleep in the scene, and the stage direction was to shoot back an espresso like I would a shot of whiskey. Only problem was, the espresso was scalding hot in the first take, so it shot out of my mouth, all over the bar and all over whoever was standing directly in front of me.

For the pilot, we didn't have Cynthia Summers as our costume designer yet and fashion was not a priority. Coming from New York, I had no idea if leather flame-throwing pants and a leather halter top, which were among the items offered to me, were Los Angeles lesbian staples. I had a pantsless scene at some point, and when I perused the rackful of underwear in the costume trailer, the least offensive ones had sewn-in spiderwebs on them. I generally tried to compromise, not wanting to be perceived as "difficult," while staying at least somewhat true to what I had in mind for the character. I ended up suggesting a white undershirt most of the time and gravitated to the few vintage Western shirts I saw on the rack. In that first fitting I realized that if Shane was more gender-fluid and less Coyote Ugly, the clothing could stay simple and not too distracting.

Another scene in the pilot required Shane taking off all her clothes and diving into Bette and Tina's swimming pool to hook up with a nameless woman, while Jenny peeps over the fence. I had agreed to do nudity, so I knew it was coming. I had been dreading the scene, but by the time we shot it, we were weeks into filming, and at that point the cast and producers were like family, so everything felt comfortable. It was, thankfully, a warm and sunny day. Rose Troche is known for being adorably nervous to shoot love scenes, and her awkwardness and my stripping down somehow canceled each other out. I thought, *If I don't make a thing of it, maybe no one else will.* One thing I learned is that the naked person on set winds up being the most powerful since no one else feels comfortable looking at you for very long, if at all. I think we maybe did the scene twice, since the resetting—drying hair, fixing makeup—would have been too time-consuming for additional takes. Rose shot it from a voyeuristic perspective through the gates of Jenny's house. The camera was so far away, I forgot it was even there. *Well,* I thought afterward, *that was painless.*

I knew going into this job that I was going to be making out with a lot of strangers. I probably shouldn't mention that one of the extras from the pilot gave me a cold sore as a wrap gift. Aside from that setback, the pilot brought me to an inevitable awakening. I was the youngest in the cast, and everyone seemed to see me as their little brother, the baby gay who would figure it all out one day. I admired how unapologetic everyone else seemed for who they were. This enclave of women were living their best, authentic lives on and off camera—a contrast with the heteronormative world I was used to. Stepping into that production felt like everything suddenly went into Technicolor and anything outside of it felt black and white. Throughout the pilot shoot the idea began to quietly percolate: Maybe there was space for me to be my authentic self too.

No one was pressuring anyone to be anything other than who they were at that moment. We weren't given a soapbox speech about how we were going to be representing the show and the gay community worldwide publicly. If anyone had, it would have sucked the joy and creativity out of the experience. Everyone's attitude was, let's just trust our instincts, have fun, and create something that's never been created before. Shane was a risk because of how far she was from typical. I saw her as something like a male character in a female body, although I did think that it was a little unbelievable when Shane, with her long hair and face full of makeup, gets mistaken for a guy during the first season at a gay club by the sleazy character Harry. Still, I eventually understood the writers were commenting on gender norms. From the very beginning, they were trusting the audience would get what they were doing without having to teach or preach, and it mostly worked.

When we wrapped the pilot, I think I developed a low-grade depression from coming off the high. It was a life-changing experience, and it felt unnatural for it to end so quickly. We couldn't imagine having this only be a one-off and never seeing each other again.

When I returned home, I realized I didn't want to be in New York anymore. I headed to LA, and Ilene graciously offered me her guesthouse. She was married, or as close to it as we could get in 2002, which was domestic partnership—and had twin girls—but told me I was welcome to stay as long as I'd like. It was very Shane of me to take her up on it and move in.

At some point I mentioned to Ilene that I needed a winter coat but didn't have the money for it. A few weeks later, when the show officially got picked up, the first thing Ilene said to me was, "I think you can go buy that winter coat."

I had no idea what was in store for us. I only knew I was one of the lucky ones who got to go for the ride.

LEISHA

About three months after we shot the pilot, Ilene threw a party at her house and invited the cast and crew. At the end of the night, a big cake was wheeled out from the kitchen. On the top, written in icing, it read CONGRATULATIONS! THE L WORD. Not only had we gotten picked up, but our show had a perfect new name. I couldn't wait to get back to Vancouver and spend every hour—every week—together, with this incredible group of women. Especially Kate. I already felt like we were two peas, one pod.

4

| | |

Lightning in a Bottle

KATE

It's hard to explain just how unbelievably special that first season felt. Maybe part of it was that we all felt like we were in on this secret that no one outside of our Canadian bubble knew about yet. I can't exaggerate the amount of joy we experienced together on set. I think it shows through in our characters' banter with each other, but even that only scratches the surface. When there was exposition, like when Alice had to explain on the van ride to Dinah Shore why it was called Dinah Shore—that it coincided with a famous golf tournament overrun by hot and bothered lesbians—it felt like we were really having those conversations with one another. I didn't even know why it was called Dinah Shore until then.

Prior to filming, I had no idea that Dinah was an original safe space. A place that a closeted teacher in the Midwest, for example, would go to so they could get their gay on for the weekend, then go home and not tell anyone. The only Dinah experience I'd had was when Erin and I were taken there by the network just before we began filming the first season, to get the word out about the show. Showtime set up a booth by the pool with *L Word* signage behind us and terrible eight-by-ten glossy promo shots from the pilot. No one seemed to care who we were or why we were there. We baked in the desert sun for hours and felt like nerds sitting on the bleachers at a school dance. Sometimes someone would come up and ask, "What's *The L Word*?" Eventually we looked at the person in charge of us and suggested we wrap things up. It was too soon.

When we began production for the first season, we had all begged Ilene and Rose to find a reason for us to sing the Indigo Girls' unofficial lesbian anthem "Closer to Fine." We ended up incorporating that into the Dinah Shore road trip scene and there couldn't have been a more fitting moment. By the fifth take Rose was probably questioning her life choices and the crew was ready to quit, but those satisfied smiles on our faces were real. We spent two days sitting in that van Alice drove to get all the coverage. Beyoncé's "Crazy in Love" had come out that summer, so we would blast that in the car in between takes to keep our energy up. The days we filmed at Dinah, we were at a hotel by the Vancouver airport in October. Everyone was freezing.

The most ridiculous storyline in that first season was probably the jail episode, when all of the characters got arrested. We knew it was a nod to grindhouse genres like *Caged Heat*, so we were in on the joke. Leisha, Erin, and I filmed a food-fight scene with the other inmates that turned into something out of *Animal House*, but it got cut. After Bette had sex with a wall, I'm sure it played like a hat on a hat.

In 2003, it was still considered a risk to play a gay character, so I have nothing but respect for all the boldface names who were brave enough to appear on *The L Word* during that first season, when no one had heard of the show. A few people turned the opportunity down for that reason.

When Ilene told me Shane was going to have an affair with a Hollywood socialite, and they landed on Rosanna Arquette to play Beverly Hills housewife Cherie Jaffe, I was elated. I was a fan of hers, since I grew up watching *Desperately Seeking Susan* and had seen *Pulp*

Fiction more than a dozen times. From the moment she showed up on set she couldn't have been more fun, kooky, and open to anything. It wasn't hard to have a crush on Rosanna and I was grateful that the script was written for Cherie to always make the first move. In the scene where I spin Cherie's chair around to look into her eyes, I copied what I did in my first audition.

Rosanna made everything look effortless. She was fearless, playing her role with abandon. She created a character that was pretty generalized on paper into something unpredictable and legendary. Maybe she saw the kid in me or what was about to happen with this show, but Rosanna quickly took me under her wing. One night we went out to dinner and got drunk on apple martinis. She wanted to know all about the show and how we all got cast, what I was planning to do after the season wrapped, and what I envisioned myself doing in my career. She gave me a copy of a documentary she directed called *Searching for Debra Winger* that I still have, about sexism, ageism, and what happens when expectation and authenticity collide for women in Hollywood. I never wanted Cherie Jaffe to leave. Whenever they'd sprinkle her back in—and they didn't do it often—I knew it would be some of the most enjoyable chaos I'd have at work.

That first season had a revolving door of remarkable guest stars. Lolita Davidovich is another one. She played Marina's wife, Francesca Wolff. In between takes she was effusive and would tell us all about her property in Santa Barbara—which she gave us an open invitation to visit—yet when action got called, she would launch into the scene without missing a beat. She was such a pro and didn't tolerate any bullshit from anyone who was trying to pull focus or make the day any more difficult than it had to be. When someone did, she promptly called them out on it in front of the entire set and it stopped everyone in their tracks.

Kelly Lynch, from *Road House*, *Drugstore Cowboy*, and a little-known gem *Three of Hearts,* played drag king Ivan Aycock. She cherished her character from the moment she arrived on set. We admired how seriously she took that role and committed to it. She never played for gimmicks and gave Ivan so much love and respect. Kelly was another mama bear. She was protective and doled out pearls of wisdom in the most unassuming way. I tried to soak it all up.

One of the most entertaining characters to come out of that first season was Tonya, played by the fearless Meredith McGeachie. On paper it read like an impossible role to pull off until we heard Meredith say the dialogue. Tonya was unapologetically opportunistic and over the top and—most terrifyingly—was probably inspired by someone one of the writers knew. To this day I can still spot a Tonya coming a mile away.

Through it all, I was absorbing not just how to play my character but all these new possibilities for how to be in the world. The show was one of the first places I saw lesbians depicted as more than two-dimensional caricatures. We're not all the same, and *The L Word* attempted to cover as many bases as it could within the world it was set in. It was refreshing to see adult women choosing to be childless, to be sex positive yet still deeply flawed, and to carry their own personal insecurities. Sex was meant to be fun and empowering, for the most part. How each character saw her own sexual identity reflected something unique yet universal. Ilene and the writers brought their gay life experiences to create this fantasy land with real-life stakes.

There were eyes watching the community inside the show, and there were characters inside the show explaining the community to other characters. It straddled the line between inside baseball and accessibility. I was learning so much of what it meant to be gay not only personally but also what it represented culturally and politically. Ilene, Rose, Leisha, Guinevere, Kim Peirce, Sandra (our first AD), and even our allies on the show who weren't part of the queer community—their support and nonchalance regarding anyone's identity and sexuality was refreshing to be around. Erin Daniels, a very heterosexual woman, always wished aloud that she was gay but said she just wasn't blessed with the gene. Jennifer, our matriarch, another straight, married woman, fully normalized Bette's queerness. She even said the challenge to playing Bette wasn't who she loved but the art research it took to understand her character's profession. Though Laurel too was married, she was open and unapologetic about having girlfriends in the past. Not one of these women ever blinked when it came to the gay content.

Ilene, her partner, and their twin girls were probably the first lesbian couple with kids I'd ever met. Like Bette and Tina, they were eloquent and smart, and their little family was just business as usual. Back in LA, they would invite us all over to their gorgeous house in the Hills—the one I'd crashed at for a little while after the pilot—with perfectly curated art on the walls and mid-century furniture. They served us farm-to-table feasts like Moroccan stew with homemade bread. It was an environment I had only seen in movies, and it seemed so idyllic and far away from my reality. Before that, I don't know what I thought a lesbian marriage would look like—I might not have ever even imagined it. Once again, my world was broken open.

We filmed the first season in the dark up in Canada, having the time of our lives but unaware of the buzz happening outside of our bubble. When Showtime started rolling out the press during that summer we started filming, nobody knew who we were or what an L word was. At one point during production that first year, our cast was invited to the Television Critics Association press tour, which is where they announce new and popular returning shows. Erin, Leisha, and I were not invited on stage, just Pam, Jennifer, Mia, and Laurel. They asked us to sit in the front row of the audience, and we looked at each other, wondering why we were even there. I think at some point near the end of the presentation, Ilene acknowledged us from the stage, and we stood up from our seats, turned around, and waved to the reporters sitting behind us like we were the runners-up.

Six months before the show even aired, our cast was invited to be part of *Vanity Fair*'s "Gay" issue with *Will & Grace*, *Queer Eye for the Straight Guy*, and *Queer as Folk*. They flew us down to LA from Canada, and we were whisked to Milk Studios in Culver City. When we walked into the shoot, no one knew who we were. We had no establishment yet, the odd thumbs sticking out of this well-known group. The shoot itself was a huge deal, and I felt like we hadn't earned our place yet. *Jennifer should be here,* I thought, *but what are the rest of us doing?* We were betting each other who would wind up stuck in the creased flap of the magazine, because it certainly wasn't going to be Carson Kressley or Sean Hayes.

In a room the size of an airplane hangar, there were racks and racks of gorgeous couture, every high-end designer you could think of. Ultimately, they put me in a black bikini with a very large, chunky, solid diamond necklace. A security guard followed five steps behind me everywhere I went. I couldn't understand why and thought I had done something wrong. I later found out they were Harry Winston diamonds. I was wearing a house in Beverly Hills around my neck.

When it comes to the cast of *The L Word*, it's a love story.
Plain and simple. Whether at base camp or someone's home, we
were always together. Pity the assistant directors who were tasked
with finding out where the hell we were. We'd be needed for touch-
ups and hear panicked voices squawking from the walkie-talkies—"I
swear I just saw them, but they disappeared!" Invariably, an exasperated AD would swing open a trailer door and find me, Erin, Kate,
Laurel, and Mia blasting Janet Jackson and learning the dance routine from the "If" video . . . led by Kate, by the way.

If we weren't camped out in someone's trailer, you could find a
slew of us in the craft service room. It was our real-life Planet, but
with every imaginable food item. Cozy and isolated from the rest
of the set, we could huddle in there two, four, or eight at a time,
gossiping away and stuffing our faces with veggies and hummus or
Mia's famous "snappies" (a single rice cracker with a dollop of tuna
and topped with a cheddar cheese cap.)

In service of bringing good energy to set, Jennifer and Mia decided we should paint the walls of the craft service room, which
were an unappetizing tan that wasn't feeding anyone's soul. I won't
name names, but someone decided it would be "really pretty" to
decorate the walls in an ombré pastel rainbow. Here was the vision:
starting at the ceiling, thick pale pink / purple stripes would fade
into beautiful baby blue / pee yellow at the floor. Who wouldn't
want to look at that while snacking? Kate and I quickly got roped
into helping because we'd been previously outed as handy. Between
buying the supplies, snapping precise chalk outlines, and the actual
painting, we labored for days. When we stood back to survey our
handiwork, it looked like a child's deranged nursery.

"A Wishing Tree!" someone exclaimed, in an attempt to salvage the project. "That's what it needs."

Mia rushed outside and returned dragging a giant dead branch. We helped her hoist it onto the main table. Under the glorified stick, she displayed some pens and paper scraps. Cast and crew was cheerily informed they could write down their secret desires and, by hanging them from the Wishing Tree, guarantee they would come true. Everyone appeared to appreciate our efforts, but as time went on, the truth about our "pretty design" found its way back to us. It became a long-running joke on set. Mostly, I felt bad for the lovely craft service woman who spent so much of her time in there. No doubt she was annoyed by the actively decaying tree taking up five feet of prime table space she would have preferred to use for one of her trademark charcuteries. Several months after our redecorating, we found a note hanging on the Wishing Tree that read, "I wish this Wishing Tree would go away."

When we weren't helping out the Neighborhood Beautification Committee, Kate would perch precariously on the back of my red and white 1971 Honda CB100 motorcycle, and we'd rip through the streets of Vancouver. We were dangerously close to looking like *Dumb and Dumber*, but fortunately, Kate was light enough that we never tipped over. One night, Erin summoned us to her apartment for a surprise. Erin is a classy lady, the refined one of the younger bunch. Whether it was her knowledge of the avant-garde Bauhaus movement or French literature, there was no predicting what rabbit she'd pull from a hat . . . but she could always be counted on to serve excellent wine. So, when she called, I hit the throttle, and we raced over. Erin welcomed us in and introduced us to her new baby grand piano. There, in the middle of her temporary living room, she had installed an elephant-sized instrument. With so much downtime, she figured she'd put her fingers to use. Kate and I burrowed into the couch and listened, enraptured, as Erin tickled both the ivories and our eardrums. While stealing the occasional drag off a cigarette from the ashtray she'd balanced on the piano's lid, Erin wowed us with Bach's Prelude in C Major. I couldn't help but feel like the crush Alice was developing on Dana was going to be super easy to play.

What was more challenging was inhabiting Alice in what we might now call a "situationship" with her on/off ex, Gabby. Played to villainous perfection by Guinevere Turner, the crushworthy femme from *Go Fish* (who was also a writer on *The L Word*), Gabby was a narcissist who was "breadcrumbing" Alice. "Cold in the streets, hot in the sheets," Alice said, rationalizing Gabby's erratic behavior. Today you can watch a thousand videos on TikTok about narcissistic personality disorder and educate yourself on how to escape a toxic relationship. Poor Alice had to figure out on her own that going "no contact" from Gabby was the only healthy option.

Then, there was Alice's bisexuality, which was introduced early on in season 1.

DANA: When are you going to make up your mind
    between dick and pussy?
ALICE: I'm looking for the same qualities in a man as I
    am in a woman.
DANA: Big tits!

The L Word serves as a time capsule for the early aughts, and this dialogue reflects the cultural attitude toward bisexuality. Neither the straight nor the gay community acknowledged a spectrum of attraction, leaving bi's ostracized by both. And if the nuances of sexuality were lost on society at that time, you'd better believe gender fared even worse.

Take, for example, when Alice dates "Lisa the Lesbian Man." This is one of the aspects of the show to have aged the least well, and those critiques are entirely valid. Throughout the series, my character was guilty of treating our transgender and nonbinary communities with utter disrespect. Though the writers and I were working with the best information we had at the time, there are scenes I can't watch today because they fill me with shame.

Lisa was based on a real person Guinevere knew, and the actor who played her, Devon Gummersal, had been in one of my favorite shows, *My So-Called Life*, so I was very excited to work with him. We talked about how Lisa was a person being true to herself and we were excited to tell the story together. After the drama with Gabby, Alice was looking for a simple man to rail her, and instead ends up with someone assigned male at birth who goes by Lisa. The friends mercilessly make fun of Lisa for acting like more of a lesbian than Alice. At Shane's yacht party, when Alice and Lisa have sex, Lisa tries to explain to Alice why she'd prefer to use a strap-on for penetration. "But you have a penis!" Alice exclaims, uncomprehending. Lisa wasn't confused about her identity, but this tight—and otherwise progressive—friend group was. Lisa was misunderstood and repeatedly thrown under the bus in service of "comedy." Yes, *The L Word* was one of the first to show a genderqueer person who wasn't a serial killer or promiscuous, and I loved that my character had a relationship with her, but I wish I could go back in time and do Lisa justice.

The L Word has had its fair share of criticism—much of it justified, starting with the fact that the very first shot of the pilot is of Tim, a straight man. Above all, though, we strove—and I think succeeded—in propelling the conversation about our community forward. The first season showed the real lives of lesbians as, for lack of a better word, "normal." We weren't on a soapbox or being killed off (yet). We got coffee with our friends and were obsessed with dating, sex, and love, like every other *Homo sapiens* our age. Our characters brought the kinds of conversations we had in real life to a mainstream audience for the first time. And not in an earnest After School Special way. We gave straight people a window into same-sex relationships, and lesbians an opportunity to see their lives reflected back at them.

Take, for example, the Chart. It's a fact of lesbian life that dating is like fishing in a catch-and-release pond: You can only cast your rod so many times before you pull in someone else's haul. The Chart came from a real diagram drawn in the writers' room to illustrate the trope that all lesbians in a certain geographical area have—or probably will—sleep together. Rumor has it I appeared on the original version—thankfully, I wasn't a "hub" like Shane. As Alice poetically explained, the Chart "connected us through love and loneliness." Alice bragged that she could link any two lesbians in six steps, and so began my character's journey into creating Facebook— years before Mark Zuckerberg.

But the storyline wasn't originally Alice's. In the pilot, Kit's character was completely different. She wasn't related to Bette and was a lesbian. She was an edgy videographer and performance artist with a giant tattoo that stretched across her back and chronicled the lives, relationships, and one-night stands of the community. Like the incomparable Catherine Opie, Kit used her skin as the canvas to tell a story and make a statement. Apparently, after reviewing the pilot, the network felt like Kit was too much of an outsider to the core group, so Pam's role was changed to be Bette's half sister, and Alice got the Chart. It's probably better that Kit was spared having to get ink every time there was a new hook-up.

One of my best friends, Ali Adler, recently texted me to say she'd found the original chart in her desk drawer. She sent me a picture of a small piece of paper with six names and lines connecting them. She claims it's the OG . . . but is it? When I showed Ali's chart to another close friend, she was irate. She vehemently insisted that the actual original was called the Booty Chart and hastily scrawled on a Swinger's Diner napkin when two previously unlinked lesbians had shown up to brunch together in an obvious "morning after" situation. That friend claims she herself had drawn it spontaneously to show her brunch date why it was fucked up that these two particular women were together because of how many connections already existed between them. So . . . who is right? Which is the original? As far as we know, the actual artifact could be locked away in a dusty government warehouse in a wooden crate next to evidence of alien life.

In addition to our core group, there were so many incredible guest stars that first season. Every week I would call Robin with stories about meeting Rosanna Arquette, Kelly Lynch, Holland Taylor, Jane Lynch, and Tammy Lynn Michaels (who was dating Melissa Etheridge, so the two of them, Erin, Kate, and I spent a whole weekend playing never have I ever. Bananas.). Perhaps the most unexpected guest star was the legend who played Slim Daddy, a hip-hop artist who samples Kit's early R&B hit. I arrived on location that morning to film the scene of the cast watching Kit's music video. Smack in the middle of our soundstage's parking lot was the tour bus of the Doggfather himself. I'd be lying if I said there wasn't smoke billowing out the windows. After finishing hair and makeup, we were escorted on set, where we would be filming with Snoop Dogg. We waited. And waited. And waited. Eventually, a production assistant named Brad rushed in looking sweaty and stressed. "He should be in momentarily," he panted. When Brad left, the news spread quickly. Apparently, Master P may have had beef with Snoop Dogg and came to our set to pay him a visit. Poor Canadian Brad had been enlisted to defuse a highly combustible situation between the crews of Master P and Snoop. And we thought lesbians had drama. When Snoop Dogg finally came to set, he could not have been more psyched to be there. "Hey, pretty ladies," he greeted us, then surveyed the scene. "I like this. I like this a lot." Then, together, we all dropped it like it's hot.

Every day on the first season of *The L Word* was a pot of honey. I couldn't believe I was a working actress on such a special show. On set and in front of the camera my confidence was growing with each scene. Looking to my heroes Carol Burnett and Tracey Ullman for inspiration, I could feel myself being more playful with the lines and taking risks with my body.

Each time the next script was released, I'd devour it front to back. We all would, the whole cast eager to see what would happen to each of the characters and what fun stuff the actors would get to do. It wasn't like it is on other shows, where actors will quickly riffle through a script until they get to their scene or count how many lines they have compared with other actors. We had a shared goal, a collective mission, and that was to do right by the characters we had the honor of playing. Ilene had a special hand in building our cast community. She would rent a house big enough to host dinner parties for all of us. No one was left out. We felt bonded and cared for, and each made efforts to pay that feeling forward. It's cheesy to say, but being there, being part of this, felt meant to be.

There were consequences to the all-encompassing nature of the experience, though. Halfway through filming, my bandmate, Heather, came to visit. We drove to a lake and were catching up, when she got serious. Heather explained that I had the show now and she needed to have her own thing, too. "Okay," I said, sympathetic to the situation I had put her in. "What do you want to do?" "This band is my whole world," she continued. "I can't put everything on pause for six months while you're filming." A pit formed in my stomach. "If you want to have your own thing," I reasoned, "how about you start a separate band? You can focus on that one while I'm here, and when I'm home we can be The Murmurs." Heather was silent. "I'll be home in three months," I lobbied her with. "Let's decide then." But Heather knew what she needed, and deep down I understood: The band was over. I was gutted. My worst fear, the reason I had initially turned down the role of Alice, had come true.

I didn't have much time to dwell, though. *The L Word* debuted on Showtime on January 18, 2004, and a million people tuned in to the premiere. This was just a couple weeks before the series finale of *Sex and the City* on HBO. The timing was kismet. Showtime had a pitch-perfect marketing department, and they utilized the hype to our advantage. Our slogan became "Same Sex, Different City." The response to the premiere was immediately overwhelming . . . we were sucked into the eye of the zeitgeist. When the show was mentioned on *The Simpsons* and *The Sopranos*, we knew people were paying attention. There was a rumor that *Saturday Night Live* wanted to do a sketch about it and had called production to take the temperature on how we would feel. We were so excited, we sat around and guessed who would play each of us. Kate wanted Jimmy Fallon to be Shane, I would have loved to see Cheri Oteri as Alice. Obviously, Maya Rudolph as Jenny, Tina Fey and Amy Poehler as Bette and Tina (but we wanted Tina to play Bette). I don't know who ultimately quashed the idea, but I would have given my left leg to see it.

KATE

When we wrapped filming season 1, Leisha and I had our cars in Vancouver, so we caravanned back to LA. We used walkie-talkies to chitchat with each other. I was heading back to an empty apartment that I had rented sight unseen. I called 1-800-Mattress somewhere near the Oregon-California border so I would have something to sleep on when I arrived. The premiere was just a few months away and everything felt like it was falling into place.

There was just one final issue. I had to find a way to talk to my parents about not only the sexual content of the show but more importantly, my own sexuality. I had dabbled enough by now to have a clear idea of who I was, but playing a lesbian and being a lesbian had been sort of separate in my mind. One was a job and the other was my life. I did my best not to think about the fact that the fearless, unapologetically sexual gay character I was playing on television was not only going to be seen by an audience of potentially millions but also by my friends and family. But I didn't want to hide it any longer. It was time for my self-imposed incubation period to end.

I was planning on spending the holidays with my parents back home. I dreaded my mom's curiosity, the incessant questions I knew were coming, but I also wanted to be open and have "the conversation." It didn't feel right if *The L Word* premiered and I didn't come fully clean to them. However, when I got home it was clear that my dad was very sick. He would retire to bed right after dinner, and I could tell he was exhausted from all the chemo and radiation treatments. I didn't want to put more on his plate. It wasn't really his opinion I was worried about anyway. By then, he had been battling cancer for so long that he didn't sweat the small stuff. Instead, I did what I had done for the past five years of our relationship: Buy a bunch of DVDs I thought he would enjoy while being on bedrest and lie with him, having movie marathons together.

On the other hand, my mom loves to stay up late into the night and catch up. It's always been our thing when I'd come to visit. We'd sit in the kitchen, she'd pour herself a glass of wine, light up a couple cigarettes, and want the gossip. My mom has always been incredibly smart with a wicked sense of humor. She's got the mouth of a sailor and she's not precious about anything. She's the kind of mom that my friends always enjoyed hanging out with because she could regale them with stories from Broadway. At the same time, she could also fully appreciate or empathize with what someone half her age was going through. She was one of the girls, in a sense.

It was on one of those nights, as we were sitting at the kitchen table drinking and smoking, that I dropped my breaking news. I genuinely thought my mom would be okay with it. I really did. I can't remember the whole conversation—I think I've probably repressed a lot of the scene. "You're just being influenced," I recall her saying. "It's just a phase."

"It's not a phase, actually," I insisted. "It's quite the opposite." That word felt disrespectful, and it stung. Like I had just decided this on whim. My mom and I are both very stubborn, and so we each dug in our heels.

My mom has always been a chronic worrier, and I know she was concerned that my life would now be harder. She wasn't being malicious, but the news threw her off more than I anticipated. I couldn't imagine why she would be surprised, considering everyone else I knew barely blinked when they found out. Which of course they soon did, since no one in my family can keep a secret. "Kid, I knew that when you were thirteen," my cousin Sean, who is the closest thing I have to a big brother, said. When my godmother, Auntie Jo, heard the news, she gave me everything I wanted to hear. "Congratulations," she said. "I love you so much. I'm so proud and excited for you, and nothing will change that." The support of the rest of my friends and family helped temper the waters, but they couldn't ease the pain from the conversation with my mom.

I was frustrated, disappointed. If she could just witness a day in the life of this welcoming and supportive community of people I had, she would understand that I felt protected, loved, and more importantly, accepted. Life didn't feel any harder; in fact, it felt brighter and bigger than it ever had. After that conversation, the conviction I had walked in with got replaced with more fear. What invisible ramifications were waiting for me due to this aspect of my identity? Was the price too high, and should I just do what I needed to make everyone else comfortable?

If my mom and I had had this conversation during a better time, when she wasn't distracted being my father's sole caretaker, I think the coming-out pill would have been easier to swallow. She was spinning a lot of plates at once, and was anxious and preoccupied, obsessively focused on my dad's health. Perhaps the fear and upheaval she was experiencing in losing her life partner became intertwined in this new change she felt I was foisting on her.

I blamed myself. I wished I had timed it all better. Why didn't I do this years earlier when things were calm and felt normal? Then again, did I actually know years earlier? Of course I did. I interrogated my own gay timeline, kicking myself for not having it all behind me already. Was this always going to be as hard as it was now? I thought of Jenna and how her parents reacted when she came out as trans. Or Leisha when she came out to her mom. I so desperately wanted my mom to be blasé about the whole thing. To congratulate me with a clink of her wineglass and make a witty comment about the future girlfriends she would have to endure as she took a drag of her cigarette. But she hadn't. I had ripped the Band-Aid off and it hurt more than I thought it would. I crawled into my shell a little bit. I needed time to get my bearings and understand what this identity, this otherness, meant to me. I could tell I was going to have to take time to come out in my own way publicly.

In February of 2004, about a month after the show premiered, my father passed away. He went from an emergency to the ICU quickly and never came home. Despite how long he'd been sick, his death felt very sudden. I didn't get the chance to say goodbye. A few months later, we put together a small memorial with the guys who worked at the violin shop and some immediate family. It was at a marina in Maryland where my dad kept his boat. He had a friend, Doug, out there, who was his unofficial surrogate son. Anytime my dad drove to Maryland to putter around on his boat, he would hang out with Doug, and they'd go sailing together. I had heard about Doug for years, but the memorial was the first time we met. Doug was chatting with everyone and asked my niece if she had a boyfriend. She said yeah. Then he looked at me and said, "Kate, do you have a partner?"

His tone didn't change when he asked, but his words spoke volumes. Although my dad didn't talk much or have many friends, if he spoke to anyone, it would have been Doug. Through Doug's question, I felt my dad's understanding, his acceptance of who I was, and it gave me some solace.

My father's death stopped everything in its tracks. I don't recall much about that season of my life. I didn't have the tools to process what I was experiencing, and once again there are gaps in my memory where I must have buried feelings and experiences, not knowing what else to do with them. My father, being a very self-effacing man, disdained anything ostentatious and was repelled by anyone who was considered a loudmouth or show-off. I can't help but think of how the timing of his death lined up with the premiere of *The L Word*. Part of me thinks that was his last little kick in the pants to say, let me knock you down a few pegs on the ladder, just so you don't get too ahead of yourself. And I respect him for it. Yet the other part of me thinks the timing's so unfortunate because my memories would be so different. But would they be better? I don't know.

The wave of excitement and celebration about *The L Word* finally being out turned to darkness and confusion. My world became very small, and I felt numb. Yet the press was only ramping up, their questions about my sexuality becoming more persistent and invasive. I had just turned twenty-six years old. I was grieving a loss I had never experienced before, was brand-new to LA, and there was no breathing room to figure things out.

It got to a point where I didn't want to talk to anyone, because I knew I'd be asked in a roundabout—or less roundabout—way if I was gay. Which I was still in the early stages of processing myself—I hadn't even had a real girlfriend at that point, so what the hell did I know? All I wanted was some quiet to understand what it all meant to me, not what it meant to anyone else. At one point a big magazine offered the cover if I came out to them, and I turned it down. What I didn't realize was that I was being accidentally outed by a few people I worked with in their own interviews. I know it wasn't on purpose, and it probably just slipped out in conversation. But it made me even more fearful and avoidant. Howard Stern asked if I would come on his show, and I was too scared to say yes.

In their defense, the smaller gay publications, like *Girlfriends* or *Curve*, were always supportive of *The L Word*. But when we premiered there wasn't really anything to talk about, outside of "So who are you and how many of you are gay?" and trying to understand where we all fell on the spectrum. They didn't even really know the characters yet. The show had impossible shoes to fill and goals to meet. I'm certain I frustrated and disappointed a lot of people. Gay press in general had tolerance up to a certain point back then, and it was obvious that they became impatient with me. It was the elephant in the room that only grew as time went on, the questions becoming more pointed, sometimes veering into passive aggression. Many thought I was closeted, that I was ashamed. The truth is, I wasn't any of those things. I was just living my life, trying to explore this part of myself privately, while facing intense pressure to put a label on it publicly. My friend Liz Feldman, who later went on to create *Dead to Me*, once shared a dream she had, where she told me, "Don't come out, just be out." It was some of the best advice I ever got, and it was the first time the coming-out process made sense. To me her words meant, take your time and live for yourself first and the rest will follow. So that's pretty much what I did. But even if that's what was best for me, it didn't always feel like enough to satisfy everyone else.

Everyone on the show did their best to protect each other when we needed it, and it was around this time that Leisha became my unofficial spokesperson. She would call and report back on questions she'd gotten about me from journalists: "So then they asked me. . . ." I never wanted her to be in that position. Maybe because she was already out, they figured she was the safest to speak with. I can only imagine how annoying it was to dance around a topic that had nothing to even do with her. She knew the strain I was under and the grief I was barely dealing with. Losing my dad was not on my bingo card for 2004, and that struggle became intertwined with the process of coming out and the overnight attention the show was getting. I didn't have the emotional bandwidth to deal with it all simultaneously, and rarely discussed my feelings. I suppose I envisioned myself as graceful and self-possessed, but I was essentially a kid navigating it all without a GPS.

Luckily, I found lifelines. I never had a mentor growing up, and that first season, I made up for lost time. Ilene, the cast, Rose—I had mentors in all different directions. One mama bear was Faye Katz, Showtime's in-house publicist. Faye was like my adoptive Jewish mother from New York. She looked out for me the moment our show was on her account. I never hired a publicist because I couldn't afford one. I got lucky having Faye in my corner. When we met, I felt like I was home. Faye treated me like a daughter, putting me in her pocket. She would accompany me to all the photo shoots and always ask "Do you like wearing that?" in her thick and unapologetic New York accent. Just to make sure I wasn't wearing something I was uncomfortable in. She simultaneously dealt with the public perception of Shane and protected me throughout those six years. Without ever putting it into words, she said, "I see you evolving into yourself and I won't let anyone disrupt that." Every phone call started with "Katie! It's Fayze!" She was five foot nothing, but her personality made her eight feet tall. Because of Faye I worked with the late, great Ingrid Sischy, who I adored, for *Interview* a few times, shot with photographer Bruce Weber, did photo shoots for *Vogue*, shot for *W* magazine with the artist Richard Prince, among others throughout the years. It felt validating that the show was being recognized in the mainstream press. We were hitting a cultural moment that we felt we'd finally earned our place in.

The show wasn't perfect. It could be outlandish, like Alice's intimate dinner date with a cardboard cutout, Shane's short-lived career as an underwear model, and Jenny calling someone a vagina wig for half a season. And melodramatic, with Tina's public table-flipping, Bette's emotional reactions to art, or Jenny's obsession with manatees. But we were unapologetic about what we were doing. Years later, a big-time A-list publicist said, "You should have hired me. I would've made you huge." "Well," I replied, "you never called, and I had Faye Katz."

Without Faye's guidance, I'm not sure how I would have survived the pressure. When the show came out, the press was trying to find the gay stereotype that fit each character. And when it came to Shane, the commonly used term was *butch*. I didn't think the character was butch, though. I didn't feel butch. I didn't look butch. I didn't think I was playing Shane butch. If the character was described as butch, I wouldn't have gotten the job. If Shane were described as butch, she probably wouldn't have made it on TV to begin with. Butch wasn't considered "TV sexy" back in those days. Even now, it's still hard to find butch characters.

But back in the first season, there wasn't much mainstream lesbian vocabulary beyond *butch* and *femme*, and butch seemed to be the easiest box to put Shane in. I wasn't well versed in representation and had just got my foot through the gay door, so I was not going to try to be a spokesperson for a community I was only beginning to feel a part of. Instead, I used the word *androgynous* to describe Shane because I had heard myself referred to that way my whole life. People would tilt their head to the side, like, "Huh, I've never thought of that before." Eventually it caught on.

It's hard to explain what it was like being in the new gay supergroup at a time when the pool was still so small. I'm not sure fans of the show even knew our real names for a while. When we got recognized, we would just hear "Alice! Shane!" If Erin was with us, people were particularly excited. "*Dana!!*" It felt like the connectivity and electricity we had together filming was fully emanating to the people watching. We weren't the Beatles by any means, but from the moment we aired, the fan base was passionate, engaged, and incredibly loyal.

The only time I felt close to being in a boy band was years into the show, when I was flown to Japan for a press junket. I was just excited to go to Tokyo with one of my closest friends, Kelly, since I was given a second ticket for the trip. I assumed I'd do an interview or two and be on my way. But when we arrived at the airport, I was greeted by a massive crowd of fans. Some were crying, others were holding banners in the air, screaming *"Shane!"* It reminded me of New Kids on the Block back in 1992. Kelly's eyes went wide, and she doubled over in laughter. I was in shock, having no idea the show had reached that far.

For me, 2004 was a year of life-changing milestones in every direction. That spring after *The L Word* premiered, three months after my father died, I fell in love for the first time. Ironically, she was a girl Leisha had wanted to set me up with a year earlier but who had been in another relationship at that time. I ended up meeting her by accident at a bar one night when my friend Brad and I were grabbing a drink with Sally Hershberger, the woman who had not only cut my hair five years earlier to play a Young American but was the person who the character of Shane was loosely based on.

The rumor floating around was that Sally resented the fact that a character was inspired by her, but she reached out to me one day and said, "Let's hang out, honey." I felt relieved that maybe she wasn't as offended as I had imagined. In LA, there's a certain group of older lesbians I've always called the Honey Gang, who have fabulous lives, clothes, with varying degrees of wealth and who seem to end every statement with "honey." My soon-to-be girlfriend, Sasha, knew everybody, including Sally, who she started chatting with once we arrived. Sasha gave off the air of a precocious and snobby trust-fund baby who didn't seem to care that she was wearing Havaiana flip-flops to the crowded, popular bar of the moment on La Brea Avenue. She barely glanced at us when we were introduced, but she, Sally, Brad, and I wound up at the same table having a drink together. She wasn't giving off any energy that she was interested in me, not that I was paying attention. In fact, most of the conversation turned into a heated CNN-style debate between her and Sally over something political that I can't remember. Brad and I sat quietly watching them, our heads moving left to right like spectators at a tennis match as they butted heads. I eventually grew tired and gave Brad a nudge so we could leave. As I was getting up, I suddenly felt a piece of paper slide under my arm. It said, "You should call this sometime," with her phone number underneath. It was smooth, but I was so out of touch that I had no idea what it meant. I learned that she wasn't a trust-fund kid after all when I saw that she drove a beat-up black 1985 Lincoln Town Car.

It got serious enough with Sasha that I finally introduced her to my mom, who was still in the throes of grief. I don't think she was ready to meet her daughter's new girlfriend. There was a lot of confusion, possibly resentment, maybe feelings of intrusion. She just wasn't ready to handle any more change, and perhaps I shouldn't have foisted that on her so soon.

Maybe I wasn't ready either. Being in a relationship at that time was probably not the best choice, but it was a source of comfort that presented itself and that I latched onto. Naturally, it went from zero to one hundred. It was that all-consuming, passionate, angsty kind of love. I was the most emotionally ungrounded I had ever been, and Sasha was twenty-one going on forty-five, but still twenty-one. There were numerous breakups and makeups. I recall her ex-girlfriend was in and out of the picture at one point.

I'd fly home on weekends from Canada, she'd come visit Vancouver a few times, and throughout this whirlwind romance there would be confessions of her cheating that would tear my heart in

Earthlings 2002

the L word

THE L WORD CALLSHEET

Earthlings Season 1 Productions Inc.
8275 Manitoba Street
Vancouver, B.C., V5X 4L8
TEL: 604 419 1300 / FAX: 604 419 1301

Executive Producer: Ilene Chaiken
Producer: Rose Lam
Line Producer: Kim Steer

Director: Clement Virgo   **P/U @ 0936**

Set cell: 604 723 9813
Set pager: 604 253 7596 #4259

EPISODE #105: "LIES, LIES, LIES"
Latest Shooting Schedule: WHITE - 28/05/03
Latest One-Liner: BLUE - 27/05/03
Latest Script: GREEN - 29/05/03

Nearest Hospital: VANCOUVER GENERAL
855 W. 12th Ave., Van. 604 875 4885

ATMOSPHERIC HAZE ON SET TODAY
Please See Safety Bulletin @ AD Office & FA/CS
SAFETY MEETING ON SET AT CALL

DATE: **Wed., June 4, 2003**
DAY: 4.5 of 8

CREW CALL: 1030
BLOCKING: 1030
SHOOTING CALL: 1100
LUNCH CALL: 1630

SUNRISE: 0510 SUNSET: 2112

WEATHER: SUNNY!
HI: 26° Lo: 12° POP: 0 % UV: 6.8

SCENE	SET DESCRIPTION	D/N	PGS	CAST	LOCATION
					8275 MANITOBA ST.
69	EXT. BETTE & TINA'S - BACKYARD	N2	5/8	1, 2, 6, 7, 8, 9	VANCOUVER, BC
	Party goes on with lies, lies, lies			11, 19	
				ATMOS A	
	SET CHANGE				
36	INT. THE PLANET	D2	2 3/8	1, 2, 5, 6, 7, 8, 11	
	Everyone congrats Bette & Tina; Lara brings Dana flower			ATMOS B	
	B CAMERA TO SPLINTER OFF:				
EP. #103-40	INT. COUNTRY CLUB-RESTAURANT	D	-	ATMOS C	
INSERT	Cell phone insert				
EP. #104-7	INT. CAC - BOARDROOM	MORN1	-	-	
INSERT	CU of plasma screen with hero photo				
					Please do not park in the neighbourhood! PLEASE PARK ONLY IN CREW PARK @ 8383 Manitoba St.
			TOTAL	3 0/8	

NO FORCED CALLS/MEAL PENALTIES WITHOUT PRODUCTION MANAGER APPROVAL

#	CAST	CHARACTER	SWF/H/TR	P/U	H/MU/WBE	ON SET	REPORT TO:
1	JENNIFER BEALS	BETTE	W	S/D	0912	1100	CIRCUS
2	LAUREL HOLLOMAN	TINA	W	S/D	0900	1100	CIRCUS
5	KARINA LOMBARD	KARINA	W	S/D	1100	1300	CIRCUS
6	KATE MOENNIG	SHANE	W	S/D	0930	1100	CIRCUS
7	ERIN DANIELS	DANA	W	S/D	0930	1100	CIRCUS
8	LEISHA HAILEY	ALICE	W	S/D	0900	1100	CIRCUS
9	PAM GRIER	KIT	W	S/D	0800	1100	CIRCUS
11	LAUREN LEE SMITH	LARA	W	S/D	0830	1100	CIRCUS
19	ANNE ARCHER	LENORE	SW	0730*	0800	1100	P/U @ HOTEL
3	MIA KIRSHNER	JENNY	TR	0900	@	HOME	COURTESY P/U

BACKGROUND PERFORMERS and STAND-INS			CALL	ON SET	REPORT TO:
STAND INS:	Suzanne (Brunette SI) Samantha (Blond SI)	Shiraine (Kit SI)	1030	1030	SET
		Rob (Male SI)	1030	1030	SET

BACKGROUND PERFORMERS:	TOTAL: 41			
ATMOS A (1):	"Jenny" Photo Double	0900	1100	CIRCUS
ATMOS B (39):	New Patrons X 35, Continuity Staff X 4	1130	1300	
ATMOS C (1):	"Alice" Hand Photo Double	F/A	F/A	

Production Manager	1st AD	2nd AD	Transport Coord.	Transport Captain	LM	ALM
Kim Steer	Alysse Leite-Rogers	Christine Derek	Gary Chibi	Doug McCord	Jamie Goehring	Rico Melnicki
604 729 0657 (C)	604 726 7019 (C)	604 328 2136 (C)	604 341 0088 (C)	604 313 1726 (C)	604 807 9010 (C)

Shane   # 109

SC.#38A1   1. $ U.S.
N.2   2. Bullet w/coke
           3. ring

Kit   # 111

SC.#22   * No personals

TINA + BETTE   #10B

SC.#16 pt. 1   1.A·TINA·Sunglasses
D.2   2.A·TINA·ring
    1.B·Bette·sunglasses 2.B·Bette·ring

ALICE   # 112

SC.# 8,9,10   1. pidk neclace
D.3 + } FLSBK
N.2 }

Shane   # 11

SC.# 16   1. ring
D.1   2. sunglasses

IVAN   # 113

SC.# 8+10   1. XX
N.1   2. Marlboro cig
        3. ring

Marina   # 109

SC. #46   1. perrier
N. 3   ☆ No personals

DANA   # 106

SC. #9   1. Wilson raquet
D. 1   P.P.

TINA   # 111

SC. #19 + 20   1. watch
D. 2   2. ring

ALICE   # 110

SC. #29   1. D.L. I.D.   5. sunglasses
             2. watch
D. 2   3. wallet
             4. cel. ph.

ALICE + DANA   # 10B

SC. #34 A   1. Blanket   No
N. 2   {turquoise:}   personals
              {set dec.}

JENNY   # 108

SC. #3   1. rings x 2
D. 1   2. Tim's ring on
                  string

VANITYFAIR

two. At one point I told Leisha I thought it was my karma for playing Shane.

Our relationship thrived off emotions, sex, and smoking. It was exhilaratingly exhausting with endless push and pull, high highs and low lows. I couldn't tell if life was imitating art or vice versa. Since Sasha had grown up in LA, she had a huge social circle. Through her I learned that practically every lesbian knew each other in one way or another, and because of that I made some amazing friends that I still have to this day. Early in our relationship, we had dinner with one of her best friends, the brilliant photographer Cass Bird, who I became very intimate with as soon as we met, as she methodically taught me the detailed mechanics of a strap-on over our sushi double date. Which then led us all on a group field trip to the Pleasure Chest on Santa Monica Boulevard after dinner to see the vast silicon exhibition for ourselves.

More than my relationship, the show increasingly provided me with much-needed security, joy, and, to an extent, an escape from my own reality. After *The L Word* was picked up for the second season, we felt like we were on a legit TV show that had staying power. There were obvious signs on set that we'd been bumped up a notch in the eyes of the network. The wardrobe budget suddenly tripled. Latching onto the show's momentum, the powers that be decided, "Let's make this fashionable!" The only person up until then who wore designer anything was Jennifer. For the first few months during the second season, our costume designer Cynthia Summers worked in tandem with stylist Ilaria Urbinati, who production had hired out of LA to shop and style us and then ship all the wardrobe to Vancouver. That strategy was short-lived when they realized it was cheaper and easier for Cynthia to just fly to LA herself with Uncle Showtime's credit card.

That began the most cherished, time-honored preseason tradition, where Cynthia would devote a shopping day to each of us individually. We would go around to all the fabulous stores in Beverly Hills that we couldn't afford ourselves and just point to all the things we wanted to wear, like Veruca Salt in *Charlie and the Chocolate Factory*. The only thing missing from those whirlwind shopping excursions was Roy Orbison playing over the whole montage. The clothes would then magically appear on our wardrobe racks.

Cynthia was Pinterest before Pinterest. She sketched these gorgeous character silhouettes herself and added a collage of photo clippings to create specific vision boards for each of us. It was always fun to see them at the beginning of every season because they would evolve each year. Shane's early inspo was seventies Mick Jagger, a lot of tight pants and half-buttoned shirts, which morphed into Hedi Slimane's Dior Homme. For Alice, it started as the girls from *Clueless*, with all their colors and pattern on pattern, then transitioned to Marni and Miu Miu. For Bette, there were the black-and-whites of Katharine Hepburn and women in power suits. Dana had movie stills from *Personal Best* and action shots of Billie Jean King and Martina Navratilova. Jenny went from ripped stockings, vintage pajama shirts, and a trash bag to Isabel Marant and Prada. It didn't matter that what these characters wore was totally unrealistic considering their (sometimes nonexistent) jobs; it was all part of the fantasy.

At the end of each season, we would "buy" our wardrobe back for 50–75 percent off. At least that's what we were told officially. What really happened was on the last day of every season, we would run into the costume department like rabid animals at the Barneys warehouse sale. Cynthia made up wildly reduced prices for the most expensive items, and we would be given the rest as wrap gifts. It felt like we won the lottery.

The show's success caught us all by surprise, and while having more recognition and fancier clothes was certainly enjoyable, it wasn't the main draw for us. Far more exciting was that being up in Vancouver was a pause on reality. We couldn't believe we got to keep doing it all, living this utopian life for six months at a time, away from everyday stresses. I likened it to prolonged vacation because it rarely felt like work. There were moments when it was impossible to think the good times were never going to end.

LEISHA

The New York Times did a think piece on **The L Word's** cultural relevance, and all my friends were calling me screaming, "Oh my god, you guys are in the paper!" They did a breakdown of lesbian stereotypes and how those visual identifiers were now the rage. Dust off your flannels, ladies, because lesbian fashion is going mainstream. The things people used to make fun of were being widely lauded as trendy. Alice was a style icon with her trucker hat and choppy hairdo. They even put a picture of Alice's 'do next to Meg Ryan's signature shag. The article talked about Shane and how her rocker look and hypersexual swagger made straight women swoon. I clutched my chain wallet, shocked. The unthinkable had happened: Lesbians were trendsetters.

That was the good part of the media hype. The not-so-good part was that every reporter asked me the same two questions: "What's it like being the only out lesbian on a lesbian show?" Immediately followed by the sly aside, "But you're not the only one, right? Kate is gay too. Come on, I'm right, aren't I?" My response was always, "I don't talk about other people's personal lives." I was badgered to out any other gay cast members I knew of, but especially my friend. Kate and I had become extremely close the previous year. We shared everything, including frank conversations about her sexuality. In our bubble, Kate was free, flourishing. I felt like I needed to be her protector. I respected that she wanted to maintain privacy and wasn't going to let someone pressure her into coming out before she was ready. The press was becoming pushy about it, as though they were aggravated no one gave them the answer they wanted, but Kate knew I would keep everything in the vault.

Like Kate, I was profoundly changed by the experience of shooting the first season of *The L Word*. As a kid, I had consumed the perpetual message that queer people were lesser than and didn't deserve human rights. It had taken years, as it often does in our community, to shake the self-hatred and to learn the basic skill of loving myself. Now, on this show, after so many years of dismantling the notion that I wasn't worthy of much, I had the chance to provide representation for someone else. With this role I could help make an impact and change archaic ideas the world had about us. It was the opportunity of a lifetime to help shape this new, more open-minded world.

There was an LA club called The Palms that screened *The L Word* on Sundays, and, for the first few episodes of season 1, Kate and I would go and stand in the back and watch as the show was projected on the wall. People were sitting on the floor, fixated, hanging on every word. When drama ensued, they would scream their inside thoughts at the top of their lungs. "Oh, fuck off, Tim!!" or "What is that eyeball on Marina's shirt!!??" Soon, viewing parties popped up everywhere, in both clubs and people's homes. Audiences would congregate to celebrate and complain. Once the show got too popular, we couldn't go to the screenings anymore. We both missed the early days where we got to witness everything.

Shane . . . Kate . . . Shane was fascinating to watch when she walked by a group of googly-eyed girls either in The Planet or when we were out roaming the streets of Vancouver together. Kate turned heads. By the end of season 1, it was evident how differently fans were reacting to Shane and Alice and, in turn, to us. Girls didn't feel like they could go up to Kate because Shane was so intimidating, brooding. On the flip side, Alice was everybody's bestie, so I was the one people approached—even if they just wanted to get closer to Kate. Alice seemed to invoke safety for fans, and they'd be strikingly comfortable opening up to me. It would take about forty seconds flat for a stranger to give me a graphic and encyclopedic rundown of their sex life.

Our popularity was skyrocketing by the end of the first season, but the new president of Showtime was unaware. He inherited the show, and we didn't know if he would renew it. We weren't *Friends* or the *90210* kids. We weren't invited to the Emmy Awards. The show was rarely acknowledged in that sphere. But even with no industry accolades, attention was growing, like a secret that people couldn't stop spilling. I'd walk into meetings and people would whisper out of the sides of their mouths, *"I love the show,"* as they passed by. It felt like *Fight Club.*

Apparently, some wonderful angel gave the Showtime CEO a copy of *New York* magazine's in-depth, thoughtful cover story titled, "Not Your Mother's Lesbians," which called our show a "wildly sexy . . . sapphic *Thirtysomething.*" *New York*'s lesbian writer, Kera Bolonik, was able to capture our cultural relevance, historical importance, and cultlike fan fervor. The time was now for a lesbian revolution. We got renewed.

When we went back to Vancouver to shoot season 2, it became clear that Kate, Erin, and I had transitioned from secondary characters to having bigger storylines. Our two-day workweeks became five-day—no more midweek road trips to Whistler for ice cream. In our expanded roles, Shane moved in with Jenny, then fell in love with Carmen. Alice and Dana had a steamy, sex-filled affair behind the back of Dana's manipulative, starfucking girlfriend, Tonya.

The L Word's increased popularity meant that the overall atmosphere on set was different in season 2 as well. Our line producer Rose Lam brought in a security company to teach us about the pitfalls of becoming famous. They told us to change our addresses and take our names off our mail and showed us how to protect our cell phones. But nothing could have really prepared us, not even the lovely rent-a-cop who warned, "Get ready. Your life is about to change."

5

|||

Land of Milk and Honeys

Kate

Filming *The L Word* in Vancouver six months out of the year was like living a second life. Someone on set eventually coined it "Gay Camp" because it was the Canadian gay Utopia. Everyone had their very distinct role in our chosen family tree. Jennifer was our protective matriarch who was always the adult in the room. The rest of us could have tears pouring down our faces while filming and she would usually be able to rise above it and stay focused with a straight face. Simultaneously, she was always curious to know what was funny and wanted to be let in on the joke, even when her maturity made her immune to our hysterics. Sometimes I'd walk into my trailer to a manila envelope sitting on the desk. Inside would be a gorgeous black-and-white photograph Jennifer had taken when we were on set. While the rest of us were laughing and eating our snappies, Jennifer always brought her camera and was quietly documenting our time together. Eventually she had so many photographs throughout our years together that she put out a book. The ones she personally gave to me, I still have framed.

Pam was the sage. Early on, we were in a van driving back from somewhere when she leaned over to me and whispered, "Start a pension now while you're young." I didn't even know what a pension was, but it was great advice. Pam, of course, was also a star, but to us she was the horse whisperer. She even brought a few with her to Canada and trained them on her days off. Production made a point of flying us to LA every season to shoot exteriors that we couldn't fake with the snowcapped Canadian mountaintops in the background. When we filmed at the Venice boardwalk in "L'Ennui" during the first season, no one there paid attention to what we were filming until Pam showed up. Suddenly, hundreds of people rushed from all directions trying to get her attention, wanting a photo or autograph. She would try to step away and barely get two feet before she was swarmed again. After having been together for a few months at that point, I forgot that the woman we all now saw as Auntie Pam was also an icon. Aside from the few overwhelmed PAs we had, there wasn't security, and since the crowds were growing around her, Pam took control of the situation herself. "Let us film this scene since we are on the clock and only have a little bit of light left, and when we are done, you and I can take photos, okay?" She handled it so graciously and in turn everyone respected her request.

Laurel was like a warm blanket. She could talk to anyone about anything and was endlessly supportive and encouraging. She always got excited when Tina was allowed to join the storyline debauchery, whether it was impulsively skinny-dipping with the rest of us in her own character's pool or dancing to the Jackson 5's "ABC" on a coffee table. By season 3, Laurel was a new mother, married and in domestic bliss. When she came to work, she would ask, "What'd y'all do this weekend? Oh my god, that sounds so fun!" I always sensed Laurel had a certain level of FOMO, and occasionally she got to join us for dinner and drinks. Inevitably she would always run into someone she once worked with. Any time I worked on something outside of the show during one of our hiatuses, without fail one of the other actors would ask me, "How's Laurel doing?"

Mia and Erin were our cool sisters. Mia was enormously talented at picking up on the subtlest things that would make us fall over in tears laughing. She astutely came up with the slogan "Bob's mumbles." Bob was our cinematographer, and until she said it, none of us had ever noticed that every time Bob walked onto set from his tech tent, he would be quietly mumbling to himself as he tinkered with the lights. We fondly called Mia "the spoon" because of her ability to stir the pot and instigate a little bit of trouble here and there. In the mornings, when Aaron, our PA who ran the base camp, would come to take our breakfast orders as we were in the makeup trailer getting ready, someone would say oatmeal, the other would say eggs or cereal. But when it got to Mia, she unveiled an elaborate order that involved tofu, salmon, kale, and miso soup. We immediately coined it "the fuck-you breakfast" since it was a pain in the ass to make. Unfortunately, Mia was onto something because word spread that it was delicious, and eventually more of us started ordering it. It got to the point where Aaron would just come up to us in the mornings and say, "The Fuck-You?" By then catering was used to it and even added "The Fuck-You" to the menu outside their food truck.

Erin was the in-house Fran Lebowitz, our personal queen of sardonic wit and cynicism. Everyone looks at Dana like she is this sweet little babe in the woods. But Erin is a sophisticated and confident wordsmith who had the fastest comebacks and always managed to drop her one-liners with a straight face. Early on, of course, Erin's costumes consisted almost entirely of athleisure. She wore Lululemon back when Lulu was just an average-looking store we'd walk by on Robson Street. We would all show up to set to film a group scene and Erin would look at what we all were wearing, then look down at what she was wearing and say, deadpan, "I look like the schmuck who can't find her dog."

One December we were in Blackpool, England, for a convention and we started chatting with one of the guys who worked at the hotel where we were staying. Earlier, he had noticed Leisha check in with her guitar and said he wanted to be a musician but the only music he could write was either very dark or horribly depressing and that he had a hard time creating anything upbeat or fun. When one of us asked him why that was, Erin, without missing a beat, dropped "Have you been outside?" For a period of time one season, it felt like Erin and Mia had an unspoken competition over who was the bigger Francophile. They both spoke over Leisha and me in French to each other every day, and neither of us could ever tell who was better at it.

Mia, Erin, Leisha, and I spent a lot of time at this bougie French restaurant in the neighborhood, indulging in our newfound job security. Erin had an appreciation for fine dining, and under her tutelage we were exposed to six-hour tasting menus and wine pairings. We'd go in for dinner at seven and be out by one in the morning. Or we would frequent the local oyster house called Rodney's in Yaletown. All the guys who worked there were incredibly friendly and looked like they were plucked out of magazines as they shucked oysters from behind the bar. It was obvious a lot of the clientele were there just to ogle or get their attention. Since Leisha and I didn't give out that kind of energy, we eventually got to know them all, and we each had a fake "boyfriend" who would slide us free drinks and dessert when we came in for dinner.

Our downtime together at night or on weekends was just an extension of what we were all doing on set during the week. All of our trailers were next to each other, and every single one of us had our dogs with us all the time—we had no other option but to bring them along. I had always wanted a dog growing up but wasn't allowed since my family lived in an apartment. A month after I moved to LA, Leisha and Erin took me to the Pasadena Humane shelter. As a cooing crowd gathered around a cage that held an adorable, picture-perfect puppy, Leisha grabbed my arm and pointed to a little guy in the next cage who immediately came over to us when I bent down to say hi. He was malnourished and all the fur around his neck was missing, presumably from being tied up. His soulful, smoky eyes looked relieved that someone was finally noticing him, and when he put his paw through the fence, trying to touch my hand, it was over. From that moment on, he never left my side for eighteen years. On his first night home, I didn't have the heart to move him as he slept directly on top of my face, blissfully snoring the entire night. His endearing lack of awareness reminded me of the stoner Floyd from *True Romance*, so that's what I named him.

Floyd went from the streets of Pasadena to being a pampered prince on a TV set. He had a cameo every year from season 2 to season 5. His debut was on the faux movie set in the season 2 episode "Lynch Pin," in which he gets fanned by a PA. Around the same time, Mia adopted a big, black, beautiful border collie she aptly named Rainbow. Leisha had her rescue mutts, Bandit and Hero, with her. Erin had her Boston terriers, Henry and Max. Laurel had Josie the corgi. Jennifer had her German shepherd and her Lab mix, and Sarah Shahi showed up with her terrier, Eddie. Our set base camp was like a dog run.

Everyone's trailer was its own little universe. Mine was the movie theater: I amassed a huge DVD collection, so if you felt like watching *Heat* or *Spaceballs*, you'd come on over to my place. Leisha's trailer was for arts and crafts, complete with a paint set and miniature canvases. Mia's trailer was the place where you'd burn incense, talk about deep things, and gossip. If you wanted your tarot read, you'd go over to Jennifer's.

We naturally found ways to stay entertained on set. We would put on wigs from the hair and makeup department and create characters if we were hanging outside base camp. Laurel did this drunk character all the time, where she would stick the back of her skirt into her Spanx like she had just come out of the bathroom and didn't know. Mia created a character that was a Russian sex therapist and would try to morph us into Gumby positions. Paul and Joanne, our hair and makeup heads, wouldn't be able to help themselves sometimes, and they would accessorize us to give these "characters" more flair. Eventually, their entire trailer-length mirror was filled with Polaroids of us posing with varying degrees of crazy.

The only people who probably weren't having as much fun in Vancouver were the ones who had to keep us focused on the task at hand. It was like wrangling cats. We were chatting so much between takes that sometimes we wouldn't even hear them call action. Sandra, our darling first AD, would come up to us on set, feeling guilty that she had to interrupt our personal party, to say, "Ladies, camera is rolling." Which of course, she had every right to do. It got to a point where breaking in group scenes became inevitable, and by then we would apologize to the director ahead of time, so they knew what they were getting into. Our camera operator Neil had probably dozed off a few times waiting for us to get through it. Eventually, our producer Rose Lam came onto set and said gently, "Girls, I know sometimes things can get really funny, but we are on the clock." Then she would leave, and we couldn't help but lose it all again.

To survive group scenes, especially at The Planet, I realized if I was reading something during the scene, I could avoid eye contact, toss my lines out, and possibly get one usable take that didn't get ruined with laughter. Inevitably one of us had a line of dialogue that would send us over the edge. It could be as simple as "hand me a napkin" but it would kill us. The combination of this chosen family and the environment we were in was like a comforting Band-Aid over the cuts from my real life. For the first time in six months, I found myself smiling again. Still, I wasn't out from the woods of grief, and the waves would hit me when I wasn't expecting it. In season 2, during our read-through for "L-Chaim," while Jennifer and Pam read their lines saying goodbye to their father, Melvin, played by the late, great Ossie Davis, I had to leave in the middle and started to have a panic attack in the production office bathroom. Mia came rushing in to check on me and put cold water on my face, holding me as I fell into her arms crying. Soon after, Leisha and Erin came in, then Jennifer, Pam, and Laurel. Suddenly this group of women enveloped me into a massive, loving hug that soon turned into laughter, since this poignant moment was happening inside a cramped bathroom.

LEISHA

Mia and I pulled a classic lesbian trope and "U-Hauled" our friendship by deciding we should live together while filming. We moved into a duplex in a quaint beach-lined neighborhood called Kitsilano, or Kits Beach, as the locals called it. Kate lived down the street in her own house and Erin lived next door. Our house was essentially a furnished short-term rental, but we painted the walls and fully redecorated it as though we'd bought the place. Mia wanted to cover the kitchen walls in plywood before cooler heads prevailed. I'm almost certain we didn't get our deposit back at the end of our lease.

Before moving in, the landlady gave me and Mia a tour of the house to explain where to take out the trash and how the appliances worked. She told us the dryer didn't have a lint screen because it went through a system in the walls. We thought it was a little strange but chalked it up to a Canadian laundry tradition. Our bedroom doors met in the corner of the hall on the second floor where the washer/dryer set did their work. One night, when I was fast asleep, my dog Bandit pawed at my head. I woke up to the smell of smoke and my bedroom aglow in orange. I screamed for Mia and we both opened our doors to find the entire dryer in a ball of fire, the flames climbing the walls and ceiling. Luckily, we got out just in time and no one was hurt. Side note for our readers, courtesy of the Vancouver Fire Department: Never go to bed or leave the house with the dryer running. It's a major fire hazard. That was a very scary event, and we felt lucky to have escaped unscathed. We owe it all to Bandit because she honestly saved our lives.

After the smoke cleared, we settled back in, and took it upon ourselves to start throwing dinner parties. Mia was always keen on having an eccentric theme anchor whatever food we'd be serving that night. One time, we had a robust Russian motif where everyone was told to wear white, and we served whole radishes with butter, salt, and eggs. We toasted with vodka while Tchaikovsky poured from the speakers. In this alternative "actresses on location" universe, I would find myself in conversations unlike any I'd had before. Karina Lombard, always so sophisticated, with her French Polynesian accent, would turn to me at the kitchen counter and say worldly things like, "Oh, you have to buy property in Big Sur or Paris." And I would think, "Oh cool, I'll keep that in mind," even though it wasn't long ago that I was making a living explaining the benefits of anti-glare polarized lenses.

People came to our duplex because we had fun stuff. Every year I would fill the bed of my pickup with the tools of my interests and hobbies: musical instruments and recording gear, brushes and canvases to indulge my inner painter, and at Mia's request, my sewing machine. (She liked me to make her custom curtains, and I happily accepted the challenge.) There were always projects and other works in progress.

According to Mia, I was one of them. She loved to play my personal stylist. "Come here for a second," she would say, while grabbing a long black ribbon, then wrapping it around my plain white T-shirt. She'd tighten it under my boobs and around my waist, then drape it across my left shoulder. "Amazing," she'd conclude. "Let's go to dinner." And off I went in my makeshift Met Gala getup into a public arena. I figured if she said it looked good, it must.

We were in our own little world and sometimes we lost track of how enclosed it was. One time a friend from Los Angeles came to visit. She'd written an episode and was expecting to watch it come to life. What she wasn't expecting was me and Mia, Erin and Kate, Laurel and Jennifer constantly scratching at our scalps and removing fistfuls of hair. Everywhere we went we left a Hansel and Gretel trail of the stuff:

on the sidewalk on the way to dinner, in the ashtray outside the Indian restaurant, next to the bowl of complimentary popcorn at the bar. Timidly, she finally asked if we had been checked for lice. I laughed and showed her the metal clip-on extensions we all wore. "They're pieces!" I exclaimed, "We all wear pieces!" I explained this sloughing off was natural and we'd be getting new hair supplements any day now.

Erin soon realized she had an aversion to the fully furnished offerings of her apartment and Kate's rent became too expensive. So Erin took Kate's place and Kate moved in with us. It was a game of musical houses that should have been set to "Flight of the Bumblebee." Thus, Kate, Mia, and I became roomies: our first platonic throuple. We'd work all day playing fictional friends, meet for dinner as real friends, then go home together. We would have the time of our lives one night and the next find ourselves in the throes of an emotionally charged, melodramatic argument that would put a sixteenth-century opera to shame. I'd be on the staircase, Mia in the kitchen, and Kate in a corner, all yelling at each other (about something ridiculous, I'm sure) like we were still on camera. It became impossible to tell whether it was life imitating art or vice versa.

Kate and I shared a paper-thin wall between our bedrooms and our emotional states began to bleed through. I was going through a vibrant period of self-discovery. My creative interests were expanding, and I was fortuitously in a place where I could explore them: I was playing different styles of music since I was solo now, painting regularly, and my acting career was on a whole new level. I thought my relationship should have been able to sustain and support this exciting personal growth, but it felt like my girlfriend, Robin, was losing interest in the parts of my life that were bringing me such joy. I did my best to stay connected, diligently checking in and remaining loyal and consistent. Eventually, the push and pull of balancing my life in Vancouver with our shared life in Los Angeles began tearing me up.

On the other side of the "wall," Kate was falling madly in love with Sasha. I thought the constant loud-sex noises from next door would drown out my muffled tears, but to my surprise I'd find Kate outside my bedroom the next morning offering to grab coffee and talk about it. We would stroll through our neighborhood and give each other the much-needed advice we both craved. She would ease my relationship anxiety, and I would give her sex advice (kidding—we all know she didn't need that). *The L Word* gang would make plans for the weekend and by Friday afternoon I'd sorrowfully bow out, again—"I can't make it. I need to go home." I felt a sense of obligation to the life I'd built with Robin and wasn't ready to let it go. But Kate would gently challenge me to stay and lean in to my new life, the one that made me feel playful and spontaneous and alive. She was becoming my rock.

Mia was largely engrossed in her own projects: she was writing *I Live Here*, a book about the lives of refugees, and she would travel to do research when she had time off. I was so impressed by what she was accomplishing. I had never met anyone who had her heart and passion for activism or who dedicated so much of her life to telling the stories of overlooked people from war-torn countries. Mia would return from Chechnya or Myanmar with piles of data and then place it around our home. Every available bit of counter or shelf space would be covered in transcripts of first-person accounts, photos, and videos. Pages lined the walls like we were at FBI headquarters and trying to find a serial killer. It became second nature to have to move aside a pile of graphic Polaroids to find the coffeepot. Mia's belongings probably took up 85 percent of that house. She had piles of shoes by the front door, and with her tiny little feet, it looked like we lived with a doll.

Kate and I eventually discovered this weird closet space off the living room that was free from Mia's piles. It felt like our own miniature clubhouse that we could hide in. Mia found us in there one morning, scanned the space, completely bewildered, and asked, "What is this adorable teensy room? Are you here all the time?" We just shrugged and mumbled, "Oh, it's nothin'." The next morning, we went into our secret fort to have coffee, and to our surprise, our sacred space had been infiltrated. Mia had colonized our lair. Her stuff was everywhere! And from then on, like kittens in a litter, we all three shared our morning rituals together in a small, uniquely decorated walk-in.

It was around this time that Mia bestowed her nickname on me and Kate: "Oh look," she said, "you're like a pair of pants—you can't have one leg without the other." And that was it: We were Pants.

KATE

While the majority of filming took place in Vancouver, we looked forward to the random adventures when an episode required us to briefly travel to another location. In season 2 we spent four or five glorious days at sea on Olivia Travel's actual, fully functioning cruise ship for "Land Ahoy." Although we all had different schedules on the boat, our cabins were lined up next to each other. When it was time to hang out, we would meander down the hallway knocking on each other's doors like a Bat-Signal. We all were assigned off-duty state troopers as bodyguards, who volunteered their time to be our security and would come with us anytime we left our cabins. One night Leisha, Sarah Shahi, my girlfriend, Sasha, and I went out dancing with ours and we all witnessed Sarah trying to teach Leisha how to dance with a sexy stink face. Leisha's assignment was to dance while looking like she smelled something terrible. She practiced with abandon—and for an entire hour—yet it turned out to be a lot harder than she thought.

Another time, when we ported in the Florida Keys, I had a two-hour break between scenes, so Sasha and I snuck off the ship with my bodyguard. The three of us rented bicycles, went swimming on a secluded beach, and had a margarita on the dock. They got me back to set with minutes to spare, and luckily no one noticed I was covered in salt water. The cruise also hosted a Halloween costume contest, which we ended up participating in. Erin, Leisha, and I dressed up as members of an eighties rock band, but we sadly didn't place. Mia brought her mom as her guest on the cruise, and she was a great sport throughout. She was even an extra in the scene where Jenny jumps into the pool in her cruise-collection couture Prada dress that turned into a life raft when it touched water.

Erin, from the moment she heard we were going on a cruise four months earlier, reminded everyone daily how she gets seasick. Somehow, though, we almost made it through the trip without incident. Almost. On the last night of the cruise, we hit a storm going into Mexico. We were in the middle of filming a fancy dinner scene in the onboard restaurant and the ship began pitching from bow to stern, back and forth. Erin was slowly turning green. She'd burst out her lines as quickly as possible, then run to the bathroom. They kept a trash can nearby.

When we arrived at our final destination, the news came out that George W. Bush had been reelected, and our fun-filled free holiday ended in a collective whimper. We were relieved to be returning to Canada, even though we only had visas to work there.

That season, production also flew some of us to LA to film scenes during the Pride parade for the episode "Loud and Proud." Alice and Shane were written to be with the Dykes on Bikes, which kicks off the yearly celebration. Leisha and I climbed onto the back of our respective Harley-Davidsons and held on to our personal dykes for dear life as they gunned down Santa Monica Boulevard. The roar of all their engines in unison was deafening. People cheered from the sidelines as this merry band of lesbians rode by. We looked at each other with tears in our eyes, both of us caught by surprise at how powerful it felt to celebrate that moment of pure and unapologetic acceptance. Jenny was written to be watching from the sidelines and her costume looked like Madonna from 1987. In between setups, we made Mia strut down the street as we sang "Papa Don't Preach." Some people around us caught on and joined in, so it quickly turned into an impromptu street performance. Between the show, living in LA, and being among this group of women, I felt like I had found my little spot in the world.

For Shane's wedding-to-be episode, the season 3 finale, production traveled the cast to Whistler, the most idyllic ski resort location, and put us all in first-class chalet hotel rooms. We were there for about a week, and on days off we went skiing and snowboarding and had drinks by the grand outdoor fireplaces. Everyone brought their girl-friends, boyfriends, husbands, whoever. It felt like a free holiday with some work sprinkled in.

Filming Shane's bachelorette scene at the lodge's restaurant, which involved practically every character, required a very long night of filming, but there was no place for cast holding. The only space they could find for us was the cramped administrative office down in the basement. Since it was a technical night, there was a lot of waiting and more waiting for setup changes and lighting tweaks. We started getting punchy around 1:00 a.m. Our cast chairs were shoved between rows of desks, filing cabinets filled with paperwork, and a copy machine. When our exhaustion and boredom took over, some of us thought it would be fun to pull down our pants, hop up on the photocopy machine, and xerox our bare asses. Which quickly led to xeroxing our bare everything and shoving them into all the files in all the filing cabinets and the unlocked desk drawers. Holland Taylor was with us that night and probably thought we were insane. I'm sure there are some very private artifacts buried there to this day.

When the season would wrap, there were some people who would go home, and we'd see them the following year. But I couldn't imagine not spending time with the girl who I now thought of as my best friend. Everything made sense with Leisha by my side. I can only liken it to a soulmate—when you know, you know. She felt like the missing link I had been unknowingly looking for. The whole cast were like sisters, but she felt like my twin, different but the same. She was a peer but also someone I looked at and thought of as a role model because of her openness, humor, and pride in who she was. Inadvertently, she was helping me grow into who I was just by being herself. I was starting to feel like the person I was meant to be with each passing day. We would bounce ideas and feelings off each other, and it always made me feel seen.

Thankfully, the feeling was mutual, and Leisha and I never stopped spending time together. We'd wrap the season and say, "All right, well, I'll call you tomorrow when I'm back in LA." There, our social circles had largely merged, and we would gravitate toward each other in group settings, sitting next to each other at dinners and hanging out together at parties. Other people at these gatherings would inevitably ask, "Haven't you seen enough of each other by now?" At one point, we each had these motorized scooters that we would zip around town on together to go vintage shopping. Even now, when we have that itch, we still call it "the shoppies." On lazier days we would zoom down the hill to get a midday coffee and cookie before Leisha had to meet Robin after work for an early-bird meal. Miraculously, a lot of the magic that was happening in Vancouver followed us home.

It really did feel like we brought a piece of Gay Camp back
with us. My friendship with Kate not only endured but deepened.
The rhythm of my life in Los Angeles, however, was very different
from Vancouver. Instead of being in a state of constant play—on set
and off—I was expected to do adult stuff. Nestled into a shady corner
at the base of a hill, Robin's house was a well-appointed haven. She'd
made a serene environment with comfortable furniture, natural materials, and soft lighting. I loved that home, and there were touches
of me throughout—a photograph here or throw pillow there—but
it was very much Robin's place. Returning to it each year after my
stint at Gay Camp was jarring, but we'd been together for years and I
thought that we would be forever. I tried to make it work because I'd
made a commitment and that's what I expected of myself.

I also expected that I would go on lots of auditions. In between
seasons was a great opportunity to land a guest spot on a different
series, ideally one that would show industry people and audience
members alike that I could play something other than a flighty lesbian. Naturally, I thought I'd hit the jackpot when I booked *CSI*. It
was the number 3 show at the time, averaging twenty-four million
viewers a week. I was to play Alison Bradford, a girl who was critical to the investigation since she'd witnessed a brutal murder but
was reluctant to come forward. Why was she shy about sharing her
story? Because she had a rare condition called hypertrichosis, more
commonly known as werewolf syndrome. *That's okay*, I thought,
imagining cute tufts of hair being glued to my chin or forehead.
I'll still be able to show I have range. Then I was in hair and makeup
for a lot longer than usual. When the stylist proudly spun my chair
for the big reveal, I was horrified to see my entire face covered with

hair. I looked like a life-sized Monchhichi but with human eyes and a mouth. So much for this being an opportunity to showcase my talents. I snuck away and called my agent. That's when I realized I could barely speak because all the hair adhesive around my mouth had hardened. Through frozen lips I mumbled, "Rmnd mmme why ths ws uh gd ideeea?" To his credit, my agent took full responsibility, then added, "Dustin Hoffman said that every actor should play a monster once in his career." *Well*, I thought, *box checked*. The only good thing about being wholly unrecognizable was that it allowed me to book *CSI* again a few years later. This time I was a party girl who, while having sex with her lover on a balcony, either accidentally or intentionally sends him plummeting to his death. It's a funny life being an actor, stepping into a role on *Grey's Anatomy* or voicing a character on *American Dad!*, and then sliding back into the familiar skin of Alice.

Before season 3, both Erin and I decided to invest in Vancouver real estate because it felt like the smart thing to do. We figured our mortgages would be a fourth of the rent we'd been paying for the furnished apartments, and I knew if I didn't invest my relatively modest earnings in something substantial, I might spend it all on nice dinners and exotic travel.

Together we checked out listings and wound up in very different places that were walking distance from each other. In Gastown, Erin fell in love with an old, soulful building. It had warm brick walls and a wonderful, old-timey view overlooking the last stop on the city's railroad tracks. She couldn't believe what a great deal she was getting, until her first night there, when she learned about shunting. This is the process of connecting and disconnecting railway cars. It sounds like a handsaw trying to cut through a rusty ship anchor and it happened at all hours under Erin's picture window.

My own apartment was very different. Vancouver looks more like *Blade Runner* or Hong Kong than any American city. There are modern glass skyscrapers everywhere and I wound up in one of them. The apartment was 1,500 square feet with two-story-high windows. The main living area was downstairs, and the bedroom was a loft above. Purchasing this place filled me with pride and a sense of security I had never known. It gave me independence as well: I hadn't lived by myself since my beloved dump in the East Village in 1990. It was exhilarating to choose all the furnishings on my own . . . especially since mid-century modern wasn't in vogue in Vancouver. I could waltz into any vintage store and snag an original Danish maple wood credenza for $150. The same piece in LA would have cost $5,000. I bought a big wooden farm table with long benches on either side in the hopes that I'd be entertaining lots of people. To fill one tall wall, I purchased an oversized abstract painting on wood, featuring shapes in hot pink, sky blue, and fog gray. I loved it. On the day it was delivered, I learned it was so big it wouldn't fit in the elevator . . . nor the doorway to the stairs. The only way to get this stunning piece of art into my apartment was to saw it in half. So I fetched my circular saw, lowered my safety goggles, and thought, *Two for the price of one.*

My loft soon became the epicenter of some wild get-togethers. At the time Canadian marijuana was hard to come by . . . unless, like us, you had a production assistant who grew the stuff. I don't know why we put so much trust in her measuring skills, but Kate was anointed the official baker of our delicious pot brownies. I'd preheat the oven, then we'd watch Kate whip up a batch of magical chocolate space cakes. Our own personal Walter White of weed. These famed parties started small but grew to include the whole cast, guest directors, writers, or whoever else was in town. They would always go off without a hitch, until we would realize someone had invited a newly cast guest star to swing by and say hello. You could see the full panic stretch across our faces when this news broke. During one brownie bender we sat at the dining table high as kites. One of our directors was describing the gnome she was seeing, surrounded by dancing squirrels, when the doorbell rang. In walked Annabella Sciorra. Now I thought I might be hallucinating. Was the actress I'd admired in *Jungle Fever* and *The Sopranos* really in my apartment? She and Dallas Roberts, who played Angus Partridge, had popped over after a civilized dinner in the neighborhood. They didn't know we were tripping our faces off and we didn't tell them because they seemed like mature adults, and we were the losers high on doobie snacks.

A frequent observer at these parties was Angela Robinson. She came on as a writer and director and brought a playful aesthetic. When editing a section of "Lesbian Phone Tree," Angela used a stylistic split screen that recalled old movies like *Pillow Talk* with Rock Hudson and Doris Day. She also had a knack for making characters and storylines well rounded. Partially, this was because Angela grounded some of the on-screen debauchery in our off-screen shenanigans. It was as if she was taking notes on our weekend adventures, because we'd come to set on Monday and see our lives reflected in that week's script. The episode in season 5 titled "Lookin' at You Kid," where Shane and Jenny throw a pot brownie party at their house, is maybe as close to documentary as *The L Word* gets.

The camaraderie of the central friend group was a signature part of *The L Word*. Beyond the fashion and the locations, I believe it was the most aspirational element of the show. To keep it spicy, the writers had us doing all kinds of things together: playing basketball, mastering self-defense, dancing, anteing in at high-stakes poker, or skiing down mountains. This meant we, as actors, had to look like we knew what we were doing. The producers hired a revolving door of experts tasked with teaching us each new skills. These after-hours classes are some of my most cherished memories.

For the episode "Layup," production did its due diligence and hired a head coach who was used to training and developing real athletes. In our first session, he ordered half of us into a line to do layups and the other half to try to block the shots. We looked at each other like, "Is he serious?" Jennifer nailed her layup like she was in the WNBA. Mia walked into the gymnasium with a cup of coffee, gave a look of dismay, then took a seat in the bleachers. Pam, Laurel, Rachel Shelley, and I earnestly tried to improve on our fifth-grade skill level, but to little effect. Kate didn't attend a single basketball lesson, so Shane's spectacular cluelessness on the court is very real. Despite the professional's best attempts, we instantly became our characters on the court and that's what ended up in the episode. My sincerest apologies to the guy who thought he was there to teach a committed group and found us numbskulls. I hope you landed your dream job as the assistant coach at UConn.

When it came to off-screen athletics, the cast could get a little competitive . . . in a friendly way. If someone was seeing great results from a certain personal trainer, we'd all start working out with that trainer. If one person got into running, biking, zip-lining, or long swims in the ocean, suddenly we were all doing it and checking each other's stats. "You're entering a triathlon? Great, I'll start stretching." "Downhill mountain biking? Fun, hold my beer." In true Bette fashion, Jennifer excelled at any activity on-screen or off. She was a beacon of health. She would bike miles and miles to get to work, while the rest of us rolled into the makeup chairs half asleep.

We tried all sorts of things together. There was an unofficial *L Word* sailing group, then a tennis club. The only thing the cast didn't rally for was an obstacle course called Muddy Buddies. Despite Mia's annual attempts to sign us up as a team, we never agreed to run and climb in mud. I do regret not following her lead on that one. We just loved spending time as a group, it didn't matter where. For a minute we frequented a sophisticated strip club called Brandi's Exotic Show Lounge on Hornby. The women who performed there were amazingly talented. They didn't just work the pole. We'd watch in awe as they incorporated fire eating or elaborate silk tricks into their routines. They were one contortion away from Cirque du Soleil. When the band Sleater-Kinney was in town to film a concert at The Planet, we took them to Brandi's and surprised them with lap dances. We knew how to show our guest stars a good time.

Another favorite haunt was Milk & Honey in Gastown. In Los Angeles we could no longer go to a lesbian bar without being recognized, so we appreciated our anonymity up north. We learned about this nondescript black box nightclub because, while filming the "Crisp-ay" scene at that location, the staff told us Saturdays were ladies' nights. They played excellent music, so we'd go dance, drink, and blow off some steam. It soon became our Cheers, and we would bring any new cast members there as a sweet initiation festivity.

With each season, new cast members either kept their distance or folded right in. Such was the case with Marlee Matlin. She and Jennifer went way back, but with us she was instantly one of the girls. She was open, loving, and funny. On set, in between takes, she'd teach us different signs (guess which cast member became fluent in sign language). After hours, Marlee was in the mix, her naughty sense of humor on full display.

While we were "oot and aboot," Mia would oftentimes find herself engaging in strange interactions because of how polarizing a character Jenny was. One night at Milk & Honey, an emboldened fan who had had too much to drink came up to her and said, "I hope you die." In perfect Mia fashion, instead of ignoring it or being offended, she calmly looked this person in the eye and said, "I'm an actor on a show and when you wish me death, it means that you're taking away my livelihood. It's just a job. It's how I pay my bills and support my family." She broke it down in the most graceful way, and the girl left, speechless.

6

| | |

Labor of Lust

Kate

As originally written, in season 3, episode 5, "Lifeline," Cherie and Shane had a love scene that involved a balcony, a chaise lounge, and acrobatics. To the best of my memory, the stage directions involved Cherie hanging off one end of the chaise, with Shane crawling on top of her from the opposite direction. At some point, they were to contort into pretzel shapes, and the grand finale would have them both in a Cirque du Soleil position for the whole neighborhood to see. If anyone tried this at home, they would be arrested for public indecency, land in urgent care, or both. Thankfully, I never had to plead my case because our director for that episode, Kimberly Peirce, had already flagged it. She didn't want to change the structure of the characters' dynamics, she only wanted to make them as realistic as possible. So Kim and Ilene made the executive decision to lose the chaise lounge and use the pool and a strap-on instead.

Now it started with Cherie having to seduce Shane from the front door and lead her all the way into the pool. We would be filming all night on a chilly Friday at a private mansion on Kits Beach, and Kim knew we had to be as uninhibited as possible. She got us a bottle of liquid courage to relax any nerves and to stay warm. Kim and I had a glass and Rosanna may have had two. Love scenes in general always have a level of anticipation prior to filming them, regardless of who they're with, and this particular one included props, cold water, and wide voyeuristic shots that didn't hide much.

The whole time Rosanna was leading me to the pool, our objective was guiding each other as gracefully as we could so neither of us would trip or, in Rosanna's case, fall backward in the dark. We couldn't help but laugh at ourselves over how unsexy and unromantic it actually was.

When it came to the strap-on, Kim liked the idea of Shane showing up at Cherie's "packing," since it would save time and feel uninhibited. My brain immediately went to the logistics: Did she swing by her house first to grab it? Does she keep it in the glove compartment? I'm wearing tight wool pants with no stretch, so how does it fit?

"It doesn't matter, Kate," Kim said. "It's television."

"Okay, so how does this all work?" Rosanna asked. She hadn't gotten to this chapter in the lesbian book of life. So, Kim, in her forthright manner, explained strap-on sex to her in detail, like a math tutor explaining long division. I watched Rosanna hang on her every word and nod along to what Kim was saying, while trying to understand. Right on cue, the props department arrived and presented the main attraction on a dessert tray like we were at a French restaurant. It took Rosanna one look for everything to click. By the end of that night Rosanna couldn't help but say, "Now I get it. I totally get it now!"

I don't know if that level of rawness would've come from anyone other than Kim. It all stemmed from her directness and unabashed honesty. Kim made what could have been a grueling and vulnerable evening into an incredibly comfortable and creative environment. We always said our show had the spirit of an indie film. We would discover things on the day that no one had thought of and live in the moment of what we had to do with the resources we had. Everyone's objective was to approach the work with honesty and integrity regardless of how outlandish certain scenarios or characters got. Our ideas came out on the fly in the most trustworthy, protective environment.

By this point, in the mid-aughts, women were being objectified daily in gossip sites like Perez Hilton and magazines like *Maxim*. For all of us working within the show, we felt like we were reclaiming women's sexuality and unapologetically owning it on our terms. *The L Word* was a fully female-dominated show on and off camera. Ninety-five percent of the time, we were collaborating with women—Kim, Rose, and directors like Angela Robinson and Lisa Cholodenko. Rose set the template and tone of the show that every other director was guided by, while simultaneously bringing their own individual vision to the project.

We all considered Rose to be the Godmother, because she was there from the very beginning. She not only wrote for the first few seasons, but she also directed too many episodes to count. She knew us, our characters, and our individual ticks so well that we had a baked-in shorthand with her. Anytime she was there, we felt like our Aunt Rose had come home.

Rose thinks fast, is unbelievably witty, yet is also incredibly sensitive. She's very good at making actors feel seen, even if they have no dialogue or happen to be in the background. In group scenes, she'd always find something specific for each individual to do that stood out from the rest, to convey their inner life. She did that with everybody so she could paint a full picture of the story in editing. She was the master of reaction shots and understood the technicalities of cameras and lenses to the point that I sometimes thought she was speaking gibberish. She always had a wealth of references to pull from and strove to dig deeper into the things that weren't spoken on the page. Like a mad scientist, she would intensely study the monitor while frantically scribbling ideas on the back of her script from behind camera, and in between takes, run onto set and deliver us those specific notes. Kim came in at the beginning of the third season and shadowed Rose for about a week. She was doing her homework and taking this little TV show of ours as seriously as she would a film. When Lisa Cholodenko came in, her approach felt more subtle and intimate, and Angela Robinson created living, breathing, joyous pop art.

A lot of fantastic ideas came from the open-door policy Ilene established with the actors and directors. Our director meeting was put in place on day one of the first season and was baked into the prep schedule. After the read-through, they would schedule a mandatory fifteen-minute sit-down with each of us to go through everything, pick out red flags, and discuss tone and theme, so we were able to get ahead of any issues and in turn create an early rapport. It was an invaluable element that nurtured collaboration.

Ilene had a lot of trust in the people she hired. Under her leadership, she invited directors to follow their instincts and generously handed us the reins to our characters. She encouraged us to make our person as real and authentic as we could, even if that meant taking them in different directions than she had planned.

Instead of being forced into this narrow idea of the character we were playing, it felt like we were creating the characters together. Which helped immensely, since every season we got a rotation of different writers. Maybe three or four were locked in season after season, but other than that, they fluctuated. It's normal that not every one of them was going to nail down the voice of every character, especially as the seasons went on. But Ilene knew that *we* knew our characters inside and out and made sure we had a say in how they would appear. She would always say, "You know your characters better than anyone, what do you think?" It felt like Ilene's trust in all of us was part of her long-game strategy in keeping the show authentic.

One example: when it's revealed to Shane and Carmen that Mark (everyone's favorite roommate) has been secretly videotaping the house, originally it was written for Shane to give him this long speech about breaking her trust. I recall her having to ask him in ten different ways "how could he do this" as he was to stand there in pathetic shame. It was easily the most words Shane had ever said out loud to anyone. I went to our director Tricia Brock with an idea, but she beat me to it. "I think you should say nothing and just punch him in the face." Ilene, who was always receptive to different approaches, trusted our instincts. So that's what we shot.

There was usually improvisation in the love scenes too, depending on our director. Rose would always come into our trailers for personal meetings to discuss those. She'd say, "So this is how I see it," and lay out the beginning, middle, and end in thorough detail. Other directors just wanted to give us the reins and see where it would lead. A lot of it was based on the chemistry we had with our scene partners and the trust we had with our team off camera.

There were times where maybe one of us had our period and felt bloated. Or didn't feel we had exercised enough or whatever thing we had in our brain that made us feel insecure on any particular day. We always felt comfortable saying, "I'd rather not be topless today." Same thing with blocking. On the day, we would figure out the positions that we each felt comfortable with and go from there. If one of us didn't like showing a certain part of our body, no problem, the other would easily step in to help give us some cover.

I had only met Elizabeth Keener and Alicia Leigh Willis in passing by the time it came to film the threesome with Dawn Denbo and her lover Cindi. We did the awkward "so we're doing this today . . ." greeting and went to rehearsal for a private blocking. Our director

John Stockwell was new to us and not the typical *L Word* hire. But any preconceived ideas I had about him soon disappeared. John instantly calmed any feeling of trepidation by being collaborative and easygoing. His sense of humor lightened the atmosphere. "I just want you guys to feel natural and the cameras will do the rest. Don't force anything," he said. He ran on instincts and never wanted to belabor the point or overshoot to the point of numbness.

A personal favorite escapade was in the episode Jamie Babbit directed, the outlandish wedding party with Shane and the bridesmaids. I always appreciated the Shane storylines that made a point of not taking themselves too seriously, and savored any moments of joyous chaos, even if they were one-offs with no follow-up. Shane was always written to have a wild side, so when those moments came around, it gave me something to look forward to, such as diving into a getaway car after being chased by the whole bridal party she had just slept with in one afternoon. Those moments that gave Shane a reason to smile and enjoy herself felt like a hall pass for my own emotions. Although I love and cherish Shane with all my heart, her emotional landscape could be complicated. There were points where my own reality had compounded with hers, and it could feel like the walls were closing in.

About a year and a half after my father died, my mom called to break the news that one of my oldest friends, Hillary, who I had grown up with, had passed away. The suddenness of her death smacked me in the face and left me in shock. One loss was already more than I could really handle, and the compounding of a second one overwhelmed me. Simultaneously dealing with Shane's demons and bottled-up emotions, along with her own abandonment issues, could be a lot to carry at once. They were obviously separate in my brain, but I don't think my body always knew that. At the same time, Shane ironically provided some valuable guidance on how to—or how not to—handle my own difficulties. From her, I learned the importance of acknowledging my own feelings and vulnerabilities, rather than stuffing them away. Over time, I came to think of my challenges not as weaknesses but as building blocks to resilience. And if there was one thing Shane and I had in common, it was this magical chosen family that collectively lifted both of us up when we needed it the most.

This family grew as new cast members joined the group. I was flown to LA to chemistry read with some potential Carmens for their studio test, and I found myself in the same conference room that I had been in two years prior. Except now it was about finding the girl who would spin Shane's head around. I didn't meet Sarah that day, and I'm not sure how they found her, but when she came on board, she and I had an immediate rapport.

Our first day together was on a rainy Monday morning, and I showed up to work with raw second-degree burns on the right side of my face from a French press that had blown up on me over the weekend. A doctor had to come to the set to assess the damage because Jules, our makeup artist, could only do so much to cover it and I was barely able to move my mouth. Any light touch on my right cheek and mouth felt like burning needles of scorching pain. Sarah had to contend with not only being the new kid but also filming her first love scene with an injured scene partner she just met. If she was feeling nervous, it didn't show. Her introductory hairstyle was a slicked-back mullet with pin-straight extensions that ran all the way down to her lower back. Did she like those and feel good wearing them? I doubt it. But she could easily laugh at herself and was a team player who didn't let these details affect anything she was doing.

From then on, Sarah and I were bonded, and we always looked out for each other. We would laugh through any of the awkward moments and trusted that we would equally commit to our on-screen relationship. If one or both of us had a flight back to LA on Friday night to visit our actual partners, and we had a love scene to film, we would focus on getting the work done as efficiently as possible so as not to miss the plane. We would go over the beats out loud together just prior to the director yelling out "action," and it reminded me of what I imagine cheer camp is like. "Okay, so I lift you here, and you grab me here, and then we move this way and I flip you over, and then you land on top. Got it? Okay. Break."

A lot of fans thought of Shane and Carmen as this hot fantasy couple together, but the truth was, Sarah and I were more like an old married couple who had been together for fifty years. We could be frank with each other without ever taking it personally. In the episode "Lost Weekend," Carmen does a striptease dance for Shane in the middle of their living room and the high heels Sarah was wearing kept getting caught in the high-pile rug. She'd lose her balance for a moment, which led to them digging into my bare feet throughout multiple takes. As I felt her heel tip grind into my baby toe for the fifth time, I finally grunted out, "Your goddamn shoes are killing me." Within seconds the frustration turned to compassion as Sarah held my sad foot and inspected my throbbing baby carrot of a toe and said, "I'm so sorry, babe, it's impossible to be a showgirl on this rug."

In "Loneliest Number," directed by Rose Troche, Carmen climbs on top of Shane and they play the "too hot" game, which I had some trouble wrapping my mind around at first.

"Is this a real game?" I asked.

"It doesn't matter if it's a real game," Rose said.

"Has someone played this before?"

"It doesn't matter. It's a seduction scene, Kate."

Sarah eventually chimed in and patted my leg, "We have flights to catch. Shut up and let's film it."

Joshanna opened my trailer door a crack, reached her arm in, and handed me a bit of fabric. I took it, then stared at the flesh-colored G-string in my hand. From the other side of the metal door, the costumer coached me: "Okay, slip it on." "I'm in," I called back. "Good," was her muffled reply. "Now use scissors to cut the sides off. To look naked, we don't want any fabric on your hip, so on each side cut from where your ovary would be to right above your crack." I giggled and did as instructed. "Use a dab of body glue on the top corners of the triangle above your crotch and one on your coccyx." After a few silent moments Joshanna asked, "You okay?" Silence. "Do you need me to come in?" I stared at my reflection, naked except for the "privacy patch," or, as I called it, "my cooter cover." Just another day at the office.

Did I spend too much time finding flaws with, or indulging insecurities about, my body? Sure. But when it came time to do a sex scene for *The L Word* I met it head on, without reservation. I approached them like a musical or dance number—an interlude that conveyed a dynamic between people that dialogue alone couldn't. I wanted to do right by the characters and by the audience. As lesbians, we had very few hot and steamy media images to enjoy. Of the few we did have, too many were of pent-up women who, when they finally gave in to temptation, would softly caress each other, then burst into tears. I felt a sense of responsibility to portray queer sex in a real—and sexy— way. We all felt a certain pressure to get these scenes right, especially those of us who were queer. Which is to say, I wanted to make it hot.

I always felt we were in the safest hands while shooting a sex scene. Ilene was incredibly welcoming, approachable, and interested in everyone's concerns or contributions. Whenever possible, she hired directors who had related life experience to bring to the material, or the sensitivity and humility to capture it. We would arrive early on set to figure it out together, and the crew was there to listen and think about how they were going to capture it. Whether it was the camera, sound, or costume department, our supportive crew helped ease any worries, and the scenes came to life with their help. With that strong foundation we could free ourselves up to fully inhabit our characters.

As actors, we protected each other and tried to help one another look our best. There was always negotiating in rehearsal, mostly over who would be the one to fight gravity: no one ever wanted to be on top because either your whole face hung down and you looked a hundred years old or your boobs dangled like cow udders.

After the first few, I started to look forward to sex scenes. They were a way to explore a different side of Alice—plus, there weren't any lines to memorize. Most of Alice's hook-ups were with people she loved, so I was able to approach them with a genuine enthusiasm: What can we do to show audiences how these characters feel about each other? For instance, Alice loves Tasha so much she's going to do this ice thing, or feed her bananas, or ice cream . . . wait, does Alice have a food kink?

It's not to say that we always got it right. There are scenes where a casual fingering looks more like a plowing. Where someone's arm resembles an aggressive oil-well pump. Or someone's elbow raises and lowers so dramatically it looks like they're trying to start an old lawnmower. Once you see it, you can't unsee it. I guess we were overcompensating for the camera and that's how the plowing began. Oftentimes there was no buildup and out of nowhere somebody would climax. Shane could have a girl in orgasmic bliss in about fifteen seconds, so she was obviously doing something right. Many of those scenes would be written on three-eighths of a page as a transition to the next, longer scene. So, you had to get in and get out. Literally.

A lot of the criticism regarding *The L Word* is that it pandered to "the male gaze." That's never sat right with me. The creators, almost all the writers, and many of the directors were gay women dedicated to capturing female desire. We wanted to show that women sexualize other women, sometimes to the point of objectification. We gaze too. We lust after a great rack or thick set of hips. Not all lesbians are looking to rent a U-Haul; sometimes we just want to give it away. I think this was inconceivable to some of the audience, so they assumed these sexcapades originated in male fantasy. For these critics, it was more comfortable to imagine men imposing their sexual appetites onto the series than it was to accept that women were writing openly about the hunger, craving, and passion we feel for each other.

We also took heat from some of our gay viewers who took issue with how white, economically advantaged, long-haired, and conventionally attractive the cast was. Could there have been a more racially, financially, aesthetically, and follicley diverse Planet posse? Absolutely. While we're at it, ideally more of the roles would have gone to openly gay actors.

But back to sex. One of my favorite scenes is when Alice is shackled in a dungeon by a vampire named Uta Refson (Nosferatu backward). Handcuffs and fangs? Fun! You're seeing me topless and tied to iron rings, but Alice is in on the joke. She knew it was ridiculous but was into it because it was about self-exploration. Alice's sense of adventure was one of my favorite qualities to delve into. I liked the idea of her dating Uta, though if that relationship had lasted more than one night, Alice would have had a hard time going for strolls on the beach in sunny Los Angeles, just saying.

The sex stakes were never higher than in "Labyrinth," in season 2, when Dana and Alice finally hook up. Erin and I met with the director Burr Steers multiple times to conceptualize and develop the different scenarios we thought these characters would be in on that long-anticipated evening. Erin and I knew that after all the buildup the release had to be over the top. We decided to reference famous sex scenes from movies like *9½ Weeks* to show that gays can do that too. We also decided Dana and Alice would be into role-playing. They were so in love that they yearned to be with each other in every scenario possible. Burr was so sweet and open to all our ideas. We walked around the apartment picking out every spot Dana and Alice could find themselves entangled. Production got the rights to the song "Finally" by CeCe Peniston, so we had the perfect score for this epic score.

Later on, imagine my reaction upon finding out I'd be having sex with Cybill Shepherd. This absolute icon plays Phyllis Kroll, a woman who realizes she has been repressing her sexuality her whole life. Alice becomes her obsession and is basically her gateway drug to a life of freedom. Cybill was excited because in her long, expansive career, she had never done a love scene with a woman. I was happy to be the actress for the job. I'll never forget the day we shot the scene in bed; she pushed me down and something came over me. I drew my hand back and slapped Cybill Shepherd's butt so hard she screamed, "What are you doing to me!?" followed by a string of expletives. I stayed connected in the scene but was dying inside. When the cameras cut, we lay there laughing about it.

When it came to sex scenes with Tasha, played by the spellbinding Rose Rollins, the two of us were really interested in exploring her and Alice's masc/femme dynamic. Working closely with our extraordinary costume designer, Cynthia, we decided Alice would start wearing dresses around Tasha and playing into the stereotypes of hetero women. Tasha leaned into the butch role, riding a motorcycle and becoming an officer in the military. She had a quiet strength that could stop a girl in her tracks. Rose and I would take tropes or scenes we've all seen a billion times in the straight world and mimic them. We shot scenes where she picked me up at the waist and I'd straddle her hips before she threw me on a table, or I'd run across the room and jump into her arms when she came home on leave from overseas dressed in uniform. It was our way of subverting expectation, showing that lesbians are different kinds of people with their own relationship dynamics, even in the bedroom.

Tasha and Alice have one sex scene that is so perfectly *L Word*. They've just come back from dinner and are having a fight about the war in Iraq . . . because nothing screams hot girl-on-girl action like a debate about foreign oil.

TASHA: Oh, come on Alice. Stop frontin', okay? That's your world. You were right in there with them with all their kneejerk liberal bullshit.

ALICE: Yeah, but, that's America. That's supposedly what you're fighting for, it's a little thing called "freedom of speech," remember?

The fight culminates:

TASHA: You know, some of the people are in the military because they want to serve their country. Okay? We believe in what we stand for. I'm sorry if we don't live our lives wearing trendy fake-ass raggedy T-shirts that scream out bullshit about why we kill people.

ALICE: You think it's trendy to not want to kill people?

TASHA: The soldiers that I served with don't want to kill
  people. Like, what the fuck? You think I want to kill
  people?
ALICE: Well, why are you there?
TASHA: The question is, "Why the fuck am I here?"
ALICE: Because we want to fuck each other!

And fuck each other they do . . . on the desk, in the bedroom, against a wall. Tasha rides Alice, Alice licks Tasha's crack, Tasha tastes Alice's toes. It's the kind of sex-a-thon that could only be inspired by war foreplay. *Ha!* Warplay!

I had always liked sex, but it wasn't until I was put in the position— well, multiple positions—of filming sex scenes for *The L Word* that I learned to see myself as a sexual woman. In intimate situations I had always been eager in the moment, but hadn't paused to consider what I could bring other than enthusiasm and technique. Several of my long-term partners had a few years on me, so in my relationships there had been a dynamic of me being younger, less professionally accomplished, basically, a girl. Being on *The L Word* helped me own and inhabit my body. I became a runner, challenging myself to five miles a day. I started taking a new level of interest in how I wanted to feel in my skin. I gave myself permission to play around with my femininity. Years ago, as a baby dyke, I had cut off my hair and wore baggy jeans. This was as much to ward off unwanted male attention as it was a flare for other lesbians—look over here! Being on *The L Word* changed my perception of what I could look like as a gay woman. In season 1, the wardrobe department tried to give Alice a bag and I was like, "We don't carry purses." I had a narrow idea of what gay could look like.

I'd always been fascinated with how clothes are the intersection of identity and presentation. I'd admired how David Bowie bent gender. He expressed himself fully, instead of contorting himself to fit into society's expectations. In my thirties, I integrated dresses and heels into my tomboy aesthetic, defining for myself what felt right in the moment. Surprisingly, playing Alice, an open, sexual being, gave me a confidence to discover and display my own sexuality in a more intentional and mature way than I ever had. What a strange and unexpected job perk.

7

| | |

Loved and Lost

LEISHA

Before we left for hiatus after season 2, there was buzz on set that one of our characters might be killed off the next year. We chalked it up to hearsay. During break, we had our one-on-one meetings with Ilene to discuss our characters' upcoming story arcs. After hers, Erin called me. "You're not going to believe it," she started, then explained that over lunch she heard the news: Dana was going to die from breast cancer.

It hit me on multiple levels at once. Professionally, I was devastated for Erin. No one wants to lose their job, but there was more to it than that. Erin loved playing Dana and felt there was so much to do with the character. Hers was a story we'd never seen before: a high-profile personality coming out from the first-person perspective. We had access to her private thoughts as she struggled with wanting to live an authentic life but knowing that meant she could lose everything. At the time of her diagnosis, Dana was ready to launch: She had a successful career, love in the palm of her hand, and a circle of friends who would go to the ends of the earth for her. Why was that the moment to take her away from the audience? From us?

Dana was *The L Word*'s way in for a lot of the straight audience and, more importantly, for those not yet out. Jenny was a voyeur, using observation and immersion to figure things out on her own.

Dana's naivete was a vehicle for the show to educate viewers on things like gaydar. She looked to Shane for sex tips, Bette and Tina as the elder stateswomen of same-sex relationships, and Alice for everything else. When Dana went to Palm Springs to come out to her Republican family, she brought Alice for moral support. Well-meaning Alice even tried to dress like a conservative. In the end, Dana had the bravery to pull her parents aside and tell them she was gay, and I believe she found that strength through Alice.

I felt terrible for my character. She and Dana were just ramping up, digging into this love story, exploring if they were meant to be. I didn't want them to be robbed of their journey. As an actor, I understood there would be a whole new range of emotion to portray. That was exciting, and a little scary, but the trade-off was depressing. Who would Alice be without her sparring partner? How would she be changed after experiencing such a seismic loss? Alice was about to grow up.

Personally, I couldn't begin to compute making the show without Erin. We had forged an incredibly special bond. The relationships you build with your peers on set can sometimes play with your heart. Of course, you know the difference between fiction and reality, but the two can get enmeshed, lines blurred. On my flight to Vancouver to shoot the pilot, Erin had been in the seat next to me. I pictured my flight home from season 3, the seat beside me empty.

Erin is probably the most different in real life from her character. She had her shit together more than any person my age that I knew. I mean, she had a diversified investment portfolio, and I barely had a savings account. Watching her transform into closeted, insecure, clueless Dana when the cameras were rolling was always a trip. In real life, Erin gave me sound advice, but in the show, Alice was Dana's lighthouse . . . guiding her out of the closet. She was like, "Follow me for happiness and fulfillment!"

Erin was a professional and showed up to do her job. Meanwhile, I was a tangle of disbelief and denial. With each episode script we got, I tore through it, praying I'd see the words, "Great news! Dana's in remission!" They never appeared. Some of us even appealed to Ilene directly. "People survive breast cancer," I lobbied. "But they also don't," was Ilene's sobering response. I carried the hope of Dana's recovery until the day we shot the final hospital scene. Only when I fell to the ground as Alice did it sink in.

There's a lot of debate about whether Alice and Dana were meant for each other. Early in the show, all they did was poke fun at each other, like kids at recess. There was definitely chemistry, but what kind? And then they shared that amazing kiss. Erin and I begged the producers to let Alice and Dana's first make-out be in the rain. Full disclosure: All of us actors were vying to have that *Notebook* moment, but of all the pairings, didn't Alice and Dana deserve it the most? It was a moot point, though, because we could never afford a rain machine.

I think Dana and Alice had to explore being together, but I don't know if it would have been sustained. There was such an honesty in their friendship, and maybe romantic relationships require a little privacy or discretion to succeed. Regardless, Alice and Dana were more themselves with each other than they even were alone. After all, in those final episodes of season 3, at her most vulnerable, Dana didn't want her girlfriend there, she wanted Alice. Maybe Alice really was her person . . . as a best friend.

I wish I'd gotten to see Dana age. I can picture her as a wonderful mom, righting the wrongs of her own childhood. Or I could see her thriving as the CEO and founder of a wellness company with a line of CBD-infused muscle repair ointments. What I know for certain is that even if she'd died at age ninety, she would want Alice by her side.

KATE

I didn't believe Erin when she told me about the cancer story-line. I remember she had to repeat "Kate, she dies" twice because part of my brain blacked out with the news. She was our sister, and without her, it felt like we were missing a vital part of our engine. It seemed wrong on every level.

To add insult to injury, Sarah Shahi was also going to be leaving us. Unfortunately, healthy relationships don't often make for interesting television. Ilene told me at some point during production that Shane and Carmen weren't going to make it, and at the finale read-through I learned Shane would be leaving her at the altar. Everything that Sarah and I had built together went out the window in one scene. I can't argue with the fact that they were too young and probably would have ended in disaster one way or another. Still, I wished we could have explored their "will they/won't they" dynamic for at least another year. I wouldn't have cared if the only option was having Carmen triangulate with Bette and Tina's nanny to make Shane jealous again. Desperate times, desperate measures.

That was the beginning of realizing that romantically, I would be starting from square one at the top of every season going forward. Up until Carmen, aside from Rosanna, I had been used to Shane's one-off conquests with scene partners I had met only an hour prior to filming a love scene. Unlike Leisha, and much like Shane, I grew numb to them since there was no built-in dynamic to work with. Carmen was the first time it felt like there was potential for a deeper connection, and after her, instinctually I knew that there wasn't a way Shane would suddenly find her perfect match.

When she left, I was heartbroken, and mourned the rhythm and unspoken understanding we had built together. The last thing I wanted was for Shane to start over with someone new and fall into yet another relationship. I had always wondered if there was a way to bring Carmen back, even if it was just for closure. Something about their demise felt not only unforgivable but unfinished. I was doing a play in New York during our hiatus while that season finished airing, and every day I was stopped in the middle of the street by people who would passionately yell at me for abandoning Carmen. I remember a school bus passing by as I walked down Lafayette Street, and some teenagers yelling out the window, *"FUCK YOU, SHANE!"* From those interactions, I knew the audience wouldn't forgive easily and I can't say I blame them. Shane needed some level of redemption after all the damage she had caused.

When Ilene and I had our season 4 meeting, I threw out an idea I had been thinking about. What if the kid brother we met at the end of season 3 could come into Shane's life and turn her world upside down? It would provide some high-stakes responsibility, show a different side of the character, and prove she actually does have a heart. At the very least, it would add new color to Shane's humanness without trying to replace Carmen. Although Paige was a brief paramour in season 4, Shane's main love story and greatest heartbreak is with the brother she never knew she had.

Clementine Ford, who played Molly, came on in season 5, and she was a breath of fresh air. In addition to being Cybill Shepherd's daughter, she was a fabulous casting choice. Molly was written to be a precocious know-it-all, and Clementine herself was naturally precocious with a sense of humor as dry as a Cabernet Sauvignon. Molly started off being conservative and straightlaced, which made the banter between our characters feel different and more innocent than what I had been used to. Molly didn't fall for Shane's charm and at least made her work for it early on, which was refreshing to play. Sex wasn't immediately on the menu. Shane had to first get past Molly's unimpressive fiancé, Richard, which wasn't difficult and didn't take long. But inevitably, once Shane conquers, the doomsday clock begins, so I never got my hopes up with Molly or any new characters. Shane's sudden commitment to any of them would have felt unrealistic without some level of closure either with Carmen or at least with herself. I knew it was a one-and-done season for the most part.

While the show was going through major transitions, I was, too, in my own life. At this point, I was out to everyone who knew me or was around me, though I still wasn't talking about it during interviews. It was around this time that I also went through my first romantic breakup that meant something. Right after the run of the play in New York wrapped up, and days before I returned to Vancouver to shoot the new season, Sasha came clean about cheating on me with a mutual friend while I was out of town. I was back in LA for only twelve hours and was already living in an *L Word* episode. The relationship was over. I was worn down from the theater schedule, and Leisha said I came back to Vancouver looking emaciated, with dark Charlie Browns under my eyes. I was physically and emotionally exhausted. At that point I had come out of the fog of grief regarding the deaths of my father and Hillary, but now these new feelings of loss were taking its place. This sensation of heartbreak felt foreign to me, like a physical weight, and I had trouble understanding let alone articulating what I was feeling.

Leisha would try to ask me how I was or what had happened, so she could help me get through it, but I didn't have the tools to express myself in a way that wouldn't make me crumble to dust. I'd simplify it all, saying, "I'm not sure, I'm just feeling . . . broken." At the same time, I appreciated Leisha's curiosity and concern, her constant questions and checking on me. Once again, the whole cast rallied around me like protective big sisters and comforted me, but I was too vulnerable to admit the truth: I felt fundamentally unlovable. The irony was that Shane was so desired and wanted, and I felt so undesired and unwanted.

LEISHA

Like world history, it felt like *The L Word* was organized into two halves around a single person—BD and AD: Before Dana and After Dana. To counter all the loss and sadness of her departure, the producers realized the salve was to have these characters laugh, enjoy themselves and each other. There was new energy on set, and that came in no small part from Rose Rollins. I read with a lot of actresses for the role of Tasha, and the producers were leaning toward picking another woman, but I knew that Rose and I had great chemistry. I fought for her to get the role.

Nobody laughs like Rose. If I could, I would bottle her chuckle and play it whenever I felt sad or just in need of a laugh track. It became my mission to make Rose laugh . . . and then I made it Alice's mission to make Tasha laugh. Her character was so serious, it was always a victory when Alice got her to lighten up.

Around this time, I realized my own life needed some levity. I was missing making music and playing live. I'd been writing on my own but was longing to collaborate with other musicians. Between seasons 4 and 5, I asked around to see if anyone was interested in starting a band. I met Cam Grey through some friends at a kickball game in West Hollywood. She had recently moved to LA from Boston, where she'd gone to the Berklee College of Music. I went to see her perform in Mellowdrone. Cam was the only woman in the band. She was at the back of the stage, hammering out sophisticated high-bass lines like she was in The Cure. It was obvious she had star power. I called her the next day to gauge her interest in getting together to write.

We hit it off and wrote songs all winter. Previously, I had only composed on a guitar, which can sometimes feel repetitive, like, okay, how are we going to arrange the chords this time? Cam was more into New Wave, so I bought a red Nord synthesizer. We'd spin knobs and flick switches, discovering sounds and tinkering with effects, then write melodies around them. It felt more like play than songwriting. Cam was proficient in Pro Tools, so she'd find a drum sample and we'd build a song around it entirely on the computer. We used our voices as instruments to layer in: I explored pedal harmonies and holding a single note while Cam sang lead. Lyrically, I would write a verse, and she'd write another. We'd put them together and often say, "Wait, what did you mean in your verse?" And the other would respond, "What did *you* mean?" No matter, we figured, it would mean something to someone. Eventually we recruited Alicia Warrington as our drummer and officially named ourselves Uh Huh Her, because PJ Harvey is an actual god.

When I was back in Vancouver for work, Cam flew up often to record our demos in a small studio I set up in my loft. We burned some CDs and sent them to a label in Vancouver called Nettwerk Music Group. They signed us right away. We got a little rehearsal space, and that's where I spent more and more of my free time. Because we weren't hitting the road yet, Alicia sadly had to step away to continue her career as a touring musician, but Cam and I kept going. I stopped flying to LA as much and devoted my extra time to building the band.

Kate loved that I was finally putting all the instruments I lugged up north every year to use. Many of *The L Word* fans weren't aware of my musical background, and I made it my mission to spread the word about this new endeavor. Of course, there was no social media, so I had to get resourceful. Kate, Pam, and I were doing an *L Word* signing at Tower Records (RIP) in San Francisco. On my way there, I stopped by Kinkos (RIP) to print hundreds of flyers with Uh Huh Her's upcoming tour dates. For each *L Word* DVD (RIP) I signed, I slipped in a flyer. That week, when the Uh Huh Her concert tickets became available, the whole tour sold out instantly. For a freshman tour, that was unheard of. We played six shows a week in six different cities, including some legendary venues. I was lucky enough to play the Knitting Factory and the Roxy in Hollywood, Irving Plaza and the Highline Ballroom in New York, and even Bumbershoot and SXSW.

What was funny was that people who had discovered me on *The L Word* thought I was an actor who started a band. They didn't know I had been in a band for ten years before *The L Word*. That year I shot a *DIVA* magazine cover where they put me in a custom shirt that said, "Nobody knows I'm a musician."

Between Rose Rollins and the other new cast members, along with Angela Robinson, we were able to bring levity to those later seasons, and in many ways managed to recapture the fun of previous years. Whenever we had a shoot on location it was like sleepaway camp. We felt like we were literally camping in the "Lifecycle" episode during season 5. We shot all night long around the campfire in the middle of a Canadian national forest and were genuinely freezing for seven hours. Rose put her Sorel boots up by the heater in the warming tent and they practically melted off her foot. All the conversations, banter, and back and forth in that episode was really us just fucking around with each other and trying to stay warm. If we got to the point of the scene or the beats we had to hit, we were allowed to basically ad-lib the rest.

For that episode, production got us all fancy mountain bikes, and we had an instructor, whose first instruction was, "Now be careful going down this hill." We took no heed, bombing down the hill with abandon and screaming the whole way. All except Jennifer, who of course took the cycling incredibly seriously. By the end of that episode, I'm sure she had her pace and pulse rate down to a science. Channeling her inner Bette, Jennifer was also doing triathlons for fun on weekends, so her athleticism and discipline was a cut above the rest of ours.

That was the same episode with the tribute to Dana, which provided yet another opportunity for impromptu hijinks. By that point it had been two years since Erin had gone, so the sting of her absence had softened a little by then. Leisha had the impossible task of taking her Dana button, which we all were wearing, and going up to attach the button to the memorial shrine. Every time Leisha went to delicately attach the pin onto the bulletin board, it would suddenly drop. And not only did the pin drop in every take, but it made this little *ting* sound every time that reverberated around the silent room during this poignant scene. By the second take, this triggered uncontrollable and convulsing hysterics. We stuck our faces in each other's hair, holding each other to muffle the sound. In the episode, it looks like we're weeping, but it was the opposite.

Also in season 5 was the "Lesbians Gone Wild" episode, which was inspired after someone on the writing staff had seen Turkish oil wrestling in Brooklyn and said it was the hot new trend. Naturally, the wrestling ring production built had to have real oil, otherwise what's the point? The director of the episode, Angela, called out, "All right, on action, just go for it." Which is precisely what we did. There wasn't much stage direction outside of us body-slamming each other into the mat. We were having the time of our lives and couldn't stand up for long because we'd slip and fall right back over onto each other anyway. I thought it would be funny to pull a hair extension from Dawn Denbo's head, but it was practically impossible to capture specific moments within the sheer mayhem of that scene. Somehow, by the grace of our lesbian god, the slow-motion camera managed to capture that moment perfectly in one take. Afterward we all were sore for days and covered in bruises that we wore proudly. It took about a week to get that oil out of our hair. Fun fact: I was wearing the first Uh Huh Her merch shirt in that scene. Leisha's new band.

For the dance episode in the last season, "Last Couple Standing," we were paired up with our partners and had to do an electric-slide-type dance. We all spent a few Sunday afternoons dicking around in this dance studio, not taking much of it seriously. The teacher assigned to us eventually gave up and it became a shuffle, if that. Out of all the dances out there, Mia and I were assigned the tango.

No matter how hard we tried, we could not get the hang of it to save our lives. We grew frustrated and asked if we could swing dance instead, but we were rebuffed. Mia's final solution was, "Just pick me up," which is what ended up in the episode because we didn't know what else to do. On the other hand, Rose and Leisha approached their Salt-N-Pepa "Push It" dance with such conviction you would think they were on *Dancing with the Stars*.

8

Let's Call the Whole Thing Off

KATE

The fifth season of *The L Word* ended on a few strategic cliffhangers—Jenny caught Shane with her girlfriend, Niki Stevens, and Bette and Tina finally got back together. Those endings could have been the unfinished yet acceptable bow to gift wrap the series after the standard five-year run on a cable show. A lot of us were assuming we were going to get canceled, so when we got word from Ilene that the show had been picked up for a sixth season, it was a genuine surprise. She also informed us season 6 was indeed the end of the line, plus we'd only be shooting eight episodes, instead of our usual twelve. Ilene didn't go into any further detail of what she envisioned that final season to be, so when we arrived back in Vancouver we were very much in the dark.

Throughout the years, the beginning of each season was always celebratory, like coming back from summer break to start the new school year. We all would arrive excited to be with each other again, equally eager to see where our characters were headed and what shenanigans we were going to partake in. This time we arrived knowing it was for the last time. For the first few weeks we kept reminding each other, "Hey, at least we got eight," to put our feelings in perspective. All things considered, we knew we were incredibly fortunate. There had always been this level of transparency and communication among all the creatives, and we, the cast, had been incredibly spoiled with that open-door policy.

However, when we arrived in Canada for the final season, things immediately felt different. Aside from the harsh yet inevitable reality of our story ending, what felt more abrupt was that suddenly there was a very clear line in the sand between what the writers knew and what the actors *could* know. Once we read the first episode, which featured a body bag on a gurney in the description and opened with a cop arriving at Bette and Tina's house, we all looked around wondering aloud if we were seeing the same thing. "Wait, wait, wait, is someone actually dead . . . again?" We didn't believe it at first and thought it had to be a dummy script.

Only Mia seemed composed. "It's going to be Jenny," she quietly stated. She did the simple math. "It's obviously not going to be Bette. It would never be Shane or Alice. Clearly, it's going to be me." But at that point none of us, including Mia, knew anything outside of that first episode. None of us knew the plan or the plot of season 6, so we were just as confused as the audience when suddenly our show about friendship, sex, and chosen family in Los Angeles morphed into a dark whodunit.

Of course, this was further complicated by the fact that in that last season, Shane and Jenny were going to get together. Per the Chart, there's the stereotype that all lesbians date each other. When Jenny caught Shane with Niki atop a hillside overlooking Los Angeles at the end of season 5, it was Mia who pitched the idea that the "you broke my heart" line should be directed at Shane, not Niki. Five seasons is a lot of television, so at some point the more ridiculous ideas we came up with suddenly seemed plausible, if only to keep things fresh. Thus, a couple was born—even though when Alice finds out, she runs into the bathroom, horrified, along with everyone else, at the thought of Shane and Jenny together.

I personally believe the Jenny/Shane combo would have been an interesting relationship to explore, had the final season not turned into *Unsolved Mysteries*. Their friendship already had history, so we could avoid the meet-cute and the "get to know you" phase that every new romance started with. The idea of crossing that line with the last person we would expect was compelling. Before I knew how that final season would unfold, I thought Jenny would at least be the one character who wouldn't try to change or save Shane from herself.

Mia and I had spent five years building their friendship, beginning when we were actual roommates. So, our off-camera dynamics informed our on-camera dynamics. We used to call Shane and Jenny's heart-to-heart conversations "whisper scenes." At one point Rose Troche yelled out behind camera, "Can we try one at a normal volume?!" Shane and Jenny felt like two broken toys who, oddly enough, understood each other. Mia and I had naturally expressed this understanding, even in Shane and Jenny's platonic friendship, through physical touch. One of us was always cuddling or hanging on the other; we held hands and displayed an intimacy that blurred the lines. Throughout the years we'd think up scenarios for Jenny to pop up out of nowhere in the middle of Shane's random sex scenes so they could have one of their deep conversations.

Although Mia came up with the idea of Jenny and Shane becoming a couple, and I welcomed it immediately, neither of us ever considered what that would entail physically. When it came time for their first kiss, I'm surprised we aren't still there trying to film it. Rose had the unbearable task of directing us that day. Everything was going smoothly right up until we had to make contact, which led to one of us running away from the other at the last possible moment. Eventually Rose came to us and said, "You've literally been hanging all over each other for six years, and now you're shy?"

By season 6, though, we were so comfortable with each other

that Mia declared a bucket list item for her character: "I want to be a top." "Fantastic!" I said. It would give my back a rest. The thought of just lying there seemed so relaxing—let Jenny do the work. However, just prior to filming, either circumstances within the scene shifted or the blocking denied Mia her wish. Once again, I was on top, and my dream of being a pillow princess ended before it even began.

Shane and Jenny were already a hard enough pill for much of the show's audience to swallow, so when Jenny got more controlling and manipulative throughout that final season, the less real it felt, and their ill-timed romance became less enjoyable to explore. One of my favorite shark-jump moments was when Jenny presented Shane with a fully equipped photography studio like it was something she found at an airport gift shop, in return for Shane's undying loyalty and possibly her voicemail passcode. It was disappointing to see Jenny morph into a cartoon villain, and in turn it felt out of character for Shane to become the out-of-touch human doormat. With that being said, I'll die on the hill that Jenny was the best character on the show. In fact, I'll double down and say I don't think *The L Word* would have worked as well without her. Although it's impossible to condone all her choices and behavior, this character that people loved to hate—or just downright hated—had so much trauma that was undiagnosed and untreated. I don't know if that was the original intention for Jenny, but Mia's fearless and unpredictable performance turned the average-girl-next-door character into this complex and complicated woman with mental health issues that people now have more compassion for, or at the very least are cognizant of.

After the initial murder mystery opener, the first episode felt like the normal *L Word*. The format for the season would be flashbacks, which we figured would lead to answering the million-dollar question of who was in the body bag. But as each episode progressed, circumstances became more unhinged. We all would try and find ways to get intel from the writers. "I just need to understand my character's arc, so I know what to play," we would plead, but it never worked—they weren't allowed to give us anything, and for good reason. Their approach was for the actors, and hence our characters, to live in real time, the events unfolding without us being influenced by how it would all end. We slowly and begrudgingly accepted the fact that we were meant to be in the dark about this.

By the time we got to that season's promo photo shoot, around the fourth episode, we realized Mia was right: Our victim was most likely going to be Jenny. By then her character had gone completely off the rails and each of our characters was exasperated and at their wits' end with her. The artwork concept for the shoot was for all of us to be standing next to each other in a police lineup, like *The Usual Suspects*. Jennifer convinced the marketing department that was the wrong message to put out there for the last season. But was it? Whether we liked it or not, that was the official ending. Instead, we stood in a row in front of our infamous hot-pink background, all holding hands and smiling like deliriously happy lottery winners. Cynthia and I decided Shane should wear a dress this time because by then, everything felt chaotic and out of sorts. The fuckery of Shane wearing a dress seemed fitting.

Once it had been confirmed how the rest of the season was going to play out, we'd commiserate about the odd direction of the final episodes with Angela, and she'd try to laugh it off and say that it was like the "Who shot J.R.?" plotline from the eighties series *Dallas*. She did her best to make light of the situation but saw the disappointment and bewilderment in our faces. I never would have thought five years earlier that not only would we be dealing with yet another character's death but that the series itself would have devolved into something like lesbian Clue. The one thing that felt like a natural evolution was that Bette and Tina would be selling their infamous bungalow and moving to New York to start over.

Midway through the season, many of us were sobering up to the reality of being jobless the following year. Ilene was developing new projects with Showtime, including a mysterious *L Word* spin-off pilot inspired by a book called *The Farm*, about a women's prison. The only reason I knew this was because I was quietly approached about possibly being in it, as Shane. Knowing this now made the whodunit make more sense, but it was impossible for me to understand how *The L Word* was going from our fabulous, fashion-forward lives in West Hollywood into this, of all things.

I suppose there were ways in which Shane in prison would've made sense, but the whole thing was difficult for me to visualize, and I had more questions than answers. It was not going to be a traditional pilot but a twenty-minute "presentation," with a smaller budget than a traditional pilot would receive. To Ilene's credit, her ideas have usually been ahead of the curve. She had the rights to *The Handmaid's Tale* and tried to get it made long before it ended up on Hulu. I was flattered that Ilene thought of me for this project and didn't want to be disrespectful to her or the offer, but I had to listen to my gut. Although it felt weird saying no to Ilene—and the prospect of a guaranteed job and salary—I just couldn't do it. It felt like it was time to move on. I had to trust fate and believe that if I was fortunate enough to get *The L Word* in the first place, a show that ran for six seasons, maybe I could use the little bit of heat from the show and trust something would come after it.

I was terrified at the unknown but, surprisingly, felt ready to face the challenge. Although our cast and crew were heartbroken that we would no longer be together, we were equally disappointed in the direction the show took, and as the weeks ticked by, it increasingly felt like most people had one foot out the door. None of us had

the appetite for a wild night out at Milk & Honey anymore, and the carefree brownie parties were a thing of the past. Now our conversations over low-key dinners or a glass of wine after work revolved around questions like "What are you doing next? When are you leaving? Have you packed?" It started to feel transient.

The usually bustling production office started to slow down as the episodes passed, and I noticed the boxes of paperwork that began to pile up in the corner, waiting to go into a storage vortex of series past. Cynthia invited us into a room where all the clothes that we hadn't already taken from all the seasons were stored. We went to our racks of clothing from the earlier years and marveled and laughed over the things we wore during the pilot that we had forgotten about (in some cases purposely). I happened to find a blazer I thought I had lost three years earlier. I even saw my infamous flame-throwing leather pants that started it all, and I still kick myself that I didn't take them as a keepsake.

The last scene that each of us had to shoot was our individual police interrogation/confession scene, so everyone wrapped separately. Those final moments were not what any of us had envisioned. Mia was the first to go, which hit hardest, since that was the catalyst for the rest of us. Tearfully, she said she hadn't made friends like this since grade school. It felt like the end of the movie *Stand by Me*. When it was my turn, a lot of the cast had already wrapped. I knew I couldn't eke out a farewell speech—it was too overwhelming—so I quietly went around to everyone separately to thank them and give them one last hug. Saying goodbye to the crew was the most difficult. They had been with us loyally for six years and were a huge part of our family. They had laughed with us and tolerated so much of our bullshit. It was hard to believe that was the end of Bob's mumbles and the *SNL* Sally O'Malley reenactments and wig characters we all invented with Joanne, Paul, and Jules in the hair and makeup trailer. No longer were we going to see the faces of our camera department—Neil, Andrew, and Eddie—who for years waited patiently for us to get through whatever laughing fit took hold of us. No more Cynthia and her cozy office chats, where we would gossip and play dress-up on our downtime. Or Joshanna, our on-set wardrobe dresser mama bear, who took care of us and always knew what we needed before we even did. Or Sandra, our first AD, with her infectious laugh, who not only wrangled feral cats nonstop for six years but kept the greatest sense of humor throughout. In a blink, all that time and work we shared was suddenly over. Perhaps the fact that the final season didn't end on a high was a blessing in disguise, since it allowed us to walk away a little easier.

LEISHA

In the last season of *The L Word*, there was scuttlebutt on set that Ilene had pitched a new show to the network. We heard whispers about it around every corner, but no one knew if it was true or not. There were rumblings that she wanted to pluck one of our characters and drop them into the spin-off. Allegedly, Ilene not only needed to find an actor who was receptive to the idea but whose character would make sense in crossing over to this alternate and antithetical universe. Kate told me she was offered the role and passed. I don't know where my name fell in the order of actors on Ilene's call sheet, but the call came. Kate and I had gone to see Michael Moore's documentary *Sicko*, and as we were eating popcorn waiting for the previews, my cell phone rang. It was Ilene, and we made a plan to meet up.

I was really curious to hear what she was thinking. Ilene explained that the new show was called *The Farm* and would be set in California's Humboldt State Farm and Prison for Women (a fictional facility). Alice in prison? It sounded a little like *The Muppets* sketch "Pigs in Space," but I kept an open mind. After being convicted of murdering Jenny Schecter, Alice would be a fish out of water in the federal prison system with no one around to save her. (Years later, of course, this scenario would make its way to TV with Piper on one of my favorite shows, *Orange Is the New Black*.) Ilene's list of actresses already in serious contention to play the other roles in the pilot was beyond impressive. As I listened to the number of ideas Ilene had, my apprehension turned to excitement. Not only would it be a sizable artistic challenge but a clever way to expand my career possibilities. No one had ever given me an opportunity like this before. Well, minus the first time Ilene had. *What did I have to lose?* I thought.

With each day of filming the last episodes, the dread of saying goodbye to the family I'd made over six seasons became hard to fathom. Of course, I knew we'd see each other, but I also knew this remarkable chapter in our lives was almost over. The work had been hard at times, with long hours, many of them spent topless, but mostly it was a fucking blast. On a daily basis I would feel enormous waves of gratitude. I knew I was lucky, made sure to cherish every moment.

By the time we shot the series finale, I had officially signed on to do *The Farm* pilot. On top of everything else Ilene had on her plate, she had the daunting task of writing the spin-off very quickly. We would be shooting it only two months after we wrapped *The L Word*. Now, was Alice actually guilty of murdering Jenny? No one, not even the writers, knew. They were trying to give every character a level of plausibility as the murderer to keep the mystery alive, so we were each told to play some sort of shady behavior. That's why to this day (minus the awful "death by suicide" explanation given in the reboot that I totally disagreed with) neither I nor anyone else in the cast really knows the truth. As actors, it was a vague way to play an ending, and I think it made for an unsatisfying experience for viewers. We were never given a fair, thoughtful, or in-depth explanation of Jenny's death. Her demise remains a mystery after all.

In the very last sequence that we filmed to wrap up the series, the cast was supposed to appear as cheerful as possible, even though their best friend had just been found dead. And because there was no storybook ending, someone had the bright idea for the last episode to end with us walking in an ethereal runway show, the cast striding effortlessly and excitedly into the great abyss. We watched, perplexed, as the set department built a huge plywood catwalk. They placed gigantic fans at the end of the platform. The cast was draped in clothing that blew behind us along with our hair. We did as we were told and sashayed into oblivion wearing expressions that morphed from suspicious to shit-eating grins. All the while we were whispering to each other, "Are we all going to heaven or the police station?" Then Dead Jenny joins the glamorous procession! I turned to Kate—"What is actually going on?" Her reaction is the sincerest smile of the entire montage.

It wasn't long after filming ended that I returned to Vancouver to shoot the spin-off. This time, though, the city was in the throes of a chilly winter. Any semblance of the "fake Los Angeles" I was so accustomed to was gone. *The Farm* was being built on the very soundstages where *The L Word* sets had just been dismantled. Everything that had been so familiar had suddenly been replaced by something foreign. A loneliness blanketed me. Could I do this without my friends? I called Kate and relayed how weird it felt. I told her how the prison shower stalls were in the place I had so often eaten Kit's famous pear polenta tart in The Planet. I was caught between the familiar and the unrecognizable. It was surreal, and the pressure was building. I called my mom for support too. "I don't know if I can do it," I said, and teared up on the phone. But my mom always had a way of reminding me I was right where I should be and that doubting myself would get me nowhere. I was so grateful to be given this chance, and the last thing I wanted was to let anybody down. I dug deep and threw myself in.

When we started, I struggled with fitting into the tone of the show. I couldn't help but worry that Ilene had made the wrong choice in picking Alice, because nothing about my character being behind bars was easy to navigate. It was a dark, serious show, like a female version of HBO's *Oz*. Where I used to be buckled over in laughter with my old castmates, I was now buckled over getting cavity searched. To say this was a change is an understatement.

In my first scene, I rolled up to the slammer aboard the transport bus, or the Grey Goose, as they called it. I was shackled in handcuffs with chains around my ankles but was wearing a brightly colored Alice outfit, a hot-pink coat, to show that I had been arrested in the middle of my normal, carefree day in West Hollywood. After roll call, I made my one allotted phone call to Tasha. "You gotta help me get out of here," I said. Rose had been approached to appear in the show if it got picked up.

Then, as prison would have it, I was paired with a crazy cellmate. This presented another issue: Sarah Strange, the amazing actress who was playing that role, had also played Jenny's best friend from college on *The L Word*. So, I was playing the same person, but she was playing a completely different person. If we were supposed to be existing in the same universe as *The L Word*, it didn't make any sense. As if that wasn't odd enough, one of the corrections officers was played by the incomparable Melissa Leo—who had also appeared on *The L Word* as Helena Peabody's ex.

That being said, I was honored to be among an ensemble that included one of my idols, Laurie Metcalf, as the warden, and other heavy hitters like Famke Janssen playing a notorious gang member.

After we finished filming, I went back to LA and was on hold for about seven months while the network decided whether or not they wanted to pick up the show. During that time, I couldn't audition for anything else because I was in first position for *The Farm*. With this restriction, I missed out on a few opportunities. As the months passed and I watched my *L Word* girls go on to do other things, I started to spiral. Cam was on tour with another band, things weren't going great with Robin, and I couldn't stop the needling thought that I might never work again. Feeling aimless and adrift, I drove to East Valley Animal Shelter where I adopted a beautiful, dirty-white junkyard dog and named her Zoo.

Finally, the phone rang. The president of Showtime told me that as much as they liked *The Farm* presentation, they were passing. It just didn't fit into the network's roster—Hollywood speak for "Yeah, it's a big fat no." A part of me was sad, but a bigger part of me was proud that I'd taken the risk . . . Now, it was time to take agency of my own life.

9

Lost and Found

KATE

I didn't have much time to process my feelings about the end of *The L Word*, since a few months later I had a job lined up on, of all places, network television. It was a huge relief: I hadn't been looking forward to falling back into pilot season, that time of year when every actor is auditioning for the new crop of potential TV shows. Lucky for me, at the last minute, I got a call about a doctor show, produced by the late Curtis Hanson, director of *LA Confidential*. That year, the theme around Tinseltown was hospitals. *ER* was ending its run, so every network wanted to fill its shoes. I had met Curtis years earlier for a film he was doing, and somehow he remembered me and reached out to discuss this lead female role, a renegade workaholic with daddy issues. It sounded promising. I was used to being on cable, where anything goes, and didn't know if I would fit into mainstream television. But since Curtis was producing it, I thought, what could go wrong?

I sat down with Curtis, his producing partner, the show's creator, and the director. They recorded the conversation we had, and when the network suits saw it, the note that came back was, "Can she come back with a different hairstyle?" That was fair, I thought—we had just finished shooting *The L Word* barely three months earlier, so my hair was still growing out from Shane and her bad decisions.

At the time, I didn't know what their expectations were, but the network paid for a very expensive stylist to put long extensions on every strand of my hair. I went back to meet with the team the second time, and when I walked into the room, Curtis took one look at me, with the most mortified look in his eyes. Nothing about this was authentic. He knew it and deep down I knew it too. What the powers that be were looking for was a straight-presenting girl, but they couldn't say that. Curtis pulled me aside. "Look, I don't give a shit about your hair, but these guys need to see something, so just get through this once, and then we can move forward." I appreciated his bluntness and thought we were just playing the game to get what we needed and then it would be more hands-off.

I wound up getting the job, and we shot the pilot in Pittsburgh a few weeks later. Easily the most fascinating aspect was the research. Production suggested we shadow some thoracic transplant surgeons at University of Pittsburgh Medical Center (UPMC) hospital to understand the level of medicine that our show was centered on. UPMC is a teaching hospital, so it's not uncommon for resident doctors to have students follow them as they make their rounds. We were given lab coats and scrubs to wear to visit patients in ICU, and we witnessed how doctors deliver bad news to families in the waiting room, which still haunts me. I scrubbed in and spent the night in the operating room, standing on a stool next to the anesthesiologist, overlooking an eight-hour heart transplant. All these years later, I still wash my hands the way I was taught in the OR prep station.

It was a complete one-eighty from what we were doing in Vancouver. All that being said, I had no expectation that this pilot was ever going to see the light of day. It was obviously trying to replace *ER* and we were just one of many vying for a chance. It was surprising when I found out at the eleventh hour that we were picked up to series, but I was even more surprised and incredibly disappointed to learn that Curtis was no longer going to be part of the show. He felt like my guardian angel and the reason I took the job in the first place. By then I was under contract and had no room to negotiate. On one hand, I was employed again, but on the other, I knew this was not what I had signed up for.

Soon after, I got called into a think tank meeting with a corporate network exec, who, in a very subtle and roundabout way asked, "How can we make you look more . . . 'accessible?'" Translation: "How can we make you look less gay?" Initially this character read as someone who was there to challenge the system, push people's buttons, and defy authority, but it was obvious those characteristics were now going to be rounded over. I looked at this executive who was tasked with having this impersonal conversation and realized she genuinely didn't give a shit what I thought about the character; she merely had to check this off her to-do list and move on with her day. Regardless, we still needed to figure out what to do with my hair. I had no desire to live with extensions that felt like a nest of painful metal bugs living on my scalp for the next six months. The solution? Flying out the most famous wigmaker in the world from France to make a mold of my head and create a custom hairpiece. The wig was my saving grace and was treated like a cast member. I think we even named her.

They moved the shoot from Pittsburgh to the Paramount lot in LA. I had never worked at home before, and it was a privilege to sleep in my own bed and only be twenty minutes away from the set. One day I was driving around in a golf cart during a break and had to stop for a commercial that was in the middle of filming. "Rose?!" I yelled out. "Oh my god, Kate?!" she yelled back. Rose Rollins was filming the commercial.

Leisha also came to visit once. She took one look at my head and couldn't believe what was happening. I had grown used to my new job by then, but she could look in my eyes and tell I was conforming to everyone else's expectations—and not just in terms of hairstyle. As I showed Leisha around this new world I was in, I felt a deep pang that she wasn't a part of it. I fantasized about dressing her in some scrubs and a face mask and throwing her into a scene so we could improvise and banter with each other like we used to, but there was too much red tape. The direction of the show became very homogenized and procedural once it was picked up to series. Any grit, edge, or risk had left with Curtis. Now, the episodic conflict was unfailingly resolved by the hero doctor of the day. My character's original rough edges were softened. I remember a request to wear my hair back for an ER scene required approval from five different people. Can we see how high the ponytail will be? No, that's too low, can it be higher? It's too messy, maybe a bun? The scene was maybe a page long. Call me dense but I was slowly realizing I was not the lead female character I had originally been pitched.

Was I feeling under-the-surface homophobia or was I just horribly miscast? By this point, I wasn't trying to hide my sexuality from anyone, though I still didn't love talking to media about my personal life (it's still something I can't say I truly enjoy). A lot of the wounds of my earlier coming-out experiences had scabbed over, including my relationship with my mom, which had become an incredibly supportive and accepting one after the bumpy start. On set, I had heard stories about discrimination in the industry, but I was the lucky one who had just spent the last six years celebrating queerness on camera. If the homophobia had been more upfront and in my face, maybe I would have been able to pinpoint where it was coming from and address it directly. Yet the subtlety of the dynamic made it feel like there was a ghost in my house that I knew was there but couldn't prove. I was under the impression there were network and production notes being passed back and forth with the higher-ups regarding my appearance. I tried not to think too much about it—I didn't have the time.

The workload was intense, the hours long, and if I had lost focus, I would have caved into myself with self-doubt. As we began filming the season, my character was more off to the side. The leading man was written to have an even more prominent hero role, and a beautiful female doctor was written in to be his potential love interest. It was a short-lived series. After the gay liberation of *The L Word*, my network experience was like jumping into a pool of cold water. The world, and our business in particular, was not ready to embrace stories or characters that didn't fit the status quo. Otherness in any form felt unwelcome. *Glee* had only just come on the air at Fox; *Orange Is the New Black* was still a few years away on Netflix. We were still very much in an era of hiding the gay away. It was fine to be loud and proud on your little cable show, but even the beauty standards for mainstream America and its thirty million viewers were completely different.

We thought we had taken some steps forward with representation. But outside that bubble, Hollywood still had a lot of catching up to do. I had to remind myself that I wasn't just imagining the popularity *The L Word* had outside of our community. I wondered where all those executives and producers went, the ones who made a point of stopping me to whisper they were huge fans of the show and never missed an episode. Was it easier for them to say that when they weren't the ones taking the risk in making it? Who was going to pick up the baton and push representation forward?

I found myself in a lull after my medical practice ended. I came close to a few projects I loved but would miss out at the last moment. When the role of Lena on *Ray Donovan* came around, it turned out to be the gift that kept on giving. It was the Energizer Bunny of TV shows. We would be in the middle of filming a season and already know when we would be back to film the next one. I finally knew what it felt like to be on a tentpole show that was the teacher's pet of the network—job security.

Being back on Showtime, the network that raised me, felt like coming home again, though under very different circumstances. With a cast starring Liev Schreiber and Jon Voight, *Ray* was very much a man's world, and I understood where I fell on the food chain immediately. I knew what I was walking into, and from day one I managed my expectations but was grateful to be employed. The woman who created it, Ann Biderman, was someone I connected with easily. She was a no-nonsense New Yorker who was a phenomenal writer with ironclad opinions, an eagle eye for detail, and excellent taste. I was just happy to be back on cable television, even if my dialogue mainly consisted of the words "yes, boss" and "no, boss." I had read something once about Jodi Foster going over scripts and flipping male characters to female characters, which I decided to experiment with: By the third season, when I asked them to consider writing for Lena like they would a man, I was allowed to come out from behind my desk and was slowly given more of a purpose. By season 6, the gloves had come off, and I was now jumping out of a window holding on to a rope that strangled my nemesis on the other end of it and blowing up cars in the middle of the day.

Lena turned out to be this unpredictable pleasure to play—not to mention the consistency of the role allowed me to usually know my schedule ahead of time. I'd walk into the read-throughs, and anyone could be there—from Susan Sarandon to Hank Azaria, Elliott Gould, and Alan Alda. The supporting cast that the show got season after season was consistently stacked. My character was pretty much an island unto herself, though, so I didn't film with the rest of the main cast that often. They had built a history and a language from all the time they had spent working together, and I didn't get to know them as well as they knew each other. Although the show was about family, for me it didn't have that family feeling. However, I did find my own personal Angel. Yes, that is her real name. She was our makeup artist, and every day we would bond and laugh over some absurd melodrama that happened against the backdrop of this testosterone-fueled world. Though I was happy to have the work, I struggled to find my place in it all. In smaller indie films I would get cast as a straight woman, while in others it would be characters with queer undertones. The descriptions usually featured the words *quirky* and *edgy*. I fit into a certain mold, and I was allowed to play in that sphere. Sometimes, I wondered if this was what my mom meant all those years ago when she was worried that my life would be harder. For the queer roles I encountered, the characters often lacked dimension or fell into obvious stereotypes. Sometimes there was no purpose to them other than superficial representation. I can still read something and quickly tell if the creatives are only filling a quota to feel like they have done their part.

LEISHA

"I bought Robin a piece of art, a series of colored circles, because she'd once described the ease and rightness of our attraction as 'the dots connecting,'" I explained to our couples therapist. "She told me she liked the painting, then leaned it against the wall by the back door. It sat there for three years." I turned to Robin and, for the first time, stood up for myself. "I feel like you want to curate everything in this relationship. There's no space for me or my things, even when it's a gift for you." The therapist gave us a knowing look.

Robin put all my belongings in the garage and told me to come get them while she was at work. You would think I'd have accumulated a lot of stuff in the ten years we'd been together, but Kate and I loaded my coffee table books and art supplies, two suitcases of clothes, a single framed photograph, and my dog Zoo into her car. Then she followed as I rode my motorcycle up that driveway for the last time.

I crashed on Mia's couch in a beautiful little bungalow she had been renting in the Hollywood Hills while I looked for an apartment to rent. She was so welcoming and wonderfully compassionate as I struggled to put one foot in front of the other. We'd sit under the stars at night, drinking wine from her small Moroccan glasses, and inspire each other with an endless supply of life's possibilities. Our lives were so different from our roommate days on *The L Word*, but the bond we'd forged then stood strong. With her and Kate and Erin by my side, I knew I could endure anything. Between running lines with Mia for whatever audition she had or driving to band rehearsal, I'd check out apartments, and finally found one in Koreatown. It had tall windows that flooded the room with light that, in the midst of my heartbreak, would help me get out of bed. I moved in and began my next chapter.

Acting professionally, even after you've been on a show for six seasons, is a constant hustle. A steady stream of auditions is a commitment and requires preparation, which can be draining. In this process, my enthusiasm for acting wavered, especially as I got back in the swing of things with Cam and Uh Huh Her. I'd go out for the occasional part, usually one with a description like "quirky, funny BFF sidekick in glasses," aka gay, but I wasn't even booking those. Two years on, it was as though my life had reverted to what it was before *The L Word*. I convinced myself that the time I spent on the show was a fluke. And then, one Friday at 6:57 p.m., my talent agent called and dropped me, explaining I hadn't booked enough jobs to keep my place on his roster. I had no representation and therefore no means of getting another job. *Time to move on*, I thought, and fully immersed myself in the band.

Cam and I were spending more time together finding and refining our sound. We'd left our record label, which gave us complete creative freedom. It was so exciting to be around her. Cam was seven years younger than me and exuded an air of "I don't give a fuck." She had the attitude of a bad girl, without the rabble-rousing behavior. Her spirit had a rebelliousness, an edge that was refreshing after the rigidity of my previous relationship.

For Uh Huh Her's second album, *Nocturnes*, the incredibly talented Wendy Melvoin of Prince and the Revolution—as in "Is the water warm enough?" "Yes Lisa"—came on as our coproducer. Wendy has a production room at Henson Recording Studios in Hollywood. Faryal, the manager, generously let us set up camp there. You know those moments when you can't believe this is your life? Going to work every day at Henson Recording Studios is absolutely one of those for me. In these hallowed halls, Carole King recorded *Tapestry*, Joni Mitchell laid down the tracks for *Blue*, and every single star in the 1980s came together for "We Are the World." And now us?

Wendy recruited Jaime Sickora, the head engineer at Henson, to record our vocals. Jaime is sunshine in human form, right down to her ring of bleach-blond curls. She is loyal, hilarious, impossibly talented—having recorded legends such as Mariah Carey, Chaka Khan, Coldplay, and Destiny's Child—but would be mortified if I told you. If you met her, you would instantly want Jaime to be your friend, but she's mine, you can't have her. Professionally, Jaime made me and Cam sound better than we ever had before, and personally she was the White Rabbit to my Alice (different Alice), leading me into a whole new Wonderland.

Uh Huh Her booked some tour dates in Europe. I had been to Paris once before with Robin. She had scheduled our itinerary meticulously and I left feeling like I'd seen so much of the city. With Cam, however, I experienced it. She told me she was going to teach me "the art of sitting." We left the hotel with no plan. We walked the city, found a café—not one recommended by a tour guide or well-traveled friend—and ate. We meandered through a park and stopped to observe, watching a couple on a bench gradually move closer to each other until they were making out. Seeing people kiss in Paris is always prettier. We noticed the range of colors on the leaves hanging overhead. Cam let the day unfold, showing me that not every minute needed to be regimented or productive. She was like freedom personified.

I found myself missing Cam when she'd go on tour with her other band. I was confused in that classic lesbian way. Was I just excited about making music with this person? Or was I falling for this girl? One day at the studio I looked up from my guitar and her face—which I'd looked at a thousand times—struck me in a different way. *Uh-oh,* I thought, *here we go again.*

Falling in love is always a drug. But falling in love with someone while on a world tour together was the greatest high I'd experienced.

I was exploring a different city every other day with someone who made colors look brighter, food taste better, and jokes even funnier. The travel was thrilling, the music was hitting, and I was all in.

During *The L Word*, Kate's and my enmeshment was wonderful but unsustainable. Outside of our Vancouver bubble, our contact lessened. As our lives were taking very different paths, we made a pact to not take our bond for granted, but there were moments where communication waned. At times five thousand miles apart, our friendship was taking a new shape.

KATE

Leisha and I would talk on the phone, but the calls were fewer and farther between. With *The L Word* in the rearview mirror, suddenly our sense of commonality was vanishing. Whatever Leisha was doing on tour was so far outside my realm of understanding. Leisha invited me to meet her a few times in San Francisco and Oregon. By then, the secret was out that she and her bandmate had fallen for each other and were in those blissfully unaware stages of love where you forget where you are. Part of me was curious to see what a day in the life of her new world looked like, but it didn't feel right to intrude. It was hard to visualize how I could visit her without taking up valuable space in a cramped bus. I was also conscious of not wanting to dampen Leisha's experience by showing up as a reminder of the past. Her present life seemed so intense, exciting, and all-consuming. Still, the connection was never fully severed. We knew that we belonged to each other to a certain extent. If we hadn't spoken by the two-week mark, one of us would pick up the phone. There was always a check-in, a grand ebb and flow.

However, when touring slowed down and we both were in LA, we would naturally pick up where we left off. In our downtime, we would throw ourselves into projects together. Leisha helped me source wood and build a twenty-foot-long built-in barbecue and taught me how to safely use a miter saw. In turn, I would get called to come over and help move some ungodly heavy piece of furniture because she suddenly had the desire to redecorate. At one point she wanted an in-ground gas-line fire pit in her backyard, so, being our industrious selves, we got to work. Beginning with snapping lines and cutting massive slabs of concrete into shapes around her pool with a deadly machine that weighed more than both of us combined.

We DIY'd our lives together long before it became popular on social media.

When one of us made a new friend, we wanted to introduce each other to them. While Leisha's band was spending long hours recording at the studio, she called to invite me over so her sound engineer and I could get a look at each other. "I really want you to meet Jaime," she said. "She grew up just outside of Philly!" As if that would seal the deal. However, sure enough, within five minutes, Jaime and I bonded over our love of Stacey Q and her B-side sleeper hits. We found ourselves having heated debates over what a water ice really is, and being an avid Steelers fan, Jaime has continuously and will always call the Philadelphia Eagles the Pigeons. To me, expanding chosen family always feels a little like house renovations. Taking what we already love and making it bigger and better.

10

||||

Long Live the Buzzsox

LEISHA

Cam and I were at a place where moving in together felt right, and Jaime was renting a guesthouse in Los Feliz. The main house was occupied by a teenage actress who loved having loud sing-along parties with her fifteen-year-old friends into the wee hours of the night . . . this is not what a recording engineer wants to hear in her downtime. Jaime would come to work with bags under her eyes, saying, "I gotta move." I started looking at house listings.

I never in my wildest dreams thought I could afford a house in LA . . . turns out, I was right. While technically the Valley is Los Angeles, it is not the glamorous part, especially not the neighborhood where I found a collection of ramshackle structures on a single lot. While Cam was sleeping one Sunday morning, I grabbed Jaime and some coffee and drove to the property. From the street, the main house looked like Grey Gardens but with more vermin than just raccoons. There were three dilapidated cars parked on the front "lawn." Though we probably should have been, neither Jaime nor I was deterred. We skulked through the alley to check out the rest of it. I couldn't see over the back fence, so Jaime cupped her hands and lifted me up. I peered over and saw a dumpy fixer-upper hidden in a field of knee-high weeds with a neglected pool that a young Tony Hawk would have killed for. When I jumped down, Jaime could see the hearts in my eyes as I blurted, "Do you know a real estate agent?"

I was filled with a new sense of purpose: to make a home for all of us. Two months—and multiple calls to exterminators—later, Cam and I moved into the front house and Jaime moved into the guesthouse. Cam and I were bouncing between life on the road and life on the compound. When we were home, I devoted my time to renovating the houses. Everyone chipped in, but I was a woman on a mission: painting, tiling, woodworking, even cement cutting. I was unlicensed and undaunted, determined to make our house a home.

There was a third dwelling on the property, and I needed to rent it out in order to make my new mortgage payment. I shook the lesbian phone tree and out fell a tiny woman with long dark hair named Sofu. She showed up for her interview in all black (a rare occurrence in LA, especially a black turtleneck on a hot summer day). She said she was Brazilian, had moved to Switzerland at thirteen to attend boarding school, and now worked in cybersecurity. After she left, Cam, Jaime, and I were convinced she was a trained assassin and therefore a great asset to our compound. We gave her the keys. Sofu maintained her status as an international woman of mystery the entire time we lived together: Between the accent and never knowing where she went at night, I remain certain she is in the CIA.

The four of us had different personalities but got along great. We were the Golden Girls if they had dildos in the dishwasher. And we always seemed to be facing a sitcom-like problem. Like the one where we found a litter of kittens behind the water heater and had to call in a lesbian Ace Ventura named Jody to come rescue them. She collected the cats, then said she'd foster them until they were old enough to be placed in forever homes . . . naturally, we called her Jody Foster.

Or the one where we decided to supplement our meager incomes by rolling joints for our enterprising neighbor. Seriously. It was 2016 and recreational marijuana had just been legalized in California. There was a woman who lived down the street who was a manager of a dispensary and who would pay a dollar per joint. Once a week she'd drop off a bag of weed and papers. We would put on a movie and see who could roll the most joints by the end credits. We'd make about $500 per movie, except for the time we rewatched *Titanic* and cleared close to $600.

Even though only four of us were living full-time on the land, there were always gobs of lesbians around. Six out of seven days a week, women were *always* over. Sometimes it would be four, sometimes fifteen, sometimes it would be thirty. We'd wake up and people were splayed out on every couch.

The compound was an entertainer's paradise: the pool was admittedly freezing but a welcome relief in the hot SoCal summer. The backyard was alive with volleyball games, barbecues, and everyone's dogs zipping around, Zoo in the lead. The cooking, whatever we'd make, was always a big to-do, from Friendsgiving to weekend potlucks. Jaime and I were like short-order cooks, doling out burgers, vegan kielbasa, and corn: "Ding, order's up."

Since sports bars never show women's games, we decided to make our own. Cam and I bought a big TV for the screened-in porch so everyone could watch Ronda Rousey wrestle her opponents into a chokehold, Sue Bird drill a three-pointer, and Abby Wambach nail a penalty kick.

As if we weren't spending enough time together, we all decided to join a gay women's softball league. We named ourselves the Buzzsox, after the White Sox and the fact that some of us would pregame with Vitaminwater discreetly infused with vodka. We were a mixed bag of rookies and "I used to play in high school" talent. We never practiced and we only won two games in three years, but we dominated the league when it came to nicknames. Kate played first base—even though Shane was known for going to fourth—and was called G-Paw because she was the lovable curmudgeon on the team. Jaime was "Cooler" because she soon realized that we needed to keep our "Vitaminwater" on ice, so she bought a rideable motorized cooler on wheels. Don't be fooled, that thing could go faster than you'd think. There was also Vanimal, Juicy, and Beast. I played outfield, and while many pop flies came my way, I could never get myself to the ball in time. They always seemed so far away (I should have taken the cooler!). In three years, I caught the ball exactly one time. The entire Buzzsox team rushed over to me, hoisted me onto their shoulders, and paraded me around the field . . . much to the irritation of the opposing team and the umpire. But who cares, it was my *Rudy* moment.

Leisha's compound had an open-door policy, and all of us who didn't live there knew the gate code. During the summers, I'd finish a boxing class and just let myself in so I could fall into the pool to cool off, and no one blinked an eye if they found me or another friend floating there.

As the core group of friends grew, so did the organized family events. Elaborate, multicourse barbecues were common, and everyone who joined pitched in to make it a collaborative feast. It became so common that by every Wednesday or at the latest Thursday, someone would ask, "So, what are we doing this weekend?" Invariably someone would suggest an art show or having a pool day. When we were offered a private court to play volley b-ball, which was our version of volleyball, we all jumped at the chance to partake in one of the most entertaining activities we invented together. We went so far as thinking that playing touch football would be a great idea one afternoon, and half of us lived on Advil the following week. One year, a few of us coined that summer as Camp. We decided was going to be three months of only blissful enjoyment.

Leisha was still on tour for another couple of weeks and was jealous she wasn't home yet. She would call to check in and ask, "What am I missing out on today?" To make up for her FOMO, when she got back, we rented a huge house on Lake Arrowhead. Friends would filter in and out through the week, depending on their own work schedules, since Arrowhead is only about an hour and a half outside of LA. Our other friend Nicol bought an inflatable boat with a motor on the back of it. The fantasy was that she and I were going to have a bountiful fishing expedition on this thing and proudly feed the whole family back onshore. She named it *The Rubber Ducky*. Leisha made a custom wooden sign that hung from the back, and everyone bid us bon voyage as we set sail. However, once we got to the middle of the lake, we heard a muffled *hiss* and our rubber lifeline started to deflate. Motorboats twice our size zoomed by, creating a wake that almost capsized us while we slowly sank. Soon our fishing poles began to drift away as we cupped our hands to scoop out the water that was rising around us. Eventually, a very nice man on a real boat came to our rescue, tossed us a line, and towed us back in. Everyone else we were with watched from the dock in hysterics and relief as the two drowned cats finally made it to safety. *The Rubber Ducky* spent the rest of her days sitting half-assed in the box she came in. However, Leisha's sign was salvaged.

In all the years of our softball team, the Buzzsox, we won two games. One of those was because the other team didn't show up. We were the D-listers of the league and no one took us seriously, but we had a lot of heart. Jaime was the captain of the Buzzsox. Which meant she had to answer for us to the people in charge. One day she was called into a very serious and time-sensitive meeting regarding a live-stream video our friend had made during one of our games that she put on YouTube. Turned out that the team we were playing that day had a player who was an FBI agent who was actively undercover on a high-level assignment, and the Buzzsox were going to blow the whole operation. It became a five-alarm fire that could only happen in a lesbian softball league.

When our outfielder, Puff, accidently caught a fly ball with her face and went limp on the ground, we all jumped in our cars and caravanned to the nearest ER. Ten of us were in the waiting room while she was getting stitched up. I remember thinking, *This is what it must feel like to have a big family.*

Without knowing it, the chosen family Leisha and I had found in Vancouver was being organically re-created at home. None of us had too many responsibilities or obligations, so we could be impulsive. Jaime would call and say, "I'm coming up your hill! Meet me outside!" and she'd whisk us to a bar she had found in the middle of a forest in a part of LA we had never known existed.

The Supreme Court legalized gay marriage during this era. We were elated to finally be given this fundamental human right, yet none of us were at a point in our lives where that seemed like the next step. I had, during this time, embarked on another relationship, one that had run longer than it ever should have. The bright red flags were there from the beginning, but I chose to ignore them, thinking that being in love, along with my high tolerance for discomfort, was enough. Somehow, along the way, I'd picked up a conviction that happiness wasn't really a prerequisite for my romantic relationships. Instead, my job was to fix what was broken, regardless of the effects on my own mental health. My own world got smaller and smaller as I focused all my energy on trying to repair things on my own. I missed my friends, I missed my interests, and more importantly, I missed feeling like myself. Still, I couldn't quite bring myself to uproot my life yet again. Should a breakup be squeezed in before or after a fifteen-hour day on set? Is it worth spoiling a holiday? Eventually the universe stopped dropping hints and just smacked me over the head with the truth I'd been trying to avoid—which, on this occasion, came in the form of Leisha. She was on tour, and we hadn't been speaking as frequently, with time changes and schedules difficult to line up. While she was away, though, she heard from a reliable source that the person I was with had been even more dishonest than I or the rest of us had already suspected. When Leisha called me after about ten days of not talking, the first thing I heard when I answered was "You have to get out of this relationship."

"What? . . . Where are you?" Turns out she was literally standing on the shoulder of a two-lane highway in the middle of Oklahoma as she unloaded every bit of information she had found out minutes before. I was driving too and had to pull over myself to keep up with it all. I was already aware of some of what she told me, but other things were news. Again, she insisted, "Please get the fuck out of this." It was a hard pill to swallow, even though it was impossible to ignore that she was right.

Maybe a week later Jaime scooped me up in her Jeep. "We are doing a surprise-by," she announced. We screeched up to the Troubadour on Santa Monica Boulevard at the exact moment Leisha was helping load in for Uh Huh Her's show that night. We all collectively screamed with excitement. The reunion was exactly what I needed at that moment and gave me the clarity to do what I had to do. My relationship came to its inevitable end, and my girlfriend moved out—but her belongings didn't. They took up my one-car garage past their expiration date, and by then even more information had filtered through our lesbian pipeline, which added to the unpleasantness of it all. Enough was enough already. Leisha and a group of friends rallied one afternoon, and before I knew it, three cars pulled up with the girls, like the Pink Ladies. They meticulously and efficiently helped me organize and remove her things. Once one car got filled up, then we stuffed the next one, and finally the last one, and we all caravanned across town to put them in a storage space.

While I was in that relationship, I had taken advantage of the high desert not being a destination spot at the time and invested in a getaway house there for dirt cheap. I had spent months renovating it with my friend Chris, who taught me how to sweat pipes, pull electricity, and frame outdoor showers. Now, between the breakup and looking around realizing there wasn't anything left to build, I knew the chances of me wanting to spend time out there now were going to be slim to none. When the house sold, Leisha was the first to say, "I'll help you." We rented our second U-Haul with boxes and tape and drove out to the desert. We managed to methodically pack up the house in less than eight hours and spent the last night eating pizza and watching *Erin Brockovich*. The following morning, reality hit me as I was looking at the view for the last time. Before I could start second-guessing myself, Leisha came out, handed me a coffee, and broke the silence with "I never liked it out here anyway." We were practiced enough by that point that we could have started a successful lesbian-owned business and called it Reverse U-Haul.

After that period of chaotic upheaval ended, I was grateful for my loyal group of friends and the stability of *Ray Donovan*, but I wanted to use this new time productively and challenge myself. Sofu offered to take me to a place she used to train at. We walked down a nondescript alley off Melrose Avenue and into an old-school, run-down gym that looked to be trapped in time—it was perfect. During that one afternoon, she opened my eyes to the magical world of boxing. Which, I came to quickly learn, was not only a sport but a mindset and art form. It provided a structure and discipline that I couldn't get enough of. I threw myself into training, and I felt not only physically better but mentally stronger than I ever had. The environment that Trinity Boxing and its owner, Martin Snow, cultivated was a melting pot of people from all walks of life who met every day to let go of wherever we had come from and devote an hour to pushing harder than we had the day before. Having a bad day? "Don't stand there, Moennig, hit the bag!" Tired from the night before? "Not my problem, get to work," Martin would bellow. With the spirit of Coach Taylor and the attitude of Mickey Goldmill, Martin inspired everyone to get out of ourselves and whatever we were feeling, whether it was fear, anger, or just frustration from a shitty day, and channel it into concentration, confidence, and then contact. Trinity became my unofficial church, and I didn't miss a day: It was meditative, brought immediate focus, and quieted my swirling thoughts. Finally, after so many years of struggle, so many ups and downs, life was this full and balanced plate. I couldn't imagine finding the time to meet anyone let alone the interest of dating anyone, and I didn't want to. Which is usually when that one person comes out of left field.

I met Ana at a mutual friend's party. It was too loud to really talk—either there, or at the next several parties where I ran into her. Eventually, she asked me out to dinner so that we could hear each other speak. I was flattered by the invite, since it felt more formal and mature than just going out for drinks or meeting up at yet another party where I wouldn't be able to hear what she was saying. I was intrigued that she had not only broken the ice but suggested the restaurant, made the reservation, and arrived on time. Still, I had zero expectations and was perfectly fine if nothing came of it. Turns out the jam-packed restaurant was loud too, but we weren't distracted this time, as our conversations flowed with the ease I would normally only feel with someone I had known for years.

My therapist once said that to really know someone's true character, you either need to spend four seasons together to see their personality and moods fluctuate throughout the year, *or* go through an unpredictable, stressful event together. We soon had a chance to test this theory, as at the exact moment Ana put the pen down after signing the bill, two police officers came into the restaurant trying to get everyone's attention. "Excuse me, everyone. Excuse me! Everyone!" The restaurant, which had previously felt like Grand Central Station at rush hour, came to a halt. "I'm going to ask that everyone evacuate the premises immediately." The staff had no idea what was going on. The police reiterated, "All kitchen staff, and anyone else in the back. Leave everything as it is and evacuate now. Please remain calm." We all spilled out onto the sidewalk to find police tape blocking off the street and the adjoining corners. Police cars lined up in all directions and more sirens were heard in the distance. An officer was outside the door directing people to his left, saying, "Get to your cars, get to your cars." Within moments, people's uneasy laughter and sarcastic one-liners morphed into demands to know what was going on. Panic and impatience grew as word spread that it was a bomb threat. The two gentlemen managing the valet were immediately overwhelmed, doing their best to meet everyone's needs as hordes of car tickets were being frantically waved in their faces, like they couldn't already see them.

I looked at Ana, who by then was leaning against a wall, away from the chaos. We watched the entitled restaurant-goers demand their cars back and the two valet guys become increasingly anxious and overburdened by the privileged, hysterical yelling in their faces. Ana calmly got up off the wall, walked over to the valet stand, and began collecting people's tickets, asking them to describe their cars so they could be more easily found. She took it a step further and spoke with the police to coordinate the best way to drive off, then told everyone, since the street was blocked off, to collect their cars in the back alley behind the restaurant. As I stood there in awe, Ana and the two valets worked in tandem and everyone began to calm down, regain their composure, and look to Ana for answers. At some point, it was our turn to finally leave, and I offered to drive Ana home. "What was that all about?" I asked. "Apparently there is a mysterious package on the corner by Magnolia Bakery, so they called in the bomb squad. No self-respecting terrorist organization would blow up Magnolia Bakery in Los Angeles at nine p.m." I fell in love with her immediately.

Uh Huh Her kicked off yet another tour promoting our latest album. We would play forty-five dates in the United States and Canada over two and a half months. The venues were packed with revved-up fans, but halfway between Milwaukee and Des Moines something in me changed. Looking out into the crowds, I couldn't help but notice that the screaming throng was mostly sixteen-year-olds. The thought struck me: *I might be getting too old for this.* Life on the road is punishing, and you get worn down faster than a pair of Birkenstocks at the Michigan Womyn's Music Festival. I was burned out.

When I told Cam I might be done with the band, she was surprised and hurt. She thought there was more life in Uh Huh Her. She also, understandably, wondered what the impact would be on our relationship. If we weren't bandmates, what were we to each other? For almost ten years, so much of our bond had been built around music—what would be left without it? I was eager to find out, excited to settle down, domesticate, and focus on our life at home.

I'm dangerous when I don't have a project . . . and even more dangerous when I do. Without the band to focus on and only the occasional guest-star role to sink my teeth into, I needed something to do. After spending the last year renovating my house from the studs, I had proven to myself that I could not only do something like that but actually enjoy it. I had been building out a workshop in my garage, filling it with tools I collected off Craigslist. It was time to challenge myself.

I became obsessed with these cute vintage trailers called Canned Hams for their distinctive shape. I spent hours watching this guy on

YouTube—a weathered old desert rat whose sole purpose in life was to pass along this valuable information to the eighteen or so viewers who might be watching—taking the trailer apart and putting it back together. This was going to be the biggest, baddest Soap Box Derby car I ever built.

I found a deal from a guy up near San Francisco who was selling his Aljoa Sportsman for $1,500. I needed help towing it to Southern California and there was only one person for the job. "Are you up for an adventure?" I asked Kate. "See ya in the morning," she replied without hesitation.

We drove her Jeep, equipped with a back tow, up north and listened to the first season of *Serial* the whole way. As we approached the house, the nice man was waiting in the driveway. The look on his face screamed, "Here come the two suckers!" Meanwhile, I was sure he was the sucker and I was getting a steal. We opened the trailer door that was barely hanging on the hinges and peered in. The entire thing was covered in black mold, and something inside of me thought a little bleach would do the trick. The windows weren't attached and/or didn't have handles. "It's beautiful," I said, beaming. "I'll take it!" I slapped some taillights on the back and off we went.

When we got back on the freeway, we realized we could only top forty-five miles per hour because the trailer's wheels were so precarious. Drivers would give us scared looks as they passed by. Kate suggested we pull over. "No, no," I assured her. "It's fine." Clang, scrape, bang! Kate shot me a look. "Leish, that whole family is frantically waving at us." I looked over and read their lips: "Your door is flapping!" We pulled over at the next gas station and bought a roll of duct tape. (In retrospect, it's shameful that between two lesbians we didn't have one on us.) We taped the door shut and everything else that was hanging on for dear life. This routine continued for the next

ten hours—a drive that should have taken no more than six—until
the poor trailer was so taped up I didn't know if I could ever get back
in. We were immensely relieved when we pulled the Ham into my
driveway at 11:00 p.m.

With Zoo, my little shadow, I worked on that trailer every day
for five months. I bent the birch veneer just so to create the curved
walls, scribed the cabinets to perfectly fit the trailer's contours, up-
holstered the bench cushions with Bolivian blankets, and installed a
hot-pink linoleum floor. It was physically demanding and mentally
taxing. Canned Hams are uniquely difficult to renovate because, as
the desert rat will tell you, you have to build them from the inside
out. Most people quit halfway through. Not this guy. Not only did
I find the manual labor meditative, but the project itself became
an escape. Cam was making music in the studio and there were so
many people around the compound that more and more I found
myself retreating to the silence of the Ham.

It was around this time that I got myself back into therapy. I was
lost professionally. I had no idea what my next move should be. Plus,
though I loved the life I'd built with Cam—her family, our house,
our sex life (even seven years in, it was the opposite of lesbian bed
death)—we'd stopped communicating. As I'd come in from the
trailer at the end of the day, she'd head out for the night. I kept trying
to tell Cam something was wrong between us, but I wasn't saying it
in a way that she could hear. At least I had the consistent company
and unconditional love of Kate and Zoo.

Until I didn't.

One random Tuesday morning, Sofu and our friend Lizzie asked
me to go with them to get a smoothie. When we got back, Zoo was
all the way across the yard, standing stiff in the corner. "Zoo, come
on," I called. She didn't come. Something was wrong. I ran to her.
Zoo was shivering and couldn't move. I went into a life-or-death-

emergency state, grabbed her, jumped into my friend's car, and sped to the animal hospital, flying a hundred miles per hour through the streets of Los Angeles.

The staff rushed her to the back. The room spun around me in slow motion. This couldn't be happening. The vet came out and told me a tumor had burst around Zoo's heart. That sweet, sweet heart. The vet told me my best friend wasn't going to make it. They let me go back and see her. I kissed and held her and was able to be by Zoo's side to say goodbye.

My life changed in a split second. My friends rushed to the hospital to hold me up. They drove me back home, and I lay in bed crying uncontrollably. My bedroom door opened, and Kate rushed in. She climbed on top of me and engulfed me in a full body hug. She didn't have to say anything. In that moment, it wasn't me who knew what I needed, it was Kate. She wasn't scared to be vulnerable and intimate with me. It was a moment in life I'll never forget because I felt so understood.

In the months following Zoo's death, I was numb. I had trouble caring about much of anything. I felt a lack of purpose and whatever I was doing felt futile. Disappearing into myself, I couldn't be the partner either Cam or I wanted me to be. Sick with despair, I was unable to address—or even articulate—our issues. I felt the compassionate thing to do was to end the relationship. Suddenly, I had no job, no girlfriend, and no direction. But I'm resilient. My working-class mentality kicked in and I realized my best option was to create an opportunity. I'd enjoyed the renovating work I'd done on my house and the Canned Ham, which incidentally, had made a less harrowing trip back to Northern California and was now enjoying life as the mascot of a beautiful cabernet vineyard. Tons of people were making oodles of money flipping houses . . . why shouldn't I?

With my friend Kelly, who designs homes for a living, I formed a partnership. We started overhauling a California bungalow in Atwater Village with the goal of building a showcase home for our company's vision. Instead of using big box store finishes, we'd source gems from salvage yards and repurpose discarded materials to keep costs down while elevating the aesthetic. It was backbreaking work. I was constantly loading and unloading my pickup truck, demolishing walls, designing and constructing custom built-ins. I can't say I was enjoying it, but I was fully committed to this new life.

I was balancing this work with increasingly frequent visits home to Nebraska. Though she'd never let multiple sclerosis define her, my unstoppable, vibrant mother now depended on a wheelchair, and her decline was rapidly accelerating. I wanted to sit with her, laugh with her, and comfort her. This was all we had. I knew this loss was inevitable and sure to undo me. I wasn't ready.

I stayed in Nebraska so my sister and I could help my father through the business of death after my beautiful mom passed. It's a strange thing when a rich life has been reduced to stuff . . . especially after a long illness when so much of that stuff is medical equipment. In a state of shock, Kaydra and I sifted through my mom's belongings. She'd always wanted to be an architect, so I kept her technical drawings as a reminder to keep dreaming. What didn't have sentimental value was sold at an estate sale or donated. A smaller house was found, and my father moved in. A memorial was organized.

There is no way to beat grief, even when you've been anticipating it for decades. Jane Phyllis Zapponi was the leader of our family, the captain of the USS *Hailey*. She brought all of the joy and creativity to our modest, warm house. And she was brave: She let me go off to New York at seventeen, a kid with neither foot on the ground, and believed that I would fly. The best parts of me come from her.

When I returned to LA, I threw myself back into the house-flipping venture. I was trying to keep myself so busy that I wouldn't have time to question where I was in life. One afternoon, I was high up on the roof, prying off an old piece of lumber, and I felt my phone pulse in my pocket. Out of nowhere, an email: *Entertainment Weekly* wanted to reunite *The L Word* cast for a special gay issue and I should be expecting details of said photo shoot. I put down my hammer, sat, and thought, *What are the chances?*

11

||

Losing the Plot

Kate

The night before the shoot, I was too excited to sleep. But when I arrived at the *Entertainment Weekly* photo shoot, there was no time for exhaustion. The room exploded with bear hugs and screams. Sarah and I naturally morphed back into that old married couple we once were as we recounted the guest spot Sarah had on *Ray Donovan* a few years earlier. We had shared a scene but didn't exchange any dialogue, so had decided to share a look as though we recognized each other, as a wink to any *L Word* fans watching. I hadn't seen Mia in years, but we instantly fell into our playful bantering selves and tried to remember all the ridiculous arguments we used to have about literally nothing that would end in fits of laughter. Finally, our Erin was back with us again and it felt like our sister had never left. For a few hours, it was as though the third season was merely a terrible fever dream.

Of course, we had all changed and grown. Some of us had gone through divorces, some had kids, yet somehow our old familiar dynamics seemed to snap back into place. It was so natural that for a moment it felt like we were just there promoting a new season. The writer from *EW* even asked coyly if this was the last people would hear from us. He said it like he knew something already, and maybe he did, since a few hours after we said our goodbyes, I found myself in Jennifer's hotel room with Leisha, hearing Ilene say the words I never expected to hear.

Throughout the early 2010s, I had sometimes found myself
wondering what Alice would be up to. Had she gone back to her
roots as a beat reporter and made a hit podcast exposing the dark
underbelly of Von Dutch? Or did she invent the prototype for the
selfie stick, pitch it to a closeted venture capitalist who loved the
product but loved Alice even more, and was now living in a geodesic
dome in Silicon Valley? Alice was such an open, curious person that
the possibilities for what she was up to were endless . . . and, if I'm
being honest, I couldn't stop daydreaming about how fun it would
be to play her again.

It didn't seem entirely crazy. In 2013, I read that *Arrested Development*, a show with a small but rabid audience (like ours), was being
rebooted after seven years. If the Bluths could do it, why couldn't
we? One day, when Kate was over at my house—as she was most
days—we agreed that bringing *The L Word* back was a no-brainer:
People still cared about the show, it ended too early, and nothing had
replaced it. But we were just actors; it's not like we had any power to
make it happen. "Should we write Ilene?" I asked. It was kind of an
insane notion; Ilene was showrunning a little series called *Empire* at
the time, so it wasn't like she was even available to take something
like this on. But just as quickly as we'd convinced ourselves it wasn't
a good idea to email Ilene, we reversed course, and I grabbed my
computer. After all, what did we have to lose? Like two schoolgirls
struggling to compose the perfect text, we nervously typed, then
deleted, then typed again: "Have you ever considered . . ."

I woke up to an email from Ilene to me and Kate, timestamped
4:00 a.m. In her ever-supportive way, she gushed that an *L Word* reboot was a wonderful idea. Before finishing the email, I grabbed the

phone to call Kate. When she picked up, she didn't even say hi, just, "Holy shit, Leish, Ilene said she's going to bring it up to the heads of Showtime." I gasped. "Oh my god."

Our dreams were crushed faster than we could say "cunnilingus." Showtime said no.

The next time Jennifer was in town, Ilene, Kate, and I met her for dinner. "Don't ask, don't tell" had been repealed, LGBTQ+ people gained legal protection against discrimination in the workplace, and the White House had been lit up like a rainbow to celebrate the legalization of same-sex marriage. In so many ways, it was a historic moment in the gay rights movement. How was there not a show on the air that could reflect these major changes? Ilene agreed, adding that she'd blazed a trail—there had never before been a show by, about, and for queer women—but no one had followed in her footsteps. Jennifer wanted to see more inclusivity and diversity. The queer experience was so much more layered and varied now. We felt we had not only an opportunity but an obligation to tell these stories. So, even though the response from the network had been a pass, we were like a four-headed dog with a bone.

For the next year and a half, our coven would convene. We'd gather evidence, articles, fan fiction—I mean, people were still writing dramatic scenarios about TiBette because they had no other lesbian couples on TV to aspire to—and present it to Showtime. No matter how compelling our case, the network wouldn't budge.

Then, in 2015, something weird started to happen. I'd be roaming through Trader Joe's searching for their unbeatable peanut butter cups or getting my hair balayaged when a young queer person would approach me and tell me how much they loved the show. I assumed they must have found their parents' dusty DVD collection in the basement, but to my surprise, I learned *The L Word* was streaming on Netflix. A whole new generation was discovering the show. They demonstrated their devotion by obsessively tweeting, posting, and memeing about it. Now it wasn't just me and Kate and Jennifer and Ilene who were willing a reboot . . . a collective consciousness was emerging.

And then it was 2016. We could all see exactly where the country was headed: With Trump at the helm, the LGBTQ+ community would be under attack. Newly won rights would be repealed and the pendulum of love and acceptance would swing back to something more hostile. During the Women's March in Washington, DC, to protest Trump's inauguration, I caught a glimpse of a poster someone had made with a picture of Erin that said "Dana didn't die for this." It was the perfect encapsulation of our fears and highlighted the danger in the absence of representation. Queer people needed to see an alternative reality to the one we were living, one that offered agency and hope. That's when we got the email from *Entertainment Weekly.*

It felt like I had hopped in a DeLorean and time traveled back to Vancouver in 2003. Though we desperately missed Laurel and Rose and Pam—due to scheduling conflicts and flight delays—*EW* had pulled off a near miracle getting this many of us together in time to make the Pride issue.

There was electricity in the air. No matter what combination of us the photographer put together, she could barely get us to stop gabbing long enough to get a shot.

During one photo we weren't in, Ilene approached me and Kate. "What are you doing after the photo shoot?" she whispered. "We need to have a discussion." Now, here's the thing you need to know about Ilene: When she comes to you like this, it's never nothing . . . in fact, it's usually something great but stranger than fiction. Like, it wouldn't be surprising if what she wanted to tell us was that she'd scored us an invite to take high tea with the queen next Tuesday.

"What's going on?" we asked. "I can't tell you here," she said. "Let's meet in Jennifer's hotel room after this."

In the bathroom of Jennifer's Sunset Tower suite, Kate and I surveyed her amazing array of skin care products. "Try this," Jennifer instructed and handed me a battery-powered face massager thingy designed to tighten muscles. There we were, the Unholy Trinity, staring at our reflection in the mirror. "What do you think Ilene is going to tell us?" I asked while buzzing the machine in circles over my cheekbones. Just then Ilene walked in.

And here lies the memory that will forever be etched in my brain. Ilene skipped the small talk: "Well, Showtime has decided to reboot *The L Word*." I could hear the words she was saying, but they didn't compute. After three whole years of campaigning, we couldn't believe it was actually happening. "Are you kidding?" we asked. "No," she said. "And not only that, I told the president of the network that because you have been such tireless advocates, I'd like you three to be executive producers this time around. You'll be my partners." Visions of the old show danced in my head. This was really happening.

KATE

The day it was announced publicly that *The L Word* was get-ting a reboot was the first time it felt real. I was sitting at the table read for *Ray Donovan* next to Kim Raver, who was a recurring character that season. She overheard people wishing me congratulations as they arrived. I was so elated I had to pinch myself to make sure I wasn't dreaming this. The possibilities with what we could do with this second chance were endless, and for once I wasn't waiting for the other shoe to drop.

"Congratulations. I read about that," Kim said cautiously. "When we did the *24* reboot, it was not at all what we expected it to be. We thought we were gonna walk right back into the exact same experience with the exact same people, with the exact energy that we had in the original. Don't want to spoil it for you, but try to manage your expectations." *Okay, Kim,* I thought.

After the announcement, Leisha, Jennifer, and I would sit with Ilene at the studio lot café, going over all the possibilities of where our characters' stories could lead. Even better, now that we were producers, we were granted access to hearing initial pitches. We met with two incredible writers, one of whom was a writer/producer who Showtime had worked with on one of their previous series. She came in with the perfect sensibility, a lot of experience, and it was obvious she had watched the original, since she knew specifics about our characters that even we had forgotten about. Unfortunately, she had a job lined up and was unavailable to even work on the pitch for the next eight months, which equates to eight years in this business. We knew we had to use all our momentum to keep our opportunity moving forward. The other main contender happened to have been a writing assistant from the original years earlier. Her first ideas would have been most people's final drafts. They were so detailed, visually exciting, and honest. She knew how to tap into our characters' conflicts in unexpected ways that made us even more inspired with where she saw things going past the first episode.

The possibilities for where the new *L Word* could lead seemed endless. We were painfully aware of the original's shortcomings and were eager to rectify them. There were so many great ideas in front of us we didn't know where to look. One of the more seamless pitches we heard was to center a couple of the new characters around Bette and Tina's daughter, Angie, who by then was seventeen years old—the reason being, kids grow up faster these days. The way it was described felt organic and well-thought-out. It was heartening to meet these writers who also had enjoyed and understood the importance of the original show and all our characters. It was also reassuring to meet with people who were just as excited about it as we were. We didn't need someone to kiss the ring, but we were somewhat taken aback during one meeting with a potential writer who only expressed criticism—it wasn't clear she'd seen the show, and if she had, we didn't get the impression she liked it. Leaving the meeting, all four of us looked at each other and said in unison, "Well, that's not it."

Once Showtime had narrowed down the candidates, they heard the writers' official pitches. Apparently, everyone brought in fancy storyboards with story arc charts and photos of dynamic character ideas printed out. We wouldn't know. We were not invited into those pitch meetings. The network felt that we would be too biased by what was said or wasn't said about our own characters and didn't trust that we could look at anything objectively. So, we sat on the edge of our seats wondering who would be chosen. A few days later, Ilene, Jennifer, Leisha, and I met at the same little café on the studio lot where we had sat with so much hope just weeks earlier. Ilene didn't break the news to us as easily this time. "Well . . . it's not who you think it is . . ."

Aside from being blindsided and now confused, we wanted to respect the network's opinion on this. Maybe they knew something we didn't? We desperately wanted them to be right, so we took it on the chin and moved forward. Probably a month or two later, we finally got our hands on the presentation that trumped the others. There were at least twenty new characters listed. Bette, Shane, and Alice were basically numbers seventeen, nineteen, and twenty. It was not going to be the reunion we had imagined. This was our first clue that Showtime's plan was to use us to bring in the audience, but otherwise keep the reboot's ties to the original minimal. Leisha said it best when she called me, crestfallen, and said, "I'm reading this . . . and wondering, when does *The L Word* start?"

It took about a year and a half for the pilot script to be finalized through several fits and starts. By January of 2019 we gave up and figured the reboot was dead. And that's precisely when we got a call saying the CEO of Showtime threw the script on a table during a meeting and declared he wanted this fast-tracked and on the air by the end of the year. They planned to announce it at the Television Critics Association conference in something like seventy-two hours and couldn't do it until our deals were locked in. Within twelve hours our whole negotiating process suddenly went from zero to warp speed. Leisha and I banded together like we always did. We felt an immense pressure to settle for less than our worth and were threatened with having the whole thing pulled if we didn't accept. We eventually caved to make the deadline because, if we could bring back the magic of the original show, we told ourselves, it would all be worth it. Still, even beyond the dollar amount, the deal we ended up agreeing to didn't feel respectful. I thought back to 2002 when Leisha and I, the two gay members of the original cast, were also the lowest paid. Now, over fifteen years later, we felt the uneasy echoes of that time.

That wasn't the only red flag. From day one, we sensed an unspoken level of resentment toward us for being there and bringing along the show's history in the first place. The divide between the new show and the old one was evident down to the nicknames we heard repeatedly. Jennifer, Leisha, and I were labeled the OGs, while the rest of the actors were called the Newbies. It's understandable to use that shorthand behind closed doors as reference but hearing it day in and out felt like a constant reminder that we were seen as two separate groups, which certainly didn't help build community. What happened to Gay Camp?

Some of my favorite moments in the reboot were when Bette, Alice, and Shane were together. When the three of us had a field trip to the karaoke stage, getting stoned with Bette in Shane's kitchen, or Alice and Shane spooning a rather large dog, it felt like the original magic showed its face again. On the other hand, more times than not, we struggled to feel like the yearslong relationships between the original characters were being honored. Our sisterhood was usually reduced to coffee shop chats and group hugs. Leisha and I had conjured up so many scenarios that Shane and Alice could find themselves in together, yet we were lucky to get a few scenes together per season. I lost count of how many times one of us said, "Why isn't she going to Shane/Alice for this?"

Years earlier, it was second nature for me to daydream up ideas of where things could potentially lead for Shane. Now, I struggled more than I had ever anticipated to find the authentic soul of this character I so cherished. Unlike Bette and Alice, Shane was a bit of a nomad. It was challenging to figure out where she could be all these years later. When she returned like Dickie Greenleaf, who just threw money at his problems like confetti to make them go away, it felt like a misstep. The inexplicable financial freedom shared by Bette, Alice, and Shane in this new story could have easily funded the government during a shutdown. I appreciated the idea that Shane had actually made something of herself since we all had last seen her, but the idea of Shane being that obscenely wealthy was particularly perplexing to me, as I was certain she would have kept all her money in a simple checking account.

Any consequence in Shane's life that didn't involve sex or cheating usually happened off camera, so her conflicts didn't feel earned or at times make much sense. As she fell deeper into the clichés, it was becoming harder to find the space to make her the complicated person she had once been.

Initially, I liked the idea of Shane being married—it felt different than what anyone would expect. But Shane's ex-wife, who was originally designed to haunt Shane's thoughts through flashbacks that would build up this mysterious woman's mythical status, was soon reduced to her pregnancy as her main character trait. The one upshot to their underwritten relationship was the unexpected gift that came from their demise: Mack the dog. It was an eleventh-hour idea that not only saved the day but also the storyline. I fell in love with the idea the moment I heard it and was adamant we use a pit bull mix, the bigger the better. Once he showed up, I would have been fine if Shane turned into the lady who never left her house and only spoke to the dog.

The friends-to-lovers evolution with Tess had so much potential to mark a real turning point in a character that desperately needed to be accountable. Their relationship was relatable in certain ways, involving navigating the pitfalls of a work-life balance coupled with the stress of an ailing, live-in mother played by the marvelous Joanna Cassidy. Yet the storyline, which was ripe with conflict, wasn't given time to be explored thoroughly and soon became predictable, with

Shane falling into her old patterns of infidelity as the only recourse. Any growth was soon stunted. I found it frustrating that Shane's challenging past was rarely touched on to give context to whatever emotional setback she was facing in the present. I squeaked in a reference here and there, but Carmen and Jenny felt like names that were not welcomed often, if ever. As if that would make the audience suddenly forget who they were. We later learned that it wasn't a requirement for the new writers to watch the original show, which helps explain why there was not only a disconnect but also seemingly a choice to distance this version from the original.

Opportunities arose that could have worked well with better planning. The creation of Dana's bar came about as a reflection of the dwindling number of queer and lesbian bars across the country. That felt like an interesting storyline; I liked the idea of Shane still working with her hands and thought there could be some interesting drama surrounding the development of a bar from the ground up. I saw the project as a chance not only for Shane to find some purpose and self-worth putting in some sweat equity but for the rest of the characters to rally around and build community and in turn actually get to know each other. If anyone knows how to DIY, it's the queers, who have been doing it since the discovery of fire. In execution, however, all the interesting elements happened off camera, only mentioned in passing or over a lunch date. It makes me laugh to think that the bar was negotiated, purchased, and renovated in a span of an episode. Maybe Shane hired Kit's contractor.

When the time came to brainstorm where Alice would be
in her life, I was ready. I had a clear vision of Alice as a household
name. It made sense to me that after Dana died and the breakup with
Tasha, Alice—ever the careerist—would throw herself into work.
The bumbling but driven girl we met in season 1, who worked as a
journalist, radio anchor, and substitute for a female-hosted morning
show, had finally arrived. The reboot would start with Alice as the
face of a successful talk show, viewers tuning in daily to get her in-
sightful, cheeky take on pop culture.

My first day on set, I felt a mix of anticipation, wonder, and trepidation; when I opened my mouth, would Alice's voice come out?
And would it sound the same? People always ask me how Alice and I
are alike, and the truth is, we aren't. The easiest way to explain how
we're different is this: If I was drinking a horrible cup of coffee and
someone asked how it was, I'd say, "It's really good, yeah, not bad
at all!" But Alice would say, "This coffee tastes like poopy shit." My
inside voice stays in, while hers spills out. It had been ten years since
I'd gotten to be disarmingly snarky . . . could I still pull it off?

This is what was running through my head as the AD yelled
"Places," and I took a seat at the breakfast table between Jennifer and
Kate. Doing my first scene with them was a momentous beginning:
If you're getting catapulted into uncharted territory, who better to
be strapped in with than your two best friends? "Okay, I got this," I
told myself. But then the director called "Action!" and Kate wasn't
Kate. This person who I'd been hanging out with incessantly for a
decade was suddenly a smoldering cool girl. Where was my couch
potato G-Paw? I panicked. Uh-oh, I better get my head in the game.
I locked in, and suddenly Pieszecki was back.

While we all had our frustrations with the reboot, there was always something special about the scenes Jennifer, Kate, and I shot together. Not just because there was so much history between us, and between the characters themselves, but also between the characters and the audience. There was an unspoken pact among us: When the trinity was united, we'd bring our best to those scenes, sprinkle a little fairy dust on them. One of these scenes was in season 1, episode 4. It's the morning of Shane's fortieth birthday, but she's got a surprise for Bette and Alice. After coffee, she makes them close their eyes and leads them next door to the bar she bought. Shane instructs them to turn around. Alice, of course, turns to face the wrong direction, but then spins 180 degrees. Shane reveals that she's named the bar Dana's. We couldn't wait to film this moment but knew someone else needed to be there. Since we were shooting the sequel in Los Angeles instead of Vancouver, that someone was only a text away. "Erin, if you're free on Friday, come to this address." She wrote back, "I think I can get a sitter, what's going on?" "Just be there," we said.

Erin showed up to holding, the area where cast waits during setups, and we were overjoyed to see her. She walked to set with us, and when she saw the bar's name, she let out an excited laugh. It was so special to show her how prominently she was being remembered, how important she was. She hung out with us for hours. There are even outtakes of the three of us taking our selfie for the show, with Erin photobombing us. I just wanted her to slap on her Lululemon Lycra and stay forever.

Call me a sap, but I also got emotional two weeks later when Laurel came back. When we're in preproduction for an episode, the department heads and creative team will come together to hear the script read aloud by the cast. It's a chance for writers to tweak dialogue and crew to ask production-related questions. I'd read the draft, so I knew what was going to happen, but at the table read, when Tina and Bette began their back and forth, I had to excuse myself. Seeing them together again just got me . . . they were the beating heart of the show.

My favorite storyline of season 1 featured new cast members. While Alice's professional life had been so obvious to me, I had no clue what her personal life would look like. As established, her dating history was a grab bag so there was no telling what she'd pull out. When the writers pitched me on Alice being in a throuple, I lit up. Bull's-eye! Who better than Alice, who always found herself in a pickle, to hilariously navigate the stickiness of a three-way relationship?

Nat (played by the comically golden Stephanie Allynne) was Alice's longtime girlfriend, and the two of them got involved with Nat's ex-wife, Gigi (played by the wildly talented Sepideh Moafi). We were so excited to dig in and explore the highs and lows of a modern-day polyamorous family with children and careers to boot. Stephanie and Sepideh and I would get cozy on the couch in my trailer and excitedly flesh out our backstories. For hours we'd concoct elaborate scenarios, giving us a shared understanding of our dynamic to bring to the scripted scenes. This storyline, to me, captured the old show's magic: It had all the juicy drama and sexiness of the original's DNA. I had so much fun playing with these incredibly gifted and creative women that I was more heartbroken than Alice when the relationship ended.

But if I had to pick one scene from *Gen Q* that was my absolute favorite, it would hands down be from season 2, episode 7. At a poker fundraiser thrown by Shane, Alice, in a baby-blue pantsuit and floppy black bow tie, is approached by Carrie Walsh, played by the one and only Rosie O'Donnell. So there's me, an enormous *Rosie* fan, playing a lesbian talk show host, having a scene with Rosie O'Donnell—the original lesbian talk show host—playing a fan of *Alice*. Here's how the scene goes:

CARRIE: I just wanted you to know, I love the show this
season, it's fantastic.

ALICE: Aw, that's really sweet.

CARRIE: I mean, a lesbian talk show host?

ALICE: That's me!

CARRIE: It's unprecedented.

ALICE: I know. Well, there's Ellen.

CARRIE: Yeah.

Awkward silence.

ALICE: But, yeah, after that I can't think of anyone. It was
like, road wide open.

CARRIE: No, you're like paving the way for everybody. It
means a lot, to a lot of people. It means a lot to me.

Can you get any more meta than that? Once we'd gotten the
scripted lines on tape, the director let us improvise. On the hour-
long drive home on the 405—LA traffic is truly as bad as everyone
says it is—I called Kate to relive the high of playing around with
Rosie. She and I often spent our commute keeping each other company like long-haul truck drivers.

KATE

The idea was that this reboot was going to be a fresh, mod-
ern version of the queer experience, but I was ironically struck by
how heteronormative everything felt. Practically every new character, even Shane, was either getting married, wanting to get married,
wanting kids, struggling with not wanting kids, or dealing with a
divorce. There was a lot of never-ending drama around weddings,
rings, and proposals. Of course, I was proud we'd gained the right to
marry who we choose, but I felt like asking, is that all we strive for
now? I never understood why these young, new characters who had
just started their adult lives spent so much of their time and energy
concerned about getting married and/or having children. Where
was that lived-in chosen family with all its history and intimacy? The
group activities and adventures, the creativity and uniqueness that
make our community so special? Where was the softball episode?

Leisha, Jennifer, and I looked forward to an honest and realistic
depiction of what our characters were now experiencing in their
middle-aged lives. Some of that happened—Bette experienced
menopause for five minutes, Alice went through her various dating
foibles and got closure from Dana, and Shane, well, she tried cos-
playing as a poker player when she acted like the Cincinnati Kid for
a season. We hoped to reflect on how fast and different the world
looked or even the experience of aging in general. We were equally
excited to explore the generational divide with our younger castmates.

The back-and-forth between these generations regarding ter-
minology, history, identity, even personal habits would have been
pure gold. I believe there was space to not only spend some time
acknowledging the progress we'd made since the last generation

kicked down some doors but also listen to and learn from the openness of the new generation. Rather than allowing these characters to challenge each other, ask hard questions, and learn through wit and nuance, the conversations about our differences were avoided out of a fear of offending anyone.

Additionally, there weren't firmly established connections between the two generations of cast members, and our on-screen introductions to one another felt glossed over and wildly unrealistic. At one point in the show, one of the characters undergoes an intervention about her drinking, and during rehearsal we quickly realized that most of the characters in the room didn't even know each other. Were they supposed to be meeting for the first time under these circumstances? Did they even know each other's names? It felt unimaginably awkward.

When Max's character, played by Daniel Sea, returned, it was long overdue. In addition to Max being one of the characters on the original show whose storyline we knew had missed the mark, he was universally beloved, and this felt like the perfect opportunity to welcome him back. It was also comforting to see him now living his best life as a father of four. The idea that Max and Shane would be the ones to run into each other and reconnect made sense. Also, that Shane would be the one to apologize for the way the original group had treated him touched on her original character's empathy. I so desperately wanted to use this rare opportunity to talk about Jenny, and Max seemed the perfect person to do it with. Why would they not bring up a traumatizing experience they both shared regarding the person who was their common thread? I thought that one of them bringing up Jenny and that time in their lives years ago could be a natural segue into acknowledging our characters' own ignorance toward Max. There was room in that scene to hit all the right notes and give specificity and context to their past. Instead, we got a conversation that stripped most of the history and nuance from the interaction.

It was always a shot in the arm to have the other original characters join us, however briefly. In those moments it felt like the band got back together. Like we always do, we found a lot of laughter and held each other up when we needed it the most. Bette and Tina walked into their well-deserved sunset together. Tasha finally returned like the hero she always was and brought Alice much-needed peace. And Shane, well, what can I say? I suppose she finally learned what nonmonogamy means, at the tender age of forty-two. Regardless of the ups and downs, we were given the gift of revisiting beloved characters that millions of people, including us, missed so desperately. I will forever treasure Shane as someone I not only grew up with but who changed my life.

We were fortunate to work with fantastic directors like Steph Green, Emil Weinstein, and Katrelle Kindred, among others. The Godmother herself, Rose Troche, even returned to direct an episode, and with her came the heart, soul, and illegible notes on pieces of paper. There was so much talent on the set, between costumes and production crews, hair and makeup teams, the camera department, plus all the ADs. And finally, a company of committed actors who threw their backs into the work every single day and strove to bring authenticity and truth into these new characters and storylines. Ultimately, though, Kim Raver was right. You can't get lightning in a bottle twice.

LEISHA

There were a lot of amazing things about *Gen Q*. The costumes, the set design, the representation of today's queer community beautifully brought to life by Ari, Ro, Jac, Jamie, Jordan, Leo, Jillian, Olivia, Sophie, and Brian. Bette and Tina getting their happily ever after. The last episode was especially meaningful to me. I recently came across a video that young Kate and I filmed after the first season of the original *L Word* in which we take turns asking each other questions written by fans. After giggling about what Shane and Alice's backstory could be—they've never hooked up, but if they had, we said, it would only be one time after they took ecstasy, then got in the bath together—Kate reads from the list, "Would you ever like to direct an episode?" I stare at her for a few seconds, then say, "I've never thought of that, ever." The handheld camera zooms in for a close-up. "Nor do I have the need to do that. But I think if I was offered, I think I'd have a blast doing it." Without hesitation, Kate says, "I could see you being great at it." Always so supportive.

Fifteen years later, I finally got to realize that vision by directing what would become the series finale. I can honestly say I loved every single thing about that job. I'd been on set for almost seventy episodes of television, so conceptually, I understood how much deliberation and intention went into every detail that shows up on screen. As an actor, I would watch a set decorator slink into frame and rotate a potted plant twenty-seven degrees, then move it back fifteen until it looked perfect in the shot. I knew every department was critical, but until I directed, I didn't know how much fun it would be to help make these choices and bring the episode to life. As an amateur painter, it's just me and the canvas—making decisions is a solo act, whether it's highlighting the green or making the brushstroke the focus. Directing an episode of TV is like having a team of brilliant minds with limitless resources and expertise consult on your painting. If I said, "What do you think about bringing out the green?" an art director might present a palette of wallpapers with twenty shades from forest to chartreuse, and the director of photography might say, "We could use a special filter to further accentuate the green." Then the prop master might suggest the character's pen being orange for contrast, or the costume designer would present a chic black silhouette so as not to compete with the background. It's a never-ending collaboration that ignited my brain with possibilities.

As director, working with the actors was especially gratifying. Between setups, I'd ask them questions about their character: "What was she doing in the two minutes leading up to this scene?" or "What do you think the subtext is behind this line?" At one point in the show, Tess falls off the wagon in spectacular form, so Jamie Clayton had some challenging material to work through. It was invigorating to collaborate with her, figuring out how to hit the right note. In one scene, Tess is so wasted that she topples into a wedding cake, but Jamie and I didn't want it to feel over-the-top. Working together, we found that the scene was most successful when Jamie kept Tess grounded and the comedy came from the reactions of the other characters. I loved jumping out from behind the monitor while we were still rolling, giving a note to Laurel in the walk-in fridge, then zipping back to see how her performance changed. (For the record, *The Bear* may be a runaway hit, but we locked our leads in a meat locker first.) All those years spent carting around books about the Stanislavski method must have paid off—I was at home in the director's chair. So, to the fan who asked if I'd ever like to direct, I owe you one.

I am—with every cell of my being—incredibly grateful that the reboot happened. Getting to inhabit Alice again and wear oh so many pantsuits, play with Jennifer and Kate on set, and work with a new crop of terrific actors was an amazing experience. If you were to ask me if I think *Generation Q* lived up to its potential as a reboot of *The L Word*, I'd probably say, "It was really good, yeah, not bad at all!" Alice, however, would tell you, "The reboot was poopy shit." She'd salute the fact that we got an army of queers back on the small screen, then rant about the challenge of gay content on a mainstream platform. To this day, the corner offices are mostly filled with cis, het, white people who still see lesbians as either butch or femme. They don't understand who we are, why we build community, and what it means to see ourselves on TV. It feels a little like executives thought, *We'll bring back this iconic title and because this audience has no other lesbian show to watch, they'll eat it up.* They didn't think through the betrayal of bringing our show back without all the characters that fans considered family. They wouldn't dare resuscitate *Seinfeld* without George and Elaine and the Soup Nazi. We have come so far, but we won't have arrived until there are multiple shows on the air depicting all the different shapes and shades of the LGBTQ+ community. Until then, I'll be on standby, ready to hop in the nearest phone booth and emerge in a pantsuit, game to play Alice if the opportunity ever comes knocking.

Way back at the beginning of *Generation Q*, I'd been single for over a year and had the occasional one-night stand, but it's fair to say I was dragging my way through the dating scene like the walking dead. I began to think about my past relationship with Kim. We were so young when we were together, and when we broke up, I didn't understand how to move on and still keep Kim in my life. I had thought a clean break was the only way, and so we lost contact. But it haunted me.

For twenty-two years, I'd occasionally see Kim out. We were always pleasant but kept it pretty surface-level. Lately, though, I had been hanging out more with the old NYC gang from the nineties. One night a bunch of us, including Kim, went to see Heather play a show. Some of the group had kids, and others were in long-term relationships, so we weren't the same bunch of misfits we had been, but when we were all together it was pure magic. That night, I was really feeling it and I jumped onstage to play a song with Heather. Gazing at the faces of these beautiful people I'd grown up with, I knew I needed them back in my life in a big way. To do that, I had to make things right with Kim.

I texted her: "Hey, this is so out of the blue, would you ever meet for coffee?" I honestly didn't think she'd write back, but less than a minute later, my phone dinged: "I'd love to." When we sat down at the café, I was so nervous. Looking across the table, I could see the wonderful woman Kim had become and could recall every formative, intimate, silly, wonderful moment of our past. Words galloped out of me.

I apologized for basically disappearing from her life. The only thing harder than owning your flaws is forgiveness, but Kim heard me out, then gracefully and kindly moved the conversation forward. She expressed her condolences for the passing of my mother and told me she'd looked into plane tickets to attend the funeral, but didn't know if it was appropriate. I reassured her that just the thought would have meant the world to my mom, who always loved Kim. In addition to our shared past, I began to hope we could forge a common present. I was so relieved and at peace when we hugged goodbye that day.

In the months that followed, I'd catch myself getting a little excited when I knew I'd see Kim. I wanted her to know that I wasn't the same immature pug person whose idea of interior decorating was an unframed Elvis tapestry tacked to the wall. I was throwing a barbecue at my house and when I saw that Kim RSVPed yes, I was determined to make everything perfect. I even recruited Jaime to help me sand and oil all three of the outdoor decks the day before. Jaime argued it was a terrible idea and the oil wouldn't dry in time. I persevered. Let the record show that Jaime was totally right . . . the morning of the party, the decks were so tacky we put fans on them to speed up the drying process. It didn't work. When everyone arrived, they slipped and slid, which made it risky to carry out drinks. So much for making a good impression. Still, Kim seemed to recognize the care and effort I had put into my home. As I led her from room to room, she commented on the use of yellow, saying, "You always did like that color." She noticed so many of the personal details I had placed and pieces I had built in my house that Jaime pulled me aside afterward and said, "Kim sees you. That's your person."

Kim and I wouldn't come to that realization until many months later. One fall night, at a party in Laurel Canyon, with twinkling fairy lights in the trees and friends all around, we looked at each other and I was home. Kim's hand reached for mine.

The universe had cast me in two reboots . . . and this one went straight to series. Our story wasn't over.

12

| | |

Liberty and Justice for All

Leisha

I'm not of the age to have experienced being broken up with in a text. Or so I thought.

We'd heard from Showtime that the chances of *Generation Q* getting a fourth season were one in a million. But it wasn't official until a friend texted me a breaking news article from Deadline.com: *"The L Word: Gen Q Canceled After 3 Seasons."* Not hearing the news directly from the network was strange, though not as strange as the rest of the headline: "New York–Set Reboot of Original with Ilene Chaiken in Works at Showtime." I called Kate immediately: "It's over."

Within minutes, Ilene texted the group chat with me, Kate, and Jennifer. She'd seen the article and was equally blindsided. That's right, the creator of the franchise had no idea there was a supposed New York iteration in the works. Oh, Hollywood.

Before I could even absorb the finality of this chapter of my life ending, Ilene's next text rolled in. "But while I have you, there is other *L Word*–related news. Press secretary Karine Jean-Pierre has invited us to the White House next month to be the spokespeople for Lesbian Visibility Week." Before I go into how many outfits I tried on for my stride through the West Wing, I have to acknowledge the complete and total insanity of this opportunity. The only way I could have imagined myself being even close to 1600 Pennsylvania Avenue would have been on an eighth-grade overnight field trip in 1984. How was this happening?

As the first Black and first openly gay press secretary, Karine wanted to recognize Lesbian Visibility Week in a significant way. According to Karine, seeing portrayals of ambitious, resilient, diverse gay women live full and complicated lives on *The L Word* had a profound effect on her in her formative years. She wanted to honor and recognize that by having the four of us appear at a press conference before the reporter pool, then do a roundtable with LGBTQ+ White House staffers.

The night before the big day, we had dinner with tech journalist Kara Swisher and some of her high-powered friends, including a woman who was described to us, in a discreet whisper, as a Washington fixer (!). Kate and I have had so many conversations about almost every topic—from candy to concrete—that we no longer need words to communicate. Over the stuffed squash blossoms course, our eyes had the following conversation: Me: "Look at us gals hobnobbing with the Whos of Whoville." Kate: "Fucking unbelievable, right, Leish?"

As the meal was winding down, Ilene casually mentioned, "If any one of you would like to speak tomorrow, Karine would love it." Tomorrow??

Lying in bed, I couldn't shake the feeling that I needed to say something at the podium. My political involvement, up until this point, had been marching in thirty-plus years of Pride parades— collecting freedom rings along the way—and leading by example. I'm not one to give speeches, but this felt different. It dawned on me that I wasn't just there as a guest, I was a representative for the LGBTQ+ community. This opportunity was too important to pass up. I wanted to do my part. I reached for my laptop.

The next morning, at the gate, we were met by the first of many incredible queer White House staffers who would show us around that day. As she led us through the campus, a maze of monumental buildings, my eyes were the size of Susan B. Anthony coins trying to take it all in. When we arrived at the base of a grand staircase, I spotted the woman who would take us on the next leg of our journey. She had dark hair pulled back, a bright energy, and was wearing the exact same Democrat-blue suit that I had labored over picking just nights before. At the instant I started to die inside, I watched mortification register on her face as well. Instead of awkwardly ignoring our obvious twinning, I acknowledged it right away. We ended up taking a stellar photo in our identical suits in identical poses beneath the portrait of Our Lady of Pantsuits herself, Hillary Clinton.

Just before the press conference, we were ushered into Karine's office. In my pants pocket, folded up, was the speech I had written. Shyly, I pulled it out and told Karine's team I had prepared a little something. My paper passed between hands as different levels of staffers approved the copy. Finally, it landed with Karine. Was I really going to do this? She smiled as she handed me back my speech. "I'll introduce you after Ilene." Suddenly, a countdown from thirty began. On the count of one, the back door in Karine's office swung open. Ilene, Kate, Jennifer, and I followed her out directly onto the stage.

I had walked onto quite a few stages in my day, but never to crickets. I'm not saying I was always met with earsplitting applause, but the audience was never totally silent. Even Karine remarked to the packed room, "Wow, you're all so quiet." Maybe this was because the press conference for Lesbian Visibility Week fell on the same day that Biden had announced his candidacy for reelection for a second presidential term. Surely, the hard-hitting journalists were expecting to hear more about that. What were *we* doing there?

Karine's opening remarks were personal and a call to arms. She spoke about the increasing threats to the liberties of queer Americans, particularly trans people, the importance of a diversity of narratives, and *The L Word*'s contribution to positive representation. Then she handed it over to Ilene.

When you've known a person so long and so well, you can forget just how impressive they really are. Watching Ilene speak, I was overcome by how remarkable she is. Composed, articulate, classy, she has poise in any situation. I felt a swell of gratitude for this exceptional woman packing us into her sidecar and bringing us along on her wild adventures.

Then it was my turn. My heart was beating out of my chest as I put on my readers. For courage, I called on my queer predecessors. I opened with how I was standing there today because, as a young gay girl from a small town in Nebraska, I was seen by my family. It was their love and support that gave me the confidence to live my life openly. I spoke about how visibility is not only the act of being seen, it is the ability to see. Directly addressing LGBTQ+ people under attack, I reassured them that we saw them and had their back.

Though my voice was shaky, I stayed present and seized the moment. As we filed offstage, I put the speech behind me and was excited to move on to the next thing on the agenda. (Because our phones had been confiscated for security purposes, it wasn't until I got back to the hotel that night that I saw how many outlets had run the story.)

We were taken on a thorough tour of the White House. We saw it all: the Rose Garden, the State Dining Room, the presidential portraits, even the flower studio and chocolate shop in the basement. Then it was time for the discussion with LGBTQ+ staffers from every branch of government. They explained the steps the Biden administration was taking toward achieving full equality for queer people. There was so much vitality and promise in that room.

Maybe it was the rush of endorphins from the speech, or the sugar high from the chocolate chip cookies that President Biden requested be baked daily and distributed throughout the White House (my kind of guy), but by the time the meeting ended, I was thinking, *Wait, should I run for office?* I was newly unemployed, after all.

On a short break, we were told we could peek into a room around the corner. Jennifer and Kate were checking out the collection of distinguished books lining the walls, when I noticed a small woman enter through what seemed like a secret door—the kind you might see in a *Scooby-Doo* episode. As she placed official-looking binders of material around the table, I realized it was none other than Janet Yellen. Feeling a little more at home than I probably should have, I chatted up the secretary of the treasury: "Hey, can I ask you a question?" Though her words were "Yes, of course," her tone was giving "Who are you and where are we going with this?" I'm not even on TikTok, but at that moment I was convinced it would make for a great post if Ms. Yellen taught me how to balance my checkbook. "Can we make a funny video together?" I chirped. Jennifer gasped, "Leisha!" Kate tried to disappear into the bookshelf, and Secretary Yellen offered a simple, dry "No." Oh well, it was a high-risk, low-yield investment.

The trip to DC gave the four of us the closure we all needed. It was the best possible thank-you and goodbye to our long and rewarding journey with *The L Word*.

KATE

It already feels like a lifetime ago that we received our security clearances to enter the West Wing of the White House. The entire time we were there it felt like time stood still. An unexpected highlight was the roundtable meeting, in which the many queer staffers within all the different departments of the administration and the four of us sat behind a thirty-foot-long mahogany table as they shared how they see the world moving forward and what they're doing to help cultivate that change. I couldn't help but wonder what three out-of-work actors from a canceled show were doing talking to these brilliant young minds. Yet hearing from them about the impact *The L Word* made in their lives was an instant reminder of what the show's legacy is all about. Since they were younger, a lot of them discovered it in their teenage years, and some had to watch it in secret. As these accomplished young people shared their stories, it was clear that for many of them, our little show really had made a difference.

I had people ask me why I didn't say anything at the podium. I never felt like I had to. There was Ilene and there was Leisha, and there was nothing I could have added that wasn't already addressed in Leisha's eloquent speech. As the four of us stood on the stage in the press room, looking down at the room of reporters who were staring back at us, most likely wondering who the hell we were, it was impossible to not embrace and feel proud of the work we had done to land in that moment.

We happened to be at the White House on a particularly busy day and the place was moving one hundred miles per hour, since the arrival of the prime minister of South Korea was imminent. We were escorted into the grand East Room, site of the state dinner, to observe the elaborate dress rehearsal.

The military orchestra was just about to perform the final run-through of their evening performance. As musicians lined up, tuning their violins and cellos, Carlos, the White House interior decorator, asked if we could be the stand-ins for President Biden, the First Lady, and their guests. "Are you sure?" we asked, as we diligently sat by their place cards before he could change his mind. The table featured soaring glass centerpieces beneath oversized cherry blossom canopies. The musicians' performance immediately enveloped the room with pitch-perfect acoustics that brought us all to tears. Seeing all the violins and cellos, I wondered quietly if any came from my dad's shop. Jennifer, being the mom she is, asked aloud, "Has anyone gotten their violins from William Moennig and Son in Philadelphia?" A girl raised her hand. "I've had this violin repaired there." She couldn't remember who it was that repaired it but she let me hold it, and for a brief moment it felt like my dad was saying hello. As we were leaving, a Secret Service agent with pitch-black sunglasses and intimidating posture came up to us. "Excuse me," she said. For a moment I froze—did Janet Yellen complain about us? "I just want to say thank you. Your show helped me so much. Can I give you something?" She handed each of us an official Secret Service pin with a rainbow flag. The same as the one she was wearing on her vest.

It's not uncommon for celebrities or a TV show cast to be invited to the White House. But they usually star in an Emmy darling that has years of clout behind it. But for us, who feel far from the celebrity world, and for a little gay show that started twenty years earlier in a small run-down warehouse by the Vancouver airport, the experience turned out to be a full-circle healing moment.

I thought back on all those years we spent nestled in Canada together, having the time of our lives while simultaneously pouring everything we had into making the original, then dreaming, planning, and working so hard to bring the show back years later. In that moment, I knew that whatever defeat we may have felt no longer mattered. Here was the clearest signal imaginable telling us to know our value and be proud of what we had accomplished. It proved that Ilene had been right: that taking risks and pushing the envelope was worth it, that if we brought our most courageous and authentic selves to this project, our audience would meet us there. Most of all, it showed once again how big of a difference representation really makes. It showed that each of us has something to contribute and that when we work together as a collective, that's when change happens. The four of us left Washington, DC, with the perfect conclusion to this profound chapter in our lives—and what we needed to move on.

Epilogue

| | |

Like a Pair of Pants

Every day, between 8:30 and 9:00 a.m., one of us calls the other for a morning check-in. Like clockwork, my wife, Ana, will hand me the phone and say, without a hint of resentment, not even looking up from her *New York Times,* "It's your other wife." My morning chats with Leisha can run from five minutes to an hour, depending on the topic. The conversations range from absurd minutiae (a detailed recap of the previous day or our double-date dinner plans for that evening) to serious (one of us is stressed, grumpy, or having a brief existential crisis and needs to be talked down), to practical (Which is better for cutting rebar, an angle grinder or a Sawzall? The answer being either, depending on the blade).

Like everyone else, we had plenty of practical (and existential) concerns to consider during the pandemic spring of 2020, as we spent our time confined inside, wiping down mail and groceries. With all our downtime, Rachel Shelley (Helena from the original *L Word*), reached out and suggested that Leisha and I try a podcast. Truth is, we had loosely tossed the idea around a few times before, but we were busy then and always lost momentum at the thought of all the technical pitfalls and disasters that could await us. Let's be honest, it's a good day if we can manage to navigate an iPhone update (and decoding the world of Microsoft Word while writing this book was a heart-stopping journey). If we manage to pull off an Instagram live without any fumbles, we think a Nobel Prize is just around the corner.

Our first idea for a podcast was doing a companion pod for the reboot, but as we imagined the potential red tape of needing or getting network approval, we lost steam. Then, we thought of doing a recap podcast for the original show. "Okay, but what happens when we run out of episodes?" we asked. As we went over each scenario, we realized we didn't want homework, we wanted spontaneity and a good laugh. Naturally, our brain trust kept coming back to one question: What were we missing? From the lack of gratifying storylines, we shared in the reboot to the isolating state of the pandemic world, we kept coming back to the same answer: friendship. More than anything else, it was a feeling of friendship and community that had made the original *L Word* so special, and we wanted to authentically find our way back to it. If we were missing those things, we thought, surely other people were too.

"Remember what Mia used to say?" Leisha recalled. "We're like a pair of pants. You can't have one leg without the other." Pants—the word felt nonsensical, yet somehow profound.

With our new objective and more free time than we knew what to do with, we bought matching microphones that looked like snow cones and took advantage of that app everyone suddenly couldn't get enough of called Zoom. We gave ourselves an eight-episode season in case our project failed miserably. Initially, I was half expecting one of us to wake up one day and admit we had made a horrible mistake in deciding to share our feelings and opinions. Would anyone even care what was going through our brains?

LEISHA

Early on, picking a theme for each episode made sense. Take music: Kate loves old-school hip-hop and I'm 100 percent riot grrrl, so there was loads to discuss. Or childhood, because we grew up so differently. Our fashion sense, or lack thereof. Television, movies, pets—there was a wide variety of topics. Then, when we ran out of themes, we just started talking. At that point, Kate and I made a conscious choice to be more open, to let listeners pick up the phone and listen in on our real, unedited, authentic conversations. We trusted each other and ourselves on where those conversations would end up. We are in many ways polar opposites, so it's not uncommon for us to disagree on the smallest of things, or go down different rabbit holes only to end up at the same conclusion. At the end of the day, we found that what other people wanted to hear from us was the same thing we wanted from each other: a phone call with our best friend.

From there, the podcast evolved naturally. Today, we talk about the mundane rituals of our lives—the kind of chitchat that would never end up in a magazine, like, "Hey, I painted my baseboards." Amazingly, people seem to enjoy it. We get a lot of comments from listeners saying, "You sound just like me and my friend!"

I love that *PANTS* is something Kate and I created together, just the two of us. We're not at the whim of a network executive or casting director . . . we made this opportunity and it's all ours to nurture and grow.

PANTS has brought us closer together. Kate and I are tighter than we've ever been, and we've come to even more deeply understand each other's lives and priorities. It's a new way of knowing each other, beyond the circumstances of our first relationship in the lesbian paradise of Vancouver, beyond all the twists and turns our lives have taken since then. I've learned that Kate hates lawn grass, and she can say no better than anyone. Kate has learned that my pantry was barren before Kim, but now I am a low-key prepper (with Kim by my side I have exponentially increased my odds of surviving the apocalypse). Kate can sense when I've had it with Los Angeles and need a dose of the wide-open skies of Marfa, Texas. And she knows that I hate body-part-shaped furnishings, like a hand bookend or a foot coffee table.

Through *PANTS*, I've come to understand myself better too. Though so much of the podcast consists of shooting the breeze, the format demands a different level of engagement. When we're talking, I'll hear myself say something and Kate respond, "Why?" It forces me to investigate or question my own opinion in a way that casual conversation doesn't require. Sometimes it makes me uncomfortable, other times I learn something.

Through all of these conversations, through this book, through these many revolutions around the sun, our friendship grows every day. So does my understanding of just how important friendship is. As queers, our chosen family is vital—it's where we get love, safety, and a sense of belonging, even under the most difficult circumstances. It's a funny thing to look back on my life and see how it all changed in a split second. How the universe sent me a loyal, forthright, pouty-lipped gal because she is who I needed to skip through the world with. How that one brief encounter set my life on a course I never imagined was possible. Thanks to Kate, I've learned to ask myself how to better show up for the people I love. Our enduring connection has made me understand that with proper tending and care a friendship can last a lifetime . . . or at least as long as it takes for us to road trip to Arkadelphia to pick up a Hammond organ I've got my eye on refurbishing.

Who knows what would have happened if twenty-three years
ago I had passed on a script titled *Earthlings* because I didn't want
to be on a spaceship? What would life look like if Ilene and Rose
hadn't fought for me so hard after I left that audition? Those couple twists of fate led to the experience that not only nurtured my
authentic self but taught me that family isn't always about what
DNA you share. It's the people you choose, who choose you back.
The ones who laugh with you, not at you, and the ones who challenge you but don't allow mistakes to define you. They invite you
to aim high, which can sometimes lead to places that originally felt
insurmountable. I never thought I would be married, yet here I am,
happily married with my mom loving and treating my wife, Ana, as
her own daughter.

For so long, I thought I had to figure everything out on my own,
that it was impossible for anyone else to relate to what I was going
through. Then, someone came into my life who showed me otherwise: a smiling Rainbow Brite in her red corduroy blazer with a
tiger leaping across the front and a plastic comb in her pocket. The
girl who proclaims *yes!* to everything, without thinking it through
or regardless of how harebrained. She taught me not to wait for permission to create my own opportunities and how to balance my independence with vulnerability. When I think about how the two of
us, who met as competitors, became coworkers, confidantes, then
family, and now business partners, it honestly catches my breath.

And what comes next? What do the next twenty years have in
store for us? Your guess is as good as mine. For all I know it could
be another Canned Ham project or fire pit. Regardless, our journey
together is nowhere near done. At the end of the day, when we

are two old biddies, sitting in rocking chairs, bickering over a lack of hearing, arthritis, and who last saw the remote, we will remind ourselves that we are still the same scrappy kids who have always found ways of working with what we have and inviting each other to dream.

I picture us like Winnie the Pooh and Piglet, walking side by side down the path, regardless of where it leads. With one of us saying to the other, "As soon as I saw you, I knew a grand adventure was going to happen."

Acknowledgments

Leisha

To my closest friends, you have filled my life with adventure, laughter, passion, and support. For that I thank you.

Katie Rhodes, my superhuman manager, friend, and visionary companion, thank you for believing no dream is too small.

Thank you to Peg Donegan, our _PANTS_ partner-in-crime.

We couldn't have done a lick of this without Tess Callero at Europa Content. Thank you for guiding us through this process with grace.

Hannah O'Grady, you did the impossible and helped me believe I belonged on the page. Thank you for your patience, insight, and expertise. Touring you through LA in the pitch-black dead of night is forever etched in my memory.

To the whole team at St. Martin's Press: the amazing Madeline Alsup, Amelia Beckerman, John Karle, Laura Clark—thank you for supporting us.

Here's to John Shealy, Rachel Zeidman, and Lindsay Porter at Gersh for getting this book on the road.

Thank you Kate Romero and Brett Freedman for taking these two old hags and making us cover girls.

Mom, Dad, Kaydra: I won the lottery being born into your arms.

Kim, may we always drive down endless country roads together.

To Kate, my comfortable, reliable, perfectly fitted pair of pants: Your friendship means everything to me.

And to every queer person I've walked beside or stood on the shoulders of . . . I am forever grateful.

KATE

The process of writing this book was nothing short of humbling, and although this is my story, it took a village to bring it to life.

Thank you to the entire team at St. Martin's Press. Our brilliant and intuitive editor, Hannah O'Grady, was our fearless backbone who not only steered but inspired us to dig deeper through each draft. Without her, this book would not exist. Thank you as well to Tess Callero at Europa Content for holding our hand throughout and believing our story was worth sharing in the first place.

To Peg Donegan, thank you for shepherding me through all these years with your blunt honesty, protection, and knowledge. Katie Rhodes, thank you for your loyalty, time, and effort you put forward with this project and all the other ones down the line.

Mom, I am proud to be your daughter. Thank you for never allowing me to be a professional child actor and always believing in me when others didn't. I hope this book brings clarity to any questions you may have had that I was unable to articulate. I love you more.

To my eccentric and creative family, chosen or by blood, whether they are still with us or not, each of you has left an imprint on me that will thankfully never fade away.

Ilene, you changed the trajectory of my life when I was twenty-four. Thank you for seeing what others didn't. Jennifer, Laurel, Mia, Erin, Pam, Rose, Sarah, and our *L Word* cast and crew, I hold a special place for you in my heart and we are forever bonded.

Jenna, without you, childhood would have felt colorless. This book only scratches the surface of what you mean to me, but I hope it conveys how special you are.

To Ana, thank you for tolerating me throughout this process and forcing me to eat when I was forgetting to. You are my North Star, and I'm the lucky one who gets to experience the world with you.

Leisha, what can I say that hasn't already been written? I hope you don't ever get sick of me because I'd be lost without you.

To our LGBTQ+ community, thank you for the endless inspiration you bring into this world through your bravery, authenticity, and artistry. I hope this book will help pay it forward and makes you feel seen.

Photos

All photos at the permissions of Leisha Hailey and Kate Moennig

INSERT 1

1. Dad, Bill Moennig
2. Dad at his workbench in the violin shop
3. Mom's headshot, which she kindly autographed
4. Father-daughter bonding
5. A short-lived violin lesson
6. Kate ate the prop after this photo was taken
7. Dressed as a German milkmaid with cousins Gwyneth and Hillary during Easter
8. Leisha's crush at Camp Kitaki
9. #77 ready to roll
10. Classic shorts-and-sweater look
11. Kaydra, Nubi, and Leisha
12. 1970s style icons
13. Learning how to use a knife
14. Hillary and Kate in Rittenhouse Square
15. Action shot of Jenna and Kate as Tigger and Winne-the-Pooh at the Free Library
16. Smoking in the nineties
17. Hanging out of Jenna's window in 1994
18. Kate and Mom in 1996
19. A couple of Young Americans
20. Heather and Leisha, touring in Norway
21. Fraggle Rock
22. Playing in LA
23. MCA Records promo shot
24. Discovered weed; made the NYC paper
25. Kim and Leisha, first limo ride; baby tees and pineapple juice
26. Heather, Kim, and Leisha in Central Park, NYC
27. Yes, we left the house like this
28. Photo booth with Jesus

INSERT 2

29. First official photo of the cast and crew during the pilot
30. Our production office in Vancouver
31. Call sheet from season 1
32. Alice's apartment with the original chart
33. Shane's drugs
34. Sisterly love
35. A yacht party to remember
36. Flashback, *Butter* the band
37. A short-lived salon
38. Kelly Lynch getting into character
39. Don't tell Jenny
40. After two lessons
41. An actor prepares
42. Rehearsing to meet Snoop
43. The food fight you never saw
44. Watching the sunrise
45. Pre-couture
46. Production office hangout
47. On location for season 5
48. Erin and Leisha behind the scenes, season 2
49. Blocking rehearsal in season 5
50. Kate and Erin in London
51. Jawlines
52. Staying warm during a night shoot
53. In between setups
54. Coyote Ugly with her juice box

Photos

All photos at the permissions of Leisha Hailey and Kate Moennig

INSERT 1

1. Dad, Bill Moennig
2. Dad at his workbench in the violin shop
3. Mom's headshot, which she kindly autographed
4. Father-daughter bonding
5. A short-lived violin lesson
6. Kate ate the prop after this photo was taken
7. Dressed as a German milkmaid with cousins Gwyneth and Hillary during Easter
8. Leisha's crush at Camp Kitaki
9. #77 ready to roll
10. Classic shorts-and-sweater look
11. Kaydra, Nubi, and Leisha
12. 1970s style icons
13. Learning how to use a knife
14. Hillary and Kate in Rittenhouse Square
15. Action shot of Jenna and Kate as Tigger and Winne-the-Pooh at the Free Library
16. Smoking in the nineties
17. Hanging out of Jenna's window in 1994
18. Kate and Mom in 1996
19. A couple of Young Americans
20. Heather and Leisha, touring in Norway
21. Fraggle Rock
22. Playing in LA
23. MCA Records promo shot
24. Discovered weed; made the NYC paper
25. Kim and Leisha, first limo ride; baby tees and pineapple juice
26. Heather, Kim, and Leisha in Central Park, NYC
27. Yes, we left the house like this
28. Photo booth with Jesus

INSERT 2

29. First official photo of the cast and crew during the pilot
30. Our production office in Vancouver
31. Call sheet from season 1
32. Alice's apartment with the original chart
33. Shane's drugs
34. Sisterly love
35. A yacht party to remember
36. Flashback, *Butter* the band
37. A short-lived salon
38. Kelly Lynch getting into character
39. Don't tell Jenny
40. After two lessons
41. An actor prepares
42. Rehearsing to meet Snoop
43. The food fight you never saw
44. Watching the sunrise
45. Pre-couture
46. Production office hangout
47. On location for season 5
48. Erin and Leisha behind the scenes, season 2
49. Blocking rehearsal in season 5
50. Kate and Erin in London
51. Jawlines
52. Staying warm during a night shoot
53. In between setups
54. Coyote Ugly with her juice box

About the Authors

Kate Romero

Kate Romero

Leisha Hailey is an actor, director, executive producer, musician, and podcaster. Hailey is best known for her beloved breakout character Alice Pieszecki in the revolutionary Showtime series *The L Word* and the reboot, *The L Word: Generation Q*. Before making her mark on-screen, Hailey cofounded the band The Murmurs in the 1990s, recording three albums for MCA/Universal Records and touring worldwide, including with Lilith Fair. More than a decade later, in 2007, Hailey cofounded the indie pop band Uh Huh Her, which toured internationally and sold albums worldwide.

Kate Moennig is a critically acclaimed actor and executive producer whose work spans film, television, and theater. She is most known for her iconic role as Shane McCutcheon in the Showtime series *The L Word* and the reboot, *The L Word: Generation Q*. Moennig has also starred in Showtime's hit series *Ray Donovan*, Freeform's *Grown-ish*, and Liz Feldman's series *No Good Deed*. Moennig's film credits include *The Lincoln Lawyer*, *Lane 1974*, and Terry Zwigoff's *Art School Confidential*.